THE

EVERYTHING®

CASINO
GAMBLING
BOOK

The Everything Series:

The Everything® After College Book
The Everything® Baby Names Book
The Everything® Bartender's Book
The Everything® Beer Book
The Everything® Bicycle Book
The Everything® Cat Book
The Everything® Christmas Book
The Everything® College Survival Book
The Everything® Dreams Book
The Everything® Etiquette Book
The Everything® Family Tree Book
The Everything® Games Book
The Everything® Get Ready for Baby Book
The Everything® Golf Book
The Everything® Home Improvement Book
The Everything® Jewish Wedding Book
The Everything® Low-Fat High-Flavor Cookbook
The Everything® Pasta Cookbook
The Everything® Study Book
The Everything® Wedding Book
The Everything® Wedding Checklist
The Everything® Wedding Etiquette Book
The Everything® Wedding Organizer
The Everything® Wedding Vows Book
The Everything® Wine Book
The Everything® Casino Gambling Book

THE
EVERYTHING®
CASINO GAMBLING BOOK

From Poker, to Roulette, to Slots—The Rules,
Strategies, and Secrets You Need to Beat the Odds

George Mandos

Adams Media Corporation
HOLBROOK, MASSACHUSETTS

An Everything® Series Book.
The Everything® Series is a registered trademark of Adams Media Corporation.

Published by Adams Media Corporation
260 Center Street, Holbrook, MA 02343

ISBN: 1-55850-762-0

Printed in the United States of America.

J I H G F E D C B A

Library of Congress Cataloging-in-Publication Data
Mandos, George.
The everything casino gambling book / George Mandos, Jr.
    p.   cm.   —(Everything series)
        Includes index.
        ISBN 1-55850-762-0
        1. Gambling. I. Title.
    GV1301.M26   1998
    795—dc21   97-32779
                            CIP

This is a *CWL Publishing Enterprises Book*, developed by John A. Woods for Adams Media Corporation. Contact CWL
Publishing Enterprises for more information at 3010 Irvington Way, Madison, WI 53713-3414, (608) 273-3710.

This publication is designed to provide accurate and authoritative information with regard to the subject matter covered. It is
sold with the understanding that the publisher is not engaged in rendering professional advice. If advice or other expert
assistance is required, the services of a competent professional person should be sought.

Product or brand names used in this book may be trademarks or registered trademarks. For readability, they may appear in
initial capitalization or have been capitalized in the style used by the name claimant. Any use of these names is editorial and
does not convey endorsement of or other affiliation with the name claimant. The publisher does not intend to express any
judgment as to the validity or legal status of any such proprietary claims.

ILLUSTRATIONS BY BARRY LITTMANN

This book is available at quantity discounts for bulk purchases.
For information, call 1-800-872-5627 (in Massachusetts, call 781-767-8100).

Visit our home page at http://www.adamsmedia.com

CONTENTS

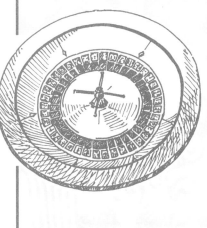

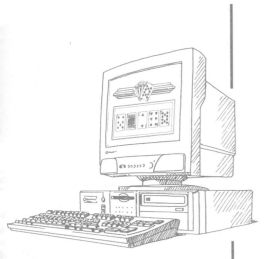

PREFACE

For many beginners, a visit to a casino is a strange and tempting experience. There are thousands of dollars changing hands all the time, people screaming with delight as they hit a slot machine jackpot, and the overall feel of the place is exciting. Then you say to yourself, I think I'll try one of these games and see what happens. There are at least two things that can happen if you don't know how to play very well. First, you are likely to lose your money, often quite quickly. Next, you might make a mistake and suffer the embarrassment of a dealer correcting you. Both of these are likely to make your time at the table a lot less fun, not to mention more expensive, than it has to be. Did you know that carefully playing the basic blackjack strategy, at worst, two hours spent at the blackjack table will cost you about as much as going to a movie?

How do you avoid losing and making a mistake? How do you make gambling fun and maybe even profitable? The answer is simple. Know what you're doing. *The Everything Casino Gambling Book* gives you the basics of each game in down-to-earth language. It describes the rules and the different bets, and it gives you the best strategy for winning. It tells you what the smart bets are and what the sucker bets are as well.

The best way to take full advantage of what this book has to offer is to find the games you're interested in and read about them before you go to the casino. Then when you visit a casino, don't start playing right away. Watch the games and how people are playing. Compare what you see with what you have read here. Pick the game in which you're interested and make small bets at first. You'll be surprised how quickly you can pick up the rules of the various games, though practicing winning strategies will take you longer. You might want to practice at home before you actually visit the casino. Deal out hands of the various games to learn their principles and dynamics. If you're connected to the Internet, there are various sites where you can play online or even download computerized versions of the various games. In fact, many of those sites are listed in this book.

Gambling can be a lot of fun, especially when you win. Making that happen is the whole purpose of this book.

ACKNOWLEDGMENTS

This book came to be through the efforts of two people. Anne Weaver at Adams Media asked John Woods, President of CWL Publishing Enterprises to develop a book on this subject for her. John contacted and worked with me throughout the development process to create the book you now have in front of you. I want to thank Anne and John for their support as I wrote this book. I also want to thank Robert Magnan of CWL Publishing Enterprises for his careful editing of the manuscript. He did a very good job. Finally, I want to thank you for buying it. I hope it works for you. Good luck!

—George Mandos, Jr.

Chapter One
GAMBLING HISTORY AND THE HOUSE ADVANTAGE

The human tendency to bet on the unknown has been around for millennia. We seem to have a predisposition to think we are better at predicting what's going to happen than someone else, and we are willing to bet on it. Confirmed gamblers are willing to bet on anything, even on which of two rain drops might reach the bottom of the window pane first.

Gambling seems to have started out in games of strength and skill between individuals or teams, with the participants betting on who would win. This led to onlookers also betting on the results. For those who were not skilled at such competitions, they created other games that involved chance, luck, and only sometimes skill. In earliest history there are stories of throwing a bone in the air and betting on which side it would land, such as we might now flip a coin. It seems clear that dice eventually evolved from such activities as a way of increasing the number of possible outcomes. Dice may be the oldest gambling device extant, as they were found in the Sumerian royal tombs of Ur dating back to the third millennium B.C. In contrast, playing cards are a relatively recent invention. It's believed that they originated in the Orient and were used in Europe as early as the 14th century.

Gambling was popular among the ancient Egyptians, as we know from evidence found in the Great Pyramid of Cheops at Giza, built around 300 B.C. In the city of Thebes, which dates from 1500 B.C., archaeologists have found dice. The Egyptians had other forms of gambling as well. A mural now in the British Museum shows two people playing a game of chance called "atep," in which two players each would bet on the number of fingers the other held behind his back. There is also evidence of a form of checkers and a game called "hab-em-hau," which involved tossing disks into a copper bowl.

Halfway around the world, in Asia, the ancient Chinese were also gambling. Confucius made references to "wei-ch'i," a game played with hundreds of pieces that were used to simulate war strategies, not unlike chess. The records suggest that the game was invented by an emperor around 2300 B.C. In India, people were gambling on dice and chariot racing by at least 1500 B.C. They bet not just money, but estates, slaves, and even wives on the outcome.

Lotteries have been around in every civilization, often to determine who would win a particular prize or suffer a horrible fate. For example, the Aztecs cast lots to chose who would be sacrificed to their gods. Greek mythology tells the story of how Zeus and his brothers Poseidon and Hades defeated the Titans and took over the universe. They then cast lots to divide it among them. Zeus won the heavens, Poseidon the sea, and Hades the underworld. If the outcomes had been different, we might associate Zeus with hell and Hades with heaven.

The Romans were great gamblers, though gambling was looked down on officially and laws were passed to make it illegal. Whether they were rigorously enforced is another question. Winners, however, could not force losers to pay off their debts. A common insult was to be called a gamester.

Throughout European history there are records of people gambling—and losing. Not unlike today, gambling came to be associated with all kinds of sins, and the church came out against it. Yet gambling continued, because people enjoy taking chances in hopes of winning.

Gambling has been in the Americas for centuries. There are records that Leif Erickson, the first European to visit America, found Indians playing games of chance and then brought these games back with him to Greenland.

New Orleans was the first major gambling center in the United States. In 1718, taverns and coffee houses provided rooms and tables for private gambling. It grew from there, until in 1811 provincial governors managed to get a law passed to prohibit gambling throughout Louisiana because of the corruption they believed accompanied it. However, this did little to stop gambling in New Orleans, and in 1823 they decided to legalize it and charge $5,000 for a gambling license to be applied toward a hospital and a college. From that point on, large public casinos came to dominate the gambling scene in New Orleans and made it America's first gambling destination city. The war between Mexico and the United States in 1846 brought thousands of troops to New Orleans, where gambling was perhaps their primary recreation. By 1850 there were over five thousand "sawdust joints" along the Mississippi River where cards and craps were

played twenty-four hours a day. Most of these places ran crooked games, and it's said that honest games could only be found in private homes. Gambling was eventually made illegal, and these houses closed down. Today, large gambling casinos are once again a New Orleans fixture.

Chicago in the 1840s was another gambling center. Gambling grew as the city grew, and as in New Orleans, it got an unsavory reputation. The historian John Quinn says of Chicago in those days, "It is not surprising that people of America descended on the city from thousands of miles distance in order to satisfy their addiction to gambling. Theirs was the thrill and the misery, the city's was the fame."

As Americans opened the frontier, gambling moved west. Such legendary figures as Wild Bill Hickok, Wyatt Earp, and Doc Holliday were well-known gamblers. Wild Bill actually died playing poker in a saloon in Deadwood, South Dakota. (Gambling, by the way, has been legalized in Deadwood, making it yet again a gambling destination for those in the Great Plains.) Wyatt Earp earned far less money as a marshall than as a gambler and owner of the Oriental Saloon and Gambling House in Tombstone, Arizona. Doc Holliday was, in fact, a dealer at this very establishment.

With the gold rush, gambling became ensconced in places like San Francisco with its Barbary Coast, and in Reno, near California's gold country. Finally, there is Las Vegas, which in Spanish means "the meadows." It was originally a camping ground for travelers going from Santa Fe to California. It remained sparsely populated until 1905, when a railroad was built that passed through the site. On May 15, 1905, a land auction was held and two thousand parcels of land were sold for a total price of $265,000. A tent city sprang up and among those tents were Las Vegas's first gambling houses.

In 1931 the state legislature of Nevada legalized gambling, and soon there were many small casinos in Las Vegas. However, there were no hotels or large casinos until 1946. That was the year Benjamin "Bugsy" Siegel opened his hotel, the Flamingo, financed with mob money on what was to become the Las Vegas Strip. This was actually Siegel's second gambling venture. He had earlier out-fitted some luxury ships as casinos that were anchored just over three miles off the California coast. However, then Governor Earl Warren got the legislature to tighten gambling laws and that was the end of that venture. If you saw the movie *Bugsy*, you know Siegel was killed about a year after his hotel opened. His successor, Gus Greenbaum, also died prematurely from similar unnatural causes.

All this prompted the Gaming Control Board to take firmer control of casinos and make licensing a more rigorous and regulated process. Soon after the Flamingo opened, several other large hotels including the Sahara, the Sands, the Desert Inn, and the Riviera also opened on the Strip. Big name entertainers, like Frank Sinatra and Dean Martin, began appearing regularly, and modern Las Vegas was on its way. Las Vegas has continued to grow in every way possible. Many of those famous old hotels that defined the Strip have been torn down. New hotel/resort/theme park/casinos like the Luxor and the Mirage, costing hundreds of millions of dollars, have opened up. The goal is to attract anyone and everyone to Las Vegas to partake of many different activities, but first and foremost, still, to gamble. Today, perhaps the only major competition for Las Vegas in terms of tourism dollars is Orlando, Florida and the many Disney attractions there.

With the success of Las Vegas, other cities began to legalize gambling as well, most prominently Atlantic City, New Jersey, which before gambling was mainly known for the Miss America pageant, a somewhat seedy boardwalk, and the source of the street names in the game Monopoly. Now its hotels and casinos have their share of glitz, even if the city doesn't quite match Las Vegas.

Many Indian tribes have recently won the right to set up casinos on their reservations, and now gambling casinos are found in nearly every state. The lure of gambling tax dollars has moved states such as Ohio, Illinois, Indiana, and Iowa to allow river boat gambling, and large, elaborate river boats have appeared along the Mississippi, Ohio, and other rivers with many of those boats never leaving port.

Gambling has been around throughout history and people around the world share the desire to bet that chance may favor one person winning at the expense of others. Millions of people enjoy playing games of chance, and it is certainly a part of the American scene. As you peruse this book, you'll learn that there are some games that are better than others to play, and by taking a little bit of time to learn the games, you'll not only have fun on your visit to a casino, but may win some money as well.

THE HOUSE ADVANTAGE

When you visit a casino, remember that although it may provide you with an entertaining experience, the only way a casino can make money is to have an advantage over you in every game you play. This allows it to generate the funds necessary to provide you with the entertainment, free drinks, and relatively inexpensive food and hotel rooms. It's in the casinos that the people who run these businesses make their money. Casinos take in billions of dollars each year, and that amount continues to grow every year.

Every casino game has an advantage for "the house." (By the way, the word casino is Italian for house.) Let's suppose a casino offered you a game where you could bet on a coin flip. You could bet on heads or tails. Either way you'd have a fifty percent chance of guessing correctly. In this game the casino would have no advantage. Half the time you would win and the other half the casino would win. You could be ahead after a short session, of course, but over time you'd lose just as often as you would win. A casino isn't guaranteed to come out ahead in this game; like you, it will only break even over time. That's why casinos don't offer games like this. Casinos only offer games where, over time, the odds favor the house.

The advantage can be as little as one percent, but even so, in time the casino will still make money. The advantage the casinos have in each game is called the *house advantage*. Throughout this book you'll see this term used regularly, in different games and on different bets in those games.

THE REAL HOUSE ADVANTAGE

Normally the house advantage is determined by the mathematical expectation of the house winning in any game. Casinos usually do much better than that in most games, because many players are not skillful and lose their money more quickly than skilled players who are more likely to win. Steve Bourie and Henry Tamburin, gambling aficionados, have calculated the actual house win percentage of the several different games covered in this book as follows:

Game	Win Percent
Keno	27.31%
Horse Race Book	15.03%
Wheel of Fortune	8.81%
Caribbean Stud	4.94%
Let It Ride	4.72%
Roulette	4.54%
Sports Pool	4.28%
Pai Gow Poker	4.01%
Baccarat	2.86%
Craps	2.85%
Blackjack	2.74%
Mini-baccarat	2.24%
Bingo	1.74%

Bingo is the game that an average customer is most likely to win playing. Clearly, keno and the wheel of fortune are not games you should play if you're looking to win. The other games with a house advantage of around two percent or so are more likely to make you a winner, especially if you play intelligently.

GAMBLING PSYCHOLOGY

From the casino's perspective, there's a lot of psychology to gambling. When you sit down at a gaming table, for example, the first thing you do is lay down the money that you want to play with. The dealer immediately gives you the equivalent amount in casino chips. It's easier for dealers to collect bets and make payoffs with chips instead of cash. But, more importantly, you're less likely to regard those bright, stackable chips as real money, and likely to risk more of them as a result.

Just because the games have a long-term advantage for the casino, this doesn't mean you can't walk away a winner. It only means that in the long run casinos will win more than they will lose. What you will learn about the games described in this book is how to play them well enough to improve your chances of winning and minimize the house advantage as much as possible. By playing the games that offer the house a lesser advantage, you'll have a better chance of playing longer with your gambling money and a better chance of coming out a winner. This will, in the final analysis, make your gambling experience more fun and less costly.

Chapter Two
HAVING FUN AT A CASINO

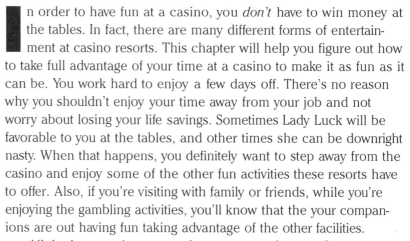

In order to have fun at a casino, you *don't* have to win money at the tables. In fact, there are many different forms of entertainment at casino resorts. This chapter will help you figure out how to take full advantage of your time at a casino to make it as fun as it can be. You work hard to enjoy a few days off. There's no reason why you shouldn't enjoy your time away from your job and not worry about losing your life savings. Sometimes Lady Luck will be favorable to you at the tables, and other times she can be downright nasty. When that happens, you definitely want to step away from the casino and enjoy some of the other fun activities these resorts have to offer. Also, if you're visiting with family or friends, while you're enjoying the gambling activities, you'll know that the your companions are out having fun taking advantage of the other facilities.

All the large casino resorts have great pool areas. Some even have small waterparks for the kids. However, be very careful when lounging around the pool in Las Vegas, because the sun is very intense in the Nevada desert. Make sure you use sunblock of at least 15 spf if you decide to take advantage of these pool areas. Better safe than sorry when you're going to be out in the sun.

A few of these pool areas have bands that play during the afternoon to keep the guests entertained. They'll also have a nice outdoor bar so you can cool off with a drink or two while you enjoy the sunshine. The Tropicana Hotel and Casino even has a swim up blackjack table, allowing you to gamble while relaxing in the pool. Gambling in the pools became popular during the '50s, but has died out in most of today's gambling resorts.

These casino resorts also attract the big names in entertainment to perform on their stages. Not only can you see the biggest names in show business, like Liza Minelli and George Carlin, but in some of the small lounges you can find the stars of tomorrow. Many of these hotels have a standard Vegas-style review show in their main show room. One of the best is the Bally's Jubilee! show in Las Vegas. The longest running of these Vegas-style reviews is the Folies Bergere at the Tropicana Hotel and Casino. It has been showing there since 1961.

Some of the newer casino resorts have chosen other alternatives as steady acts in their main show room. At the Mirage Hotel and Casino you can find the magicians Siegfried and Roy. While the tickets are expensive ($80 a seat), their show is well worth the price. Also in Las Vegas you can find magician Lance Burton doing a regular show at the Monte Carlo Resort and Casino. The best new show to hit Vegas in the past few years is Cirque du Soleil at Treasure Island Hotel and Casino. This is a modern-day circus without any animal acts. Don't get turned off by the word circus. It's the closest comparison one can make to this show. This is a fun show for all ages. The flounes, a combination clown and mime, have colorful costumes and continuously entertain the audience while groups of talented performers perform unbelievable stunts. If you're going to see just one show in Las Vegas, make sure it's Cirque du Soleil. But if you want to see this show, remember to order your tickets in advance because they always play to a full house. Tickets for this show go on sale ninety days in advance.

If you've had a tough day at the tables and you need help unwinding, you can also choose to use the hotel's spa. A good massage can do wonders to take your mind off the money you might have just lost at the casino. Or, if you've been a winner, maybe you can use some of your winnings to indulge yourself a little. Most of these spas are offer a full range of services, including massages, mud packs, saunas, and steam baths. If you'd rather work out your frustrations in a gym, most resorts offer completely equipped facilities. Some of the best spas and gyms are located in these hotels: Caesar's Palace, the Mirage, Golden Nugget, and Bally's.

If golf is your game, then casino resorts have some of the best courses you'll find. Be ready to pay higher than normal green fees for these courses, but they're usually worth it if you enjoy top-notch golf courses. Just imagine how expensive it is for the courses to remain green throughout the summer heat in Las Vegas. They do a great job with the courses in Las Vegas and attract some major golf tournaments in the spring and fall.

Even though this book is for the gambler in you, the casinos certainly won't neglect the rest of you or your family or friends. Gambling has come a long way from the gambling dens of the past. Although the desire to take chances may be universal and eternal, you can gamble in comfort and style at today's casinos.

Now, let's start working on making you a winner!

Better Than Movies

What would you rather do, go to the movies or gamble for two hours? If it's a close decision, you might want to base your choice on price. Movies these days run about $7 for two hours of fun. The following games can all be played for two hours and the average player will lose less than $7:

Game	Expected Loss
$5 Blackjack (basic strategy used)	$0–$3.60
$11 Sports Wager	$0.50
$1 Keno (live game only)	$3.50–$4.50
$5 Craps (pass line)	$4.25–$5.50
$0.25 Video Poker (9/6 Jacks or better)	$6.26

part **2**

CASINO

TABLE GAMES

Chapter Three
BLACKJACK

Blackjack is the most popular table game in casinos. One reason blackjack is so popular is because it gives the player a better chance at winning over the long haul than all other casino games. The house advantage in blackjack is only 0.5 percent. That means if you play basic blackjack strategy, the casino will only win 0.5 percent of your money over time. This is an average, so there are times when you can actually make money. If you were to gamble $100, the casino is going to pay you back $99.50 on average over time. So it's going to cost you about fifty cents per hundred dollars to play blackjack in a casino, on average, if you play intelligently.

You may remember from Chapter 1 that the actual house win percentage is 2.74 percent. That percentage is significantly higher than 0.5 percent. Why? Because many players don't know how to make the most of the odds. This chapter is going to teach you how to play intelligently and maybe even improve on that percentage.

Blackjack is played with a standard fifty-two-card deck. A casino game of blackjack can be played with one, two, four, six, or eight decks. The casino determines the number of decks it uses for its blackjack games. As a player, the fewer decks the better. Why? It's easier for players to count cards (that is, keep track of the cards that

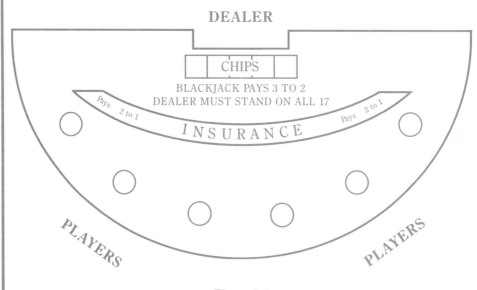

Figure 3-1
A typical blackjack table.

have been played) when there are fewer decks in use. Also, the fewer the decks, the fewer hands per hour you play because the dealers need to shuffle the cards more often. So the more time they spend shuffling, the less time they have to deal and play. The house also has an advantage in the way the cards are dealt when more than two decks are used. Figure 3-1 shows a typical blackjack table at a casino.

THE RULES

Blackjack is a simple game to learn. Many people have played black-jack or twenty-one growing up as kids. The rules in casino blackjack are the same, for the most part.

Each card has a numerical value. A five is worth five, a seven is worth seven, and so forth. All face cards are worth ten, as are all tens. Aces are worth either eleven or one. If you're dealt an ace, it's up to you to decide which value you want it to have. For example, if you have an ace and seven in your hand, it can be counted as eight or eighteen: it's your choice. You can also switch the value of that ace in the middle of a hand, if it's to your advantage. Because you have the option of playing the ace either way, a hand containing an ace is called a *soft hand*. A hand with no aces is called a *hard hand*. A hard hand can only be counted one way, since all cards other than aces have a set value.

At the beginning of the game, each player lays down a bet. The dealer then gives each player two cards, dealing them one at a time starting with the player at his left and continuing clockwise. In single- and double-deck blackjack games, the cards are dealt face down. In blackjack games that use a shoe (four or more decks), the cards are dealt face up. (A shoe is a container that holds the cards for the dealer. It got this name because it looks similar to a shoe.) The dealer also deals himself two cards, one face up and one face down, no matter what the number of decks are being used. (The face-down card is also called the hole card.)

Each player must add the value of his or her cards to determine what the hand is worth. For example, if you have a five and a seven, your hand is worth twelve. If you have a nine and a jack, your hand is worth nineteen. (Remember: all face cards are worth ten.) If you have an ace and six, you have a total of seventeen or seven. (Remember: aces may be used as one or eleven.) If you have a queen and an ace, you have twenty-one. That total is called a blackjack. Getting a blackjack on the deal is called a *natural*.

The object of blackjack is to beat the dealer. You compare the total of your hand with the dealer's total. Each player plays against the dealer and not each other. No matter how many players are sitting at your blackjack table, your object is to beat the dealer, so don't worry about the other players' hands. You can beat the dealer in two ways. If your cards total twenty-one or lower and that total is higher than the total of the dealer's hand, you win. If the dealer goes over twenty-one, then you win. Any value over twenty-one is called a busted hand. Of course, the same applies to you: if your hand total is over twenty-one, then you've busted and automatically lose.

That's fairly simple so far. There's a little more to the game than that round of two cards. But first, we'll explain the layout so you can more easily follow what happens next.

A blackjack table consists of six or seven spots for players and one dealer. In front of each player there's a betting circle where you place the chips you want to wager. Each table will have a sign indicating the minimum and maximum betting limits. Those limits are usually $5 minimum and $2,000 maximum. The casinos change the minimum/maximum sign according to how busy they might be. If they get really busy, then they might raise the limits, to restrict the game to the higher rollers and allow them to bet more money. If things are slow, they might lower the limits to attract more players to the table. It's the basic economic principle of supply and demand.

The dealer always plays his hand last. That means his face-down card remains unknown to the players until he turns it over to play his hand. It would be no challenge to the players if both the dealer's cards were turned face up at the beginning. In turn, it would also be unfair to the players if both the dealer's cards were face down. The players need to judge how to play their hands based on the dealer's face-up card and the total of their hand.

The reason the dealer deals the cards to the players face down when using one or two decks is that the use of only 52 or 104 cards makes it easier for the players to keep track of the cards that have been

played. By dealing the cards face down, the dealer makes it tougher for players to count cards. By using three or more decks, which makes it more difficult to count cards, the house increases its advantage, so it allows the players to see each other's hand to compensate for the greater house advantage. The house only gains anywhere from .30 percent to .60 percent, depending on the number of decks being used.

The game begins when the dealer deals every player and himself two cards each. When the cards are dealt face down, you may only use one hand to pick up your cards; this rule is to prevent cheating. When the cards are dealt face up, you're not allowed to touch the cards at all. Play begins with the first player to the dealer's left (called *first base*). Each player in turn decides whether to *take a hit* (get another card) or to *stand* (stick with his or her two cards). You're allowed to hit your hand as many times as you like, until you decide to stand or you bust. The dealer will ask each player, usually with a hand signal, if he or she wants another card. As a player, you *must* respond with a hand signal.

The signals differ according to the number of decks in use, that is, depending on whether the players are holding their cards (in one hand only) or the cards are lying on the table. In single- or double-deck games, if you want to take a hit, you scrape your cards toward you on the table, as if flicking crumbs. If you want to stand, then you tuck the cards under your chips, using just the one hand. In games using more than two decks, since you can't touch the cards, you use your fingers to signal. To signal a hit, you scrape the table in a pulling motion towards you. To stand, you wave your hand over your cards.

These hand signals are very important and must be used when playing blackjack. The reason for the hand signals is to prevent cheating by the dealer and/or the players. The casino security personnel use cameras in the ceiling for surveillance of the games. Since the security cameras used in casinos don't have sound, personnel would be unable to monitor spoken questions and answers. By making the players use hand signals, the security personnel can make sure dealers and players aren't cheating.

After receiving your two cards, you may have four choices to make before proceeding to play your hand: split pairs, double down, surrender, and take insurance. Let's go through each of these options.

Knowing What You'll Lose

If you play perfect basic blackjack strategy for eight hours straight at a $1 table, you can expect to lose only about $2.50. Remember that this is an average over time. Of course, you'll have a tough time finding a $1 blackjack table as the lowest table in most casinos is a $2 table. On a $5 table, your expected loss on average in eight hours would be $12.50.

Splitting Pairs

If you have two cards of the same value (two sixes, two tens, a king and a jack, and so on), you may split the cards into two separate hands. In order to do this, you must place an equal bet on each of your hands. In essence, you're cloning yourself and becoming two players. So, you just place a second pile of chips in the betting circle right next to your initial pile, in the same amount. If you're playing a single- or double-deck game, you'll also have to turn over your cards to prove you have a pair. After you've split your pair and doubled your wager, you now have two hands. Both hands are treated separately, meaning you play one hand out before proceeding to the next hand.

It's very important to know when to split pairs and when to leave them together. The strategy of splitting pairs will be covered later in this chapter.

Double Down

Before you decide to hit or stand, you may double down if you believe that your hand has a much better chance of beating the dealer's hand. Some casinos allow you to double down only if your first two cards total 9, 10, or 11. Other casinos will allow you to double down on any total for your first two cards. The best way to find out the casino's rules is to ask the dealer.

Doubling down is adding to your initial wager. You may double the amount of your wager or you may "double down for less." The dealer then deals you a third card. You cannot stand on the two and you cannot take another hit.

For example, let's say that you wager $25, you get an eight and a two (a total of ten), and the dealer has a six showing, so you decide to double down. You put a $25 chip next to your initial wager (doubling down) and you receive one card. By deciding to double down, you feel your hand has enough chance to beat the dealer's hand that you want to increase your potential winnings. By letting you double your bet, the house gives you just a single additional card, not the usual unlimited hits or the option to stand on two cards. Doubling down can be a very powerful tool for the players, and will be covered in more detail later in this chapter.

Surrender

Surrendering can also be a powerful tool for players. Unfortunately, most casinos don't offer this option. If you do find a casino that offers it, you have a better advantage than if you were playing at a casino that doesn't offer it.

If you don't like your two cards, simply tell the dealer "surrender" and turn in your hand, forfeiting half of your bet. In other words, you're dropping out and keeping half your bet, rather than risk losing all of it. The reason for surrendering is that you don't think you have much chance of beating the dealer. This can help the smart player save a lot of money when Lady Luck is turned the other way.

Insurance

When the dealer's face-up card is an ace, he offers the players a chance to take insurance. This means that you're allowed to insure your hand against the possibility of the dealer having a natural twenty-one with his two cards. To take insurance, you must place a bet on the insurance line equal to half of your wager. This is a side bet. You're betting that the dealer has a blackjack. If the dealer makes the natural, your bet pays off at two to one.

In actuality, this is a very bad bet and should generally be avoided. When the dealer has an ace, he has a very good chance of getting a *pat hand*, that is, 17, 18, 19, 20 or 21. (It's called a pat hand because the dealer stands pat.) So if the dealer has a good hand but not a blackjack, you lose your insurance bet and probably your initial wager as well. This is bad.

The only time you should make this bet is if you're counting cards and are almost sure the dealer has a ten-value card underneath his ace. If you make an insurance bet and the dealer has a natural, then you win twice the amount of your insurance bet but lose your initial wager. Therefore, you'd *push* on this hand. (A push is when you don't win or lose money on a hand.)

Never take insurance. It's a sucker's bet.

Playing the Game

Each player in turn, starting from the dealer's left, gets to finish out his hand. If a player decides to stand, to not try to get closer to a total of twenty-one, then play passes to the next player. If a player decides to take a hit, the dealer gives him or her an additional card until he or she decides to stand or busts (goes over twenty-one). If that happens, the dealer removes his or her wager and cards. If you're playing single- or double-deck blackjack, you must turn over your cards immediately if you bust. After a player busts, the dealer removes the used cards and places them in a discard rack face down.

Once all the players get their chance to play their hands, the dealer gets his turn. By always making the players play out their hands first, the casino gains its advantage over the players. Even if the dealer busts his hand, any player who busted still loses because he or she busted first.

The dealer flips over his face-down card and determines whether to hit his hand or to stand. The dealer doesn't have a choice: he must follow strict rules. The dealer must take a card if he has less than seventeen and must stand if he has seventeen or higher. Some casinos require the dealer to hit his hand if he has a soft seventeen (one of his cards is an ace). It's better for the players if the casino requires the dealer to stand on all seventeens. If a dealer is required to hit a soft seventeen, then there's a chance he can improve his hand (get closer to twenty-one) but no risk of busting, because the ace would then be worth only one.

After the dealer finishes out his hand, he makes a sweep of the players' hands from his right to left. He evaluates each player's hand against his, then takes the bet if the player has a lower count, pays off the player if he or she has a higher count, or gives a push sign (indicating a tie or standoff), meaning that neither wins the bet. The usual push sign is for the dealer to pat the table in front of the player's wager. Then, after taking care of all the bets, the dealer ends the hand by removing all the used cards and placing them in a discard rack face down.

Payouts in blackjack are simple. If you win, you get paid even money or the amount you bet plus your bet remains. The only exception to this rule is when you win with blackjack. You get paid three to two if you win with blackjack or your bet plus half your bet. For example, if you win with eighteen and you have $25 bet, then you win $25 and your original $25 chip remains in the betting circle. If you win with a natural or blackjack and you have a $25 bet, then you win $37.50 and your $25 chip remains in the betting circle.

If you win after doubling down, then you win the total amount of money you wagered. For example, if you initially bet $25 and then doubled down (adding $25), then after you received one additional card you won with a total of twenty, you'd receive $50 plus your two $25 chips would still remain on the table. If you doubled down with only $10 on your initial $25 bet, you'd win $35 and your $35 bet would stay down.

That's all there is to learn about the rules of blackjack. However, it's applying the basic blackjack strategy that seems to confuse players and keeps them from minimizing the house advantage. To become a good blackjack player, you must be able to use proper basic blackjack strategy. You may get lucky and win without using the basic blackjack strategy, but over time the player who uses a good strategy will win more than the player who doesn't.

BASIC BLACKJACK STRATEGY

Basic blackjack strategy has been developed by testing millions of hands on a computer simulating casino blackjack. Some of the parts of the strategy may seem strange and sometimes suicidal, but to maximize your chances of winning, you must follow the basic blackjack strategy guidelines. Nobody can guarantee that the strategy will make a winner out of you no matter what. This strategy is mainly designed to help players win more money in the long haul, as well as lose less money in those situations where they have less chance of winning.

There are minor differences in strategy used between multi-deck and single- or double-deck blackjack. Since most casinos use multi-decks (more than two) in their blackjack games, the multi-deck basic blackjack strategy will be covered first. Memorize the table below to play proper multi-deck basic blackjack strategy.

MULTI-DECK BASIC BLACKJACK STRATEGY

Player's Hard Hand Total (no aces)	Player's Decision Based on Dealer's Up Card
5	Hit no matter what the up card.
6	Hit no matter what the up card.
7	Hit no matter what the up card.
8	Hit no matter what the up card.
9	Double down (only on first two cards) against an up card of 3 through 6. Hit against everything else and don't double down.
10	Double down (only on first two cards) against an up card of 2 through 9. Hit against 10 or ace.
11	Double down (only on first two cards) against an up card of 2 through 10. Hit against an ace.
12	Hit against a 2 or 3. Stand against 4, 5, or 6. Hit against 7 through ace.
13	Stand against 2 through 6. Hit against 7 through ace.
14	Stand against 2 through 6. Hit against 7 through ace.
15*	Stand against 2 through 6. Hit against 7 through ace.
16**	Stand against 2 through 6. Hit against 7 through ace.
17, 18, 19, 20, or 21	Stand against everything.

* Surrender (if that option is available) against a dealer's ten.
** Surrender (if that option is available) against a dealer's nine, ten, or ace.

Use this strategy at all times. After you take a hit, retotal your hand and look to see what you should do according to the chart above. For example, if you have a two and four on your first two cards (a total of six), then you look at the chart for six. (It tells you to hit.) Your new card is a three. Now you have a total of nine. You look at nine and it tells you to hit against everything. (Remember: you may only double down on your first two cards.)

Use the table below if you have a soft hand (you hold an ace). Note: A soft hand becomes a hard hand when you can no longer count the ace as eleven, because that value would put you over twenty-one and bust your hand.

Player's Soft Hand	Player's Decision Based on Dealer's Up Card
Ace and 2	Double down against 5 and 6. Hit against everything else.
Ace and 3	Double down against 5 and 6. Hit against everything else.
Ace and 4	Double down against 5 and 6. Hit against everything else.
Ace and 5	Double down against 5 and 6. Hit against everything else.
Ace and 6	Double down against 4, 5, and 6. Hit against everything else.
Ace and 7	Double down against 3, 4, 5, and 6. Hit against 9 and 10. Stand on all else.
Ace and 8	Stand against everything.
Ace and 9	Stand against everything.
Ace and 10	Blackjack! Stand on everything. Don't take insurance.

The table below reveals when you should split pairs and when not to.

Player's Pair	Player's Decision Based on Dealer's Up Card
Aces	Split against everything. Note: When splitting aces, you're entitled to only one card on each ace (a total of two cards for each hand). This is a rule that most casinos follow.
Twos	Split against 2 through 7. Hit against everything else.
Threes	Split against 2 through 7. Hit against everything else.
Fours	Hit against everything.
Fives	Double down against 2 through 9. Hit against 10 and ace.
Sixes	Split against 2 through 6. Hit against everything else.
Sevens	Split against 2 through 7. Hit against everything else.
Eights*	Split against everything.
Nines	Split 2 through 6 and on 8 or 9. Stand against 7, 10 or ace.
Tens	Stand against everything. Don't ever split tens!

* Surrender (if that option is available).

Once you've split the pairs, play each hand separately. After you've split your hand, refer to either the hard hand chart or the soft hand chart, depending upon whether or not you hold an ace.

By memorizing and practicing the basic blackjack strategy, you'll become a better blackjack player. The strategies outlined in the basic strategy tables for multi-deck blackjack may be used in single- or double-deck blackjack with the following exceptions. If you can't find your hand in the charts below, use the multi-deck basic strategy chart.

■ ■

SINGLE- OR DOUBLE-DECK BASIC BLACKJACK STRATEGY

Player's Hard Hand	Player's Decision Based on Dealer's Up Card
8 total	Double down against 5 or 6. Hit everything else.
9 total	Double down against 2–6. Hit everything else.
11 total	Double down against everything.

Player's Soft Hand	Player's Decision Based on Dealer's Up Card
Ace and 2	Double down against 4–6. Hit everything else.
Ace and 3	Double down against 4–6. Hit everything else.
Ace and 6	Double down against 2–6. Hit everything else.
Ace and 8	Double down against an 8. Stand on everything else.

Player's Pair	Player's Decision Based on Dealer's Up Card
Twos	Split against 3–7. Hit everything else.
Threes	Split against 4–7. Hit everything else.
Sevens*	Split against 2–7. Hit against 8, 9, and ace. Stand against a 10.

* Surrender (if that option is available).

■ ■

Card Counting

Card counting—keeping track of the cards that have been played—is not illegal, but if you become a good card counter who wins at blackjack regularly, then you could be banned from casinos. Why do people count cards? People count cards to give them an idea of what cards are remaining in the deck. The basic blackjack strategy is based on the dealer's face-down card being a ten-value card. If a lot of high cards have been played, that is, if the deck has a large number of low cards, it's more likely the dealer's face-down card won't be a ten-value card, so the basic blackjack strategy will

The Man Who Won a Million and Lost It

On a Sunday in April of 1995, a man walked into the Treasure Island Resort and Casino with his social security check of $400. The Treasure Island Resort and Casino is upscale, something this man was obviously not. He proceeded to cash his social security check and started playing blackjack at a $5 minimum table. No matter which dealer dealt to him, he was rude and nasty. Apparently his wife had thrown him out and instructed him never to return. This man got on a lucky streak most of us would only dream of. He used no particular strategy and didn't count cards. He was just lucky. He kept increasing his bets and moving up to higher limit tables. Eventually the owner of Treasure Island Resort and Casino gave

be less useful. It's to the player's advantage if a greater number of ten-value cards (tens plus all face cards and aces) remain in the deck. It's bad for the players when there are a large number of low-value cards (2, 3, 4, 5, and 6) remaining in the deck, because the dealer has a better chance of making a bad hand good.

By counting cards, you can vary your bets according to what's remaining in the deck (including any cards currently face down on the table). Bet more when there are more ten-value cards remaining and bet less when there are more low-value cards remaining.

Why assume the dealer's hole card is a ten? Look at all the cards in a deck. Each standard fifty-two-card deck is composed of four suits (clubs, diamonds, hearts, and spades) with thirteen cards per suit. In each suit you have one of each of the following cards: ace, two, three, four, five, six, seven, eight, nine, ten, jack, queen, and king. Four of those thirteen cards have a value of ten. Therefore, in a fifty-two-card deck sixteen cards have a value of ten (four in each of the four suits). So in a standard fifty-two-card deck, just over 30 percent of the cards are ten-value cards. That's a large percentage of ten-value cards, so the inventors of the basic blackjack strategy assumed the dealer's hole card to be a ten. This is a principle you should remember in order to become a good blackjack player.

Counting cards is a very difficult task and not to be recommended for beginners, especially in a casino where the game moves pretty quickly and where there are a number of distractions. Beginners should play at a low-limit table and get comfortable playing basic blackjack strategy. Try to get to the point of playing like a robot where your play is automatically determined by the dealer's up card and by the total of your hand. To get to that point you'll need to spend a good deal of time playing at a casino blackjack table. Only after you get comfortable playing basic blackjack strategy should you begin to learn to count cards.

It's good for the players when the deck has more tens remaining than low-value cards. So how do you know what cards remain in the unplayed deck? To figure that out, count the cards that have been played. For every low-value card (2, 3, 4, 5, and 6) that's been played, count plus one (+1). For every ten-value card (ten, jack,

queen, king, and ace) that's been played, count minus one (-1). Don't worry about the mid-value cards (7,8, and 9).

To correctly estimate what cards have not been played, apply this counting method not only to your own hand, but to all the other players' cards including the dealer's. Let's take an example, starting with the first hand dealt from the deck. If you're holding 6, 5, and 8, that would be a total of plus two (one for the 6 and for the 5). If the dealer has a king and ten, that would mean minus two. The count would then be zero: plus two for your hand and minus two for the dealer's hand. This example assumes you're the only player at the table. If there are other players, then count their cards as well.

Continue to count the cards in subsequent games. The more games played from the deck before the dealer shuffles again, the more accurately you can assume what values remain to be played.

That's all there is to counting cards. It sounds simple because the math is simple, but in reality it's very difficult. This is because it's hard to keep track of several people's hands and concentrate on the game at the same time. If you become a good card counter who applies perfect basic blackjack strategy, then you can vary your bets according to the count remaining in the deck.

If you get a positive count, meaning that more low cards than ten-value cards have been played, you want to increase the size of your wager. If you get a negative count, then there are fewer ten-value cards remaining in the deck so you want to decrease the size of your wager. Here's a good rule of thumb. If the count gets to plus five, then increase the size of your bet one unit. For every count above five, increase your bet an extra unit. If the count gets to minus five, then decrease your bet one unit. For every unit below minus five, decrease your bet another unit. If the count goes too far into the negative, get up from the table and wait for another shuffle. Winning isn't likely in the cards at that point.

All of this is based on three basic facts. Counting cards yields a better idea of the values of the cards remaining in the deck. By having a better idea of what's remaining, you can increase or decrease your bets. By having certain points at which to increase

The Man Who Won a Million and Lost It
(continued)

this man a complimentary suite in the hotel. He lived life like a king for about a week or ten days. His lucky streak ran his bankroll up to around $1.5 million dollars. The whole time this man was extremely rude to the staff at Treasure Island and to their other customers. Many of the dealers were cheering for this man to lose his money because he was chasing good tipping customers away from their tables. Eventually he lost all but $50,000 of the $1.5 million dollars he had won. At that point, the owner told the man he had to leave his property and never return. It was rumored he went to downtown Las Vegas and lost the rest of his $50,000 and later died of a heart attack.

or decrease your bets, you can maximize your profits or minimize your losses.

When you're using basic blackjack strategy, you are assuming the dealer's face-down card is a ten-value card. When the count gets to plus five or higher, your chances of this being true are greater. When the count gets into the negative, the chances of the dealer's face-down card being a ten-value card are lower, making the assumptions underlying basic blackjack strategy less valid. That's why you want to lower your bets when the count is negative and increase your bets when it's positive.

Those are the basics of blackjack, along with a little bit of advanced schooling on the strategy. If you know these basics and apply the strategy, you can have a good time at a casino playing blackjack without spending too much money.

Some Points to Remember When Playing Blackjack

The point of this section is to bring some reality to playing blackjack. Some people feel they can quit their jobs and make a living playing blackjack. Very few can do this. The ones who can usually get banned from casinos. By using the techniques described in this chapter, you can expect to win sometimes in blackjack—or at least minimize your losses and have a good time playing. What follows are some mistaken notions people have about blackjack. Don't fall victim to these.

♠ *By knowing the basic blackjack strategy and applying it perfectly, I can always win at blackjack.* This is not true. By applying the basic blackjack strategy, you can cut your losses to a minimum, not guarantee winning. The rules of casino blackjack favor the house. By using basic blackjack strategy, you can lower the house's advantage over you. You can never get the upper hand by only using this basic strategy.

♠ *By counting cards, I can always win at playing blackjack.* This is not true. By counting cards you can get an idea of what's remaining in the deck, but you certainly can't predict what cards are going to be played next. By knowing what's remaining in the deck, you can cut your losses and maximize your profits. Be warned, though, casinos carefully watch players who vary their bets by large margins. They take such variations as evidence that a player is counting cards. Play it safe. If you're counting cards, be sure to only increase your bets by a couple of units at most when the deck is in your favor. A sure way to get banned from a casino is to bet the minimum until the deck gets a high positive count and then bet a couple hundred dollars.

♠ *Really good basic blackjack strategy players who count cards can make a living playing blackjack.* In most cases this is not true. If you think grinding out $20,000 from a casino is easy, then you're sorely mistaken. After all, your bankroll must be able to take large losing streaks. A professional blackjack player claimed he averaged just over $18,000 a year from playing blackjack for sixteen years. (Also, for every professional blackjack player who might be able to make a living at the game, there are thousands of players who are losing, some small and some big.) Remember that casino blackjack is geared for the casino to win. For short periods of time players can win against the casino, however, over the long haul the casino will always win against the player.

ETIQUETTE

Blackjack is a very simple game to play. However, when playing casino blackjack, even though you might be playing for low stakes, the player right next to you might be playing for high stakes. It's important to observe the proper blackjack etiquette.

The first thing is to check the table minimum-maximum sign. Please make sure you read the sign correctly. You don't want to try playing $5 at a $25 minimum table. If the dealer has dealt your cards to you and didn't notice you hadn't bet the minimum until after the deal, you may have to drop out of the game, which is likely to upset the players to your left, because your cards (now discarded) would have gone to them.

Basic blackjack strategy has become a universal approach to helping people play blackjack. When you're playing with a table of strangers, the dealer will expect you to play the basic blackjack strategy. If you stray from this strategy, the other players may start making comments, even though you're allowed to play however you want. If you're playing at a table with your friends, then feel free to play however you want. However, when playing at a table with at least one stranger, then try to play basic blackjack strategy to the best of your ability.

Here's an example. If you're the last player before the dealer's turn and you have a two-card total of fourteen with the dealer showing a six, then basic blackjack strategy tells you stand because the odds are in favor of the dealer busting (exceeding twenty-one). Let's say you hit instead of stand and you draw a ten and bust. Now the dealer turns over his face-down card and has a total of sixteen (basic blackjack strategy always assumes the dealer's face-down card is a ten-value card), so he has to hit. Now he draws a five, giving him twenty-one. Most players will lose when the dealer has twenty-one. If you had played basic blackjack strategy, you would have stayed and the ten that busted you would have gone instead to the dealer, busting him and making winners out of all the players remaining in the game—including you. When this happens, players who know the strategy may get upset and may say something to you for not playing basic strategy. It's to your advantage to play proper basic blackjack strategy, and it will make your time at a blackjack table fun and enjoyable.

Chapter Four
CRAPS

Craps is the fastest game in the casino. In fact, to run a craps table a casino generally assigns four workers. Because there's a lot of action, it's particularly important to know the rules and strategies so as not to get lost or slow down the game.

Craps is believed to have derived in the United States from a game popular in England in times past. The basic game is quite simple, requiring only two dice and a little open area to toss them. The popularity of craps peaked during World War II, as many soldiers enjoyed playing the game whenever and wherever they could gather a few comrades with some money. While craps is no longer as popular, it still draws crowds of players in a casino. If you hear a group of people in a casino making a lot of noise, they're probably playing craps. On a single throw of the dice, players can win a lot of money or lose a lot of money, so you'll often hear either cheers or loud groans of disappointment.

Craps is played with two dice on a table that's about twelve to fourteen feet long and looks kind of like a giant bath tub. Each half of the table has an identical craps layout. Figure 4-1 shows a typical craps layout. In the middle of the table is an area that's shared by both sides of the table. A game of craps can involve anywhere from one to sixteen players, with eight on each side of the table being about the maximum.

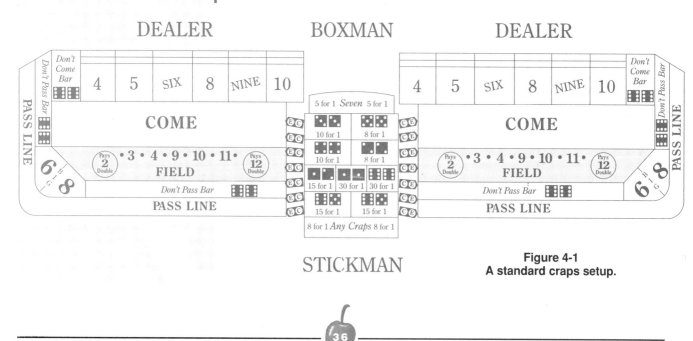

Figure 4-1
A standard craps setup.

THE RULES

A craps game is run by four casino employees: a boxman, two dealers, and a stickman. The boxman (or boxperson) is responsible for counting all cash that'll be changed by the dealers, arranging the bank of casino chips, and supervising the game. The two dealers each work half of the table and are responsible for taking losing bets, paying winning bets, and helping players make bets. The stickman (or stickperson) is responsible for keeping up the pace of the game, moving the dice to the shooter (using a rattan stick), calling the dice (what was rolled), and instructing the dealers to make payoffs for winning proposition bets.

Each player at the table gets a turn at throwing the dice. The player who's rolling or throwing the dice is called the shooter. The game starts with the stickman offering the shooter a choice of two dice out of five. The shooter must use only one hand to choose the two dice and roll or throw them to the opposite end of the table against the back wall. Everybody at the table bets on the outcome of those two cubes of plastic.

The shooter's first throw is called the come-out roll. If the dice come up seven or eleven (called a *natural*), he or she wins. If they come up 2, 3, or 12 (*craps*), he or she loses and the next player takes over as shooter. Either outcome is known as a decision roll. But if the dice total anything else (4, 5, 6, 8, or 9), that total becomes the shooter's *point*, which the dealers mark on the table with a puck—a black and white marker placed white side up in that numbered space. The shooter then continues rolling until one of two things happens: he or she throws his point again and wins (called a *pass*) or throws a seven and loses (called a *miss-out*). It's that simple. It's the bets and the terminology that complicate the game.

Everyone at the table bets on the shooter. There are many bets you can make in a craps game. Refer to the layout in Figure 4-1 to understand where the various bets are placed.

Pass Line and Don't Pass Bets

Players may bet on the basic outcome of a shooter's turn, that is, on whether the shooter will pass (win) or not pass. These opposite bets are called pass line and don't pass. If you think the shooter will make his or her point, put at least the table minimum in chips on the spot in front of you marked "pass line." If you think the shooter won't make his point, put at least the table minimum in chips on the spot just above the pass line marked "don't pass."

On the come-out (first) roll, any player who bet the pass line will win if a 7 or 11 is rolled and lose if a 2, 3, or 12 is rolled. Any winning pass line or don't pass bet gets paid even money or one to one. On the come-out roll, any player who bet the don't pass will win if a two or three is rolled, push (tie) if a twelve is rolled, and lose if a seven or eleven is rolled. Any player may bet either way, including the shooter.

Consider the following example of how the betting works. A shooter on the come-out roll throws a seven, so the two dealers take all the don't pass bets and pay off all the pass line bets. Then, the same shooter throws the dice for a new come-out roll. This time the shooter throws a five. Now the dealers will each mark the five box on their half of the layout with a puck, white side up. This indicates to all the players that the point is five. Now in order for the pass line players to win their pass line bet, the shooter must throw a five and avoid throwing a seven. For the don't pass bets it's just the opposite: for them to win, the shooter must throw a seven and not throw a five. Any other outcome of the dice won't affect the pass line or don't pass bets.

The shooter throws the dice a few more times, then sevens out—that is, he gets a seven before he can make his five. This shooter is now done and the dealers clear (collect) all pass line bets and pay all don't pass bets. The stickman next offers the player to the left of the shooter an option to roll the dice.

The pass line and don't pass bets provide the house with a small advantage—1.4 percent. The casinos get that edge by not paying the don't pass when a twelve is rolled. If they paid the don't pass when a twelve is rolled, then playing either the pass line or don't pass would be a fifty-fifty chance. For example, if you bet $100 on either the pass line or don't pass, over the course of a craps game your expected return would be $100, according to the true odds. But with the house advantage, your expected return *on average* is $98.60. The casinos are in business to make money, so they need to get their cut somewhere on each game they offer.

Come and Don't Come Bets

A come bet and the pass line bet are virtually the same bet. The only difference is when each bet can be made. A pass line bet can be made only on a come-out roll. If the shooter rolls a 4, 5, 6, 8, or 9, play continues but players cannot place any pass line bets. That's where the come bet enters into the picture. Think of it as a second chance to make a pass line bet. To make a come bet, put at least the table minimum bet directly in front of you in the large area marked "come."

On the next roll, you win if the shooter throws a seven or eleven, just as on the first roll on a pass line bet. You lose if the shooter rolls a 2, 3, or 12. If any other number comes up, then the dealer for your half of the table will move your bet from the large "come" area to the smaller box with that number, positioning it by where you're sitting. After your bet gets moved to a numbered box, you will win if the shooter rolls that number and lose if a seven turns up—whichever comes first. It's your responsibility to keep track of your come bets. If the dealer pays off your come bet, it's up to you to grab your chips or another player may do so. If your bet loses, don't worry. The dealer will surely take care of it!

Just as a come bet is similar to a pass line bet, a don't come bet is similar to a don't pass bet. You can make a don't come bet only when the shooter has established a point. To make a don't come bet, place at least the table minimum in the box marked "don't come," which is located next to the other numbered boxes closest to the dealer.

On the next throw, you win on your don't come bet if the shooter rolls a two or three. If the shooter rolls a twelve, you push or tie. (Remember the house advantage!) If the shooter rolls a seven or eleven, you lose. If any other number is rolled, a dealer moves your don't come bet behind that number in a don't come box. This bet says you think a seven will come up before the number your bet is next to. It stays there until a seven is rolled and you win or the number is rolled and you lose. All payoffs on the don't come are even money or one to one.

The house advantage on come and don't come bets is the same as pass line or don't pass bets—1.4 percent. With the house advantage that low, craps players have a reasonable chance at winning a

The Law of Diminishing Probability

One prominent gambling writer observes that he believes in a "law of diminishing probability." By this he means that if, for example, a shooter has had up to eleven straight passes, there is a greater and greater chance of not passing. In fact, he suggests that after about seven recurrences in any game, there is a much higher than 50 percent chance that this will not continue. The actual laws of probability treat each throw separately, since there is no scientific basis for any cumulative effect. But people will believe what they believe and behave accordingly.

little money. In fact, the low house advantage is one reason craps is still popular in casinos today.

Odds Bets

The odds bet (also called taking odds) is the best bet to make in a casino. It's the only bet in the casino where the casino has no advantage over the player. The casino pays the player true odds when he or she wins an odds bet.

You can make an odds bet only after you make a pass line bet, come bet, don't pass bet, or don't come bet and a point is established. Once a point is established for your pass line bet or come bet, you can place up to two times your bet behind (outside) the pass line bet or tell the dealer to put odds on your come bet. To understand how much you'll get paid for your odds bet, look at Figure 4-2.

Let's review this true odds chart. By the chart, you can see that the number most likely to roll is a seven. Why? Because the two dice can total seven in six different combinations. All the other totals are less likely to roll than a seven because they come from fewer than six combinations of the two dice. Since craps revolves around the number seven rolling, all the other numbers are compared with the seven when figuring out the true odds.

For example, the true odds of rolling a four or a ten (they each have three combinations, so the odds of rolling them are the same) before a seven are two to one. Why two to one? Let's look at the number of combinations for a seven to roll (six) and the number of combinations for a four or ten to roll (three). That's six chances to three chances, a ratio that we simplify to two to one. Since a seven is twice as likely to roll before a four or a ten, the true odds for a four or ten are two to one. The true odds for a five or nine are three to two. The true odds for a six or eight are six to five.

Odds bets are not marked on the craps layout, probably because the house has no advantage over the player on these bets and therefore has no reason to encourage them. To take odds on a pass line bet, just set an amount up to twice the amount of your pass line bet directly outside your pass line bet. If the shooter rolls the point before a seven, you'll get even money for your pass line bet and

DETERMINING TRUE ODDS

True odds are the number of ways a 7 can be made, as opposed to the number of ways any other combination of points can be rolled at a given time.

2	one way		1/36
3	two ways		2/36
4	three ways		3/36
5	four ways		4/36
6	five ways		5/36
7	six ways		6/36
8	five ways		5/36
9	four ways		4/36
10	three ways		3/36
11	two ways		2/36
12	one way		1/36

Using these figures, you get the following true odds of rolling your point before rolling a seven:

Points	True Odds
4 and 10	2 to 1
5 and 9	3 to 2
6 and 8	6 to 5

Figure 4-2
True odds of rolling different numbers with two dice.

true odds for your odds bet. Figure 4-3 illustrates how to make an odds bet on a craps layout.

For example, if the point was five and you had a $5 pass line bet with $10 odds behind it, you'd win $5 for the pass line bet and $15 for the odds bet when the shooter rolled a five before a seven. The true odds on five rolling before a seven is three to two. So to figure out what you should get paid, multiply your $10 bet by one and a half or 1.5. That's $15. You can see how important it is that you know what the true odds are for each point. That way, you'll know if you get paid correctly. Believe it or not, dealers make mistakes.

To take your odds on come bets, you must wait until the dealer moves the come bet to a number, then tell the dealer you want odds on your come bet and put down the amount you want for odds in the come area. Make sure the dealer puts your odds on the correct come bet. When there are several players this can get confusing, so watch where your come bet goes.

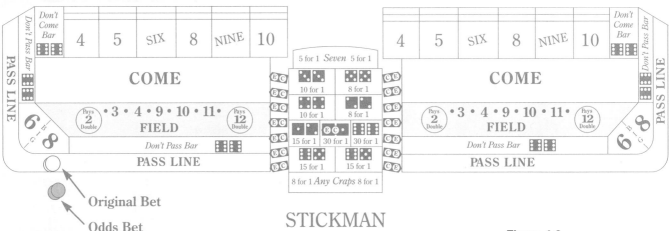

Figure 4-3
Placing chips on an odds bet.

Odds on the Don't Come or Don't Pass Bets

Laying odds is the opposite of taking odds. When you've bet the don't pass or don't come, you want a seven to roll before the point. Laying odds gets you paid at the true odds, only you have to bet more money than you'll win because the odds are in your favor that a seven will roll before the point.

For example, if the point is four and you have a $10 don't pass bet with a $20 odds bet and the shooter throws a seven before a four, you'll win $10 for your don't pass and $10 for your odds bet. The true odds of a seven rolling before a four is one to seven. A seven is twice as likely to roll as a four. Therefore, you get paid one to two on your lay bet, or half your lay bet, when the seven rolls before the four.

To make it fair to all players, the casino allows the players betting the don't side to lay an amount that they'd win if they had won a pass line bet with full odds. Players playing the don't pass and don't come can lay up to four times their don't pass or don't come bet when the point is four or ten. When the point is five, six, eight, or nine, you're allowed to lay up to three times your don't pass or don't come bet.

To lay odds on the don't pass, set the amount you want to lay in odds next to your don't pass bet. To lay odds on a don't come bet, set the amount you want to lay in odds in the come area and tell the dealer you'd like to lay X amount on your don't come bet.

Place Bets

Place bets are very similar to come bets, except you don't have to place a bet in the come or pass bar first (as with odds bets). If you want to do a place bet on the four, for example, you tell the dealer you'd like to place X amount on the four. In order for your place bet on the four to win, you need the shooter to roll a four before a seven. The only numbers you can place are the possible point numbers: 4, 5, 6, 8, 9, or 10. Place bets on the 4, 5, 9, or 10 must be made in $5 increments. Place bets on the six and eight must be made in $6 increments. The reason for this is the odds of seven to six do not make it easy to pay off $5 bets on those numbers. The payoffs on place bets are the following:

- ♠ four or ten place bets get paid nine to five: for every $5 bet, you'll win $9.
- ♠ five or nine place bets get paid seven to five: for every $5 bet, you'll win $7.
- ♠ six or eight place bets get paid seven to six: for every $6 bet, you'll win $7.

Your place bets remain on the number after that number is rolled and the dealer counts your winnings out in front of you. If you don't want your place bet to stay on that number, you have to tell the dealer to take your place bet down and return the chips to you.

Remember, for a place bet to win, the number you selected must roll before a seven. If a seven rolls, then your place bet will lose. Making place bets gives the casino a larger house advantage than it has with pass line bets or come bets. The house advantage on placing the four or ten is 6.67 percent. The house advantage on placing the five or nine is 4 percent. The house advantage on placing the six or eight is 1.52 percent. The reason for these differences is the likelihood of one of these numbers being rolled, as shown in Figure 4.2.

Buy Bets

A buy bet is similar to a place bet, only you pay a 5 percent vigorish (commission, sometimes called a vig) in order to get true odds. The only numbers that are smart to buy are the four or ten. Buying the 5, 6, 8, or 9 will only raise the house advantage higher than if you placed them. No one buys the 5, 6, 8, or 9.

To buy the four or ten, you must make a bet of at least $20. On a $20 buy bet the vigorish charged is $1 (5 percent of $20), which is paid at the time you make the buy bet. In order for your buy bet to win, you need that number to roll before a seven. If a seven rolls before that number, you'll lose the buy bet. If your number rolls, then the dealer will pay you two to one on a buy bet of four or ten.

If you want to keep the same buy bet after it wins, then you'll have to pay another vigorish of 5 percent of the bet.

The house advantage on a buy bet on the four or ten is 4.76 percent, which is lower than a place bet on the four or ten, but still not as good as a pass line or come bet.

Lay Bets

A lay bet is different from laying odds on your don't pass or don't come bets. A lay bet is the opposite of a buy bet. When you have a lay bet, you're hoping a seven will roll before the number you made the lay bet on. While it's not smart to buy the five, six, eight, or nine, it's OK to lay those numbers.

Here's an example of a lay bet. You tell the dealer you want to make a lay bet on the six. The dealer will put your chip on that number. This means you are betting that a seven will be rolled before a six comes up. If any other number besides a six or seven is rolled, nothing happens to your bet. If a six is rolled, you lose. If a seven is rolled, you win.

When you make a lay bet, you pay a vigorish (commission) of 5 percent, just like you do on a buy bet. The vigorish is 5 percent of the amount you'll win if the lay bet is successful. The minimum amount you can lay on the four or ten is $40. The minimum amount you can lay on the five or nine is $30. The minimum amount you can lay on the six or eight is $24. By paying the vigorish on lay bets, you get the true odds if a seven rolls before number you lay.

If you have a lay bet on the four or ten and a seven rolls before the number you lay, then you'll get paid one to two, or $1 for every $2 bet. If you have a lay bet on the five or nine and a seven rolls before the number you lay, then you'll get paid two to three, or $2 for every $3 bet. If you have a lay bet on the six or eight and a seven rolls before the number you lay, then you'll get paid five to six, or $5 for every $6 bet.

The house advantage on lay bets on the four or ten is 2.44 percent. The house advantage on lay bets on the five or nine is 3.23 percent. The house advantage on the six or eight is 4 percent.

Casino Dice

Casino dice are very precisely machined and true to a tolerance of 1/5,000 of an inch. The dice are made of special plastic. Spots are drilled and then filled with a paint material that is the same weight as the plastic removed from the holes. The dice are then buffed and polished so no recessions remain. The standard size dice used in nearly all casinos are 3/4 inch.

While most people only lay the 4 or 10, on occasion some people will lay the 5, 6, 8, or 9. With the higher house advantage on laying the 5, 4, 8, or 9 (because there are more combinations that yield these numbers), you're better off playing the don't pass or don't come instead of making lay bets on those numbers.

Big 6 or Big 8

On each side of a craps table there is an area near the corner with a big red six and eight. This is called the Big 6 or Big 8. This bet works the same as a place bet on the six or eight. The only difference is you get paid even money instead of seven to six. When you bet the Big 6 or Big 8, you want whichever of the two you select to roll before a seven. The minimum amount bet on the Big 6 or Big 8 is the table minimum. The house advantage on the Big 6 or Big 8 is 9.09 percent. Avoid this bet at all costs.

Field Bet

This is a bet that on the next throw of the dice one of seven numbers will roll: 2, 3, 4, 9, 10, 11, or 12. You lose if 5, 6, 7, or 8 is rolled.

To bet the field, place an amount of at least the table minimum in the area marked "field" (between the don't pass bar and the come area). Place your chips in the field directly in front of where you're standing. If any of those seven numbers rolls, you win even money or one to one. If 5, 6, 7, or 8 is rolled, you lose. If you get lucky and bet the field before a two or twelve is rolled, you'll get paid two to one on your field bet. In some casinos, they'll pay you three to one for the twelve. If you're going to bet the field, you'll want to try to play in casinos that offer three to one on the field bet.

On the surface, the field looks like a good bet. However, let's look at the true odds of one of those seven numbers rolling compared with the odds for one of the other four. On two dice there are thirty-six different combinations that can be rolled. Out of those seven numbers there are sixteen of the thirty-six combinations that can be rolled. The four losing numbers have the other twenty combinations. So the odds are once again in the casino's favor that you'll lose money on that bet in the long run. The house advantage on the field bet is 5.5 percent.

Proposition Bets

Proposition bets are located in the center of the table, directly in front of the stickman. To make a proposition bet, you toss the chips to the center of the table and call out to the stickman how much you want to bet and on what you want bet. The stickman is responsible for setting up the proposition bets in the proper place and instructing the dealers on how to pay for the proposition bets.

Proposition bets are the worst bets you can make at a craps table. The house advantage on the proposition bets ranges from 9.09 percent to as high as 16.67 percent. You'd be better off trying your luck at a slot machine in hopes of hitting a high payoff. Keep in mind that you don't have to bet the table minimum on proposition bets; sometimes you can bet as little as one dollar.

Any Seven

This is a one-roll bet that the shooter will throw a seven on the next roll. The casino pays you only four to one for this bet. The true odds of throwing a seven are five to one. The house edge on this bet is 16.67 percent. You'll often see that the table for this bet says "5 for 1." This means that for every chip you play and win, you will receive five chips (including the one you played). This is the same as four to one, but it sounds more enticing.

Any Craps

This is a one-roll bet that the shooter will roll a 2, 3, or 12 on the next roll. The casino pays you seven to one if 2, 3, or 12 is rolled. The true odds of a craps roll (2, 3, or 12 are called crap dice) are eight to one. The house advantage on this bet is 11.1 percent.

Twelve

This is a one-roll bet that the shooter will roll a twelve on the next roll. This bet attracts a large number of novice players because of its high payoff of thirty to one. Remember, there are thirty-six possible combinations on two dice, only one of which is a twelve. The true odds the casino should pay you are thirty-five to one, not just thirty to one. The house advantage on this bet is 13.69 percent.

Two

This is a one-roll bet that the shooter will roll a two on the next roll. Since the odds of throwing a two are the same as for a twelve, the casino pays you thirty to one. The true odds the casino should pay you are thirty-five to one. The house advantage on this bet, as for the twelve, is 13.69 percent.

Eleven

This is a one-roll bet that the shooter will roll an eleven on the next roll. In a craps game, eleven has the nickname of "yo." Why? Because in the noise and action, it would be easy to confuse "seven" and "eleven." So, the stickman and the dealers call out "yo" instead of "eleven." The payoff for a yo bet is fifteen to one. The true odds of an eleven coming up on the next roll are seventeen to one. The house advantage on this bet is 11.1 percent.

Three

This is a one-roll bet that the shooter will roll a three on the next roll. Since the odds of rolling a three are the same as for an eleven, the payoff is fifteen to one, although the true odds of rolling a three on the next roll are seventeen to one. As for the eleven bet, the house advantage on this bet is 11.1 percent.

Horn Bet

This is a one-roll bet that a 2, 3, 11, or 12 will come up on the next roll. There's a $4 minimum on horn bets. All this bet is doing is combining the four above bets—2, 3, 11, and 12—into a single bet. The payoff for the horn bet? If three or eleven is rolled, you get three times the amount of your bet. If two or twelve rolls, you get paid seven times the bet minus one quarter of the bet. Do yourself a favor and stay away from this bet. The house advantage on this bet is 11.1 percent.

Hard Ways

When both dice come up with the same number it's called a hard way. For example, if the shooter rolls two fives, this would be ten the hard way or a hard ten. Two and twelve are not called hard ways because the only way to make either is with a double: two ones or two sixes. The only numbers that can be rolled hard are 4, 6, 8, and 10.

Hard 4

When you bet a hard four, you're hoping for a two to come up on both dice before any other four combination or a seven. If the shooter rolls one and three, your bet loses. If the shooter rolls a seven, you lose this bet. The only way you'll win is on a double two before any other combination of four or any seven. The payoff on this bet is seven to one. The true odds of this happening are eight to one. The house advantage is 11.1 percent.

Hard 10

When you bet a hard ten, you're hoping for a five on both dice to be rolled before any other ten combination or a seven. The payoff is the same as for a hard four—seven to one. The true odds of this happening are eight to one. The house advantage is 11.1 percent.

Hard 6

When you bet a hard six, you're hoping for a three on both dice to be rolled before any other six combination or a seven. The payoff for a hard six is nine to one. The true odds of a hard six rolling before any other six combination or a seven are ten to one. The house advantage is 9.09 percent.

Hard 8

When you bet a hard eight, you're hoping for a four on both dice to be rolled before any other eight combination or a seven. The payoff for a hard eight is the same as a hard six, or nine to one. The true odds of a hard eight rolling before any other eight combination or seven are ten to one. The house advantage is 9.09 percent.

Craps-Eleven (C & E) Bet

This is a one-roll bet that the shooter will throw any crap dice (2, 3, or 12) or an eleven on the next roll. The payoff for this bet is three times the amount you bet if craps rolls (2, 3, or 12) and seven times the amount you bet if an eleven rolls. The house advantage on this bet is 11.1 percent.

There are some more obscure proposition bets that aren't listed on the craps layout. Very rarely do you see players make these other obscure bets. There are more than enough ways to bet on craps without getting into these obscure proposition bets. Also, these additional proposition bets have a high house advantage.

BASIC CRAPS STRATEGY

Craps is a very fast-paced game, especially for beginners. Stick with the basics until you get comfortable with the game. Craps is the most difficult game to learn in a casino. As a newcomer to the game, watch a game for a while before making any bets.

Once you understand what's going on, make a basic pass line or don't pass bet. If you've noticed the table to be cold (meaning shooters aren't making their point before they throw a seven), then bet the "don't" side (don't pass or don't come). If the table has been hot, bet with the shooter (pass line or come bet). After the point is established, make sure to take your full odds (the maximum in odds) bet. This is the best bet in the casino.

If you feel like you need to have more money in action, then make a come bet or don't come bet after the point is established. Be sure to take the odds on your come bet or don't come bet when it gets moved to a number. Having two numbers in action should supply you with enough excitement while you learn the game of craps.

Like every other casino game, craps tends to move in streaks. The table could get hot, where every shooter is making points, or it could be cold, where the shooter sevens out every couple of rolls. Bet with the current trend. Don't fall for the trap of "Well, the pass line is due this time." The previous results have no bearing on the outcome of the next roll.

Remember to set a realistic limit on how much you want to win or lose at a session of craps. Once you've reached either mark, quit. Hopefully you'll be able to cash in your chips for a profit.

Top Ten Craps Superstitions

1. *Never call out the number seven.* It's like the dice have ears and since most players play the pass line, seven is bad after the point is established. It's also a good way to get the other players at the table mad at you. If you need to call for it, then call it by its nickname, big red.

2. *Don't let the dice hit you when they are rolling.* The shooter at the other end of the table has the dice and tosses them to your end while you're making a bet. The dice hit your hand and come up a seven. Another bad mistake. Everyone at the table will be mad at you. Make your bets early and listen for the stickman to call out "the shooter has the dice" or something to signal to raise your hands.

3. *When the dice go off the table, always request the same dice.* Many people believe that changing the dice will cause a disruption in the flow of the game and therefore cause a seven out. To avoid this, they request the same dice. If the dice are hot, then stick with the same dice.

4. *When calling for an eleven to be rolled, call for it by its craps nickname, yo.* The only time you really want an eleven to be rolled is on the come-out roll. Calling it by its nickname seems to make it more likely the eleven will be rolled. At least it gets you involved in the game with the other players and hides the fact you're a beginner.

5. *Craps rolls come in pairs.* It seems like once one craps roll occurs, then the very next roll will be another craps. You'll often see people make the "any craps" bet after the first craps roll.

6. *A woman who's a beginner will always have a good first turn as the shooter.* Lady Luck will shine when a woman playing craps for the first time throws the dice. You should bet the pass line if the shooter is a woman, just in case she's a rookie.

7. *Never play at a craps table by yourself.* The reason no one is playing at that table is because it's cold. Playing alone won't change the table's luck. Instead, find a table with a good number of players and a lot of noise. These are the tables that are hot.

8. *Try to throw the dice so they roll as a little as possible.* It's believed that the more the dice actually tumble, the more chance they have of coming up seven.

9. *You have better luck when you throw the dice off the mirror on the table.* Many craps players believe that if you shoot the dice off the mirror, the dice will land favorably for the players. The mirror on the craps table is located on the opposite wall from the dealers. Casino personnel will discourage this activity because it damages the dice and the mirror.

10. *After the point is established, you always place the points opposite.* The odds are the same as hitting the point or hitting its opposite, so many believe that the opposite will have a greater chance of coming up than the point. Here are the possible points and their opposites: point of four, opposite ten; point of five, opposite nine; point of six, opposite eight; point of eight, opposite six; point of nine, opposite five; and point of ten, opposite four. Pairs of opposites always add up to fourteen.

ETIQUETTE

Craps can be a game where the players bond and develop a camaraderie. Usually this occurs when all the players are betting for the shooter or betting the pass line and come bets. These are known as "right bettors." If you want to feel like a part of this group instead of feeling like an outsider, then bet with them. By betting the way most of the other players bet, you'll take less criticism.

However, if you like to be a "wrong bettor" (one who bets the don't pass and don't come), then make your bets as quietly as possible. Just blend in and don't say too much. Especially don't rub it in if you win.

There are two very big common courtesy rules when playing craps. The first one is to never let your hands interfere with a roll of the dice. Players will yell at you if the dice hit your hands. Make your bets as quickly as possible after a roll so you're less likely to interfere with the next roll. It seems more often than not that when the dice hit your hands it ends up being a seven. This will cause the whole table to be angry with you.

The second rule is to never say the word "seven." It's a superstition that almost all craps players respect. By saying the word "seven," craps players believe the dice will come up seven. There is no valid truth to this superstition, but, why get everybody mad at you?

The casino would like you to obey a few rules when playing craps. If you have a drink, don't drink it over the table. Set it on the shelf below your chip rack. A drink spilled on a craps table is quite messy.

When shooting the dice, handle the dice with one hand only. Both dice must be thrown at the same time to the opposite end of the table. The casino would prefer you don't set the dice (arrange them on certain numbers) before you throw them. Some casinos will strictly enforce this preference, while others will let it pass. The casino also doesn't want you rubbing the dice on the layout before you roll them. Enough rubbing of the dice could cause them to become unbalanced. All casinos will enforce this rule.

Craps is a fast game, so take caution when playing. Money can be lost and won quickly. Keep your eye on your chips in the chip rack and on the table. With all the commotion, it's easy for players or onlookers to steal some of your chips.

If you use the conservative strategy outlined above and obey these etiquette rules, you'll have fun learning and playing craps.

This chapter will cover the American roulette wheel and not the European wheel from which it was derived. What's the difference? In Europe, the roulette wheel has the numbers one to thirty-six and a zero slot. The American roulette wheel adds a slot—double-zero. That added slot means the chances of winning are one out of thirty-eight in American roulette, a little worse than the one in thirty-seven for the European version.

The numbers are arranged around the roulette wheel in a way that seems arbitrary, even random. However, there is a method: high, low, odd, and even numbers are as mathematically balanced as possible. The zero and double-zero are at opposite sides of the wheel, odd and even numbers alternate, and the colors of the numbers alternate between black and red, with zero and double-zero standing out in green. All of the numbers offer the same chances of winning.

THE RULES

The basic action is simple. The dealer, also known as the croupier, spins the roulette wheel in one direction and rolls a small ball in the opposite direction. When the ball stops bouncing and stays in a slot, that number wins. It's a simple game with certain complications.

When sitting down at a roulette table, first take notice of the sign indicating the table minimum and maximum. Nothing is more embarrassing than betting the wrong amount of money and being scolded by the dealer. A typical roulette table minimum-maximum sign might indicate something like "$2 minimum, $500 maximum." That's fairly clear: a player has to bet at least $2 but no more than $500 per spin of the roulette wheel.

Sometimes the table minimum-maximum sign will be a little more involved, such as "Inside minimum $1, Outside minimum $2, $500 maximum." In roulette, "inside" refers to all the numbers on the betting layout (0, 00, 1–36) and "outside" refers to all the other betting areas on the roulette layout, as shown in Figure 5-1.

ROULETTE
LAYOUT

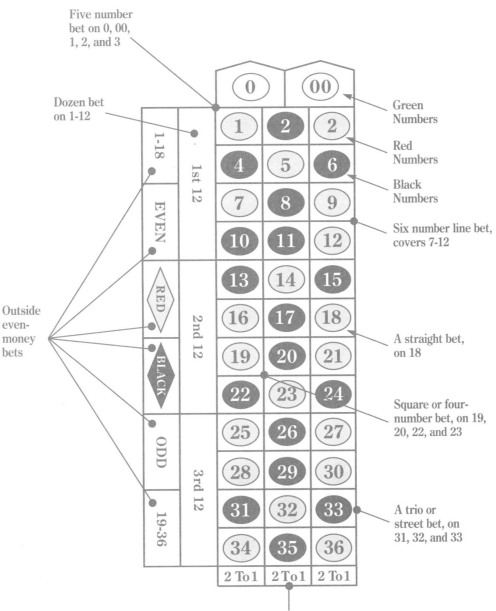

Five number bet on 0, 00, 1, 2, and 3

Dozen bet on 1-12

Green Numbers

Red Numbers

Black Numbers

Six number line bet, covers 7-12

Outside even-money bets

A straight bet, on 18

Square or four-number bet, on 19, 20, 22, and 23

A trio or street bet, on 31, 32, and 33

A column bet on 2, 5, 8, 11, 14, 17, 20, 23, 26, 29, 32, and 35

Figure 5.1
The betting layout for roulette.

55

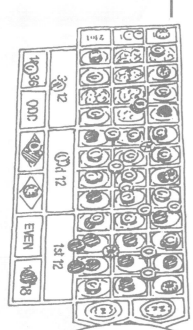

After noting what the table minimum-maximum is and making sure it's within your gambling budget, find an open seat and get roulette chips. Roulette chips are different from casino chips in that they are color-coded to differentiate between the roulette players, not according to their cash value. "Inside bets" are those made on the thirty-six number and zero and double-zero layout. "Outside bets" are all those made outside the number layout. Sometimes the betting is fast and furious, and the different chip colors make it easier to keep track of the action. Most casinos have eight colors of roulette chips. If more than eight people want to play at any one time, the extra players have to use the regular casino chips. This can become quite confusing when a few people start playing with casino chips, so the dealer may limit the number of players using casino chips.

The dealer marks the roulette chips to indicate the value the player would like for each chip. Unless the player says otherwise, the chips are usually valued at the table minimum, such as fifty cents or one dollar each. All roulette chips should remain at the roulette table. The roulette dealer will cash in your roulette chips with casino chips when you are ready to leave the table.

After getting your roulette chips, you are now ready to make some bets. Refer to Figure 5-1 to follow where the various bets are placed. Bets can be placed up until the moment when the dealer drops the ball and announces, "No more bets." In the explanations below, "chips" refers to roulette chips. Also, for each payoff indicated, remember that the bet remains on the table.

The Inside Bets

Straight Bet

This is betting that one number on the roulette layout will hit on the next spin. The payoff for a straight bet is thirty-five to one. For example, to bet $2 on the number 35, you would place $2 in chips on the number 35 on the roulette layout, making sure the chips aren't touching any lines. If 35 hits on the next spin, you win $70.

Split Bet

This is betting that one of two numbers adjacent on the layout will hit on the next spin. The payoff for a split bet is seventeen to one. For example, to bet a $5 split bet on 28 and 31, you would place $5 in chips on the line between 28 and 31. If either 28 or 31 hits on the next spin, you win $85.

Trio Bet

This is betting that one of three numbers in one row of the table layout will hit on the next spin. This is sometimes also called a street bet or a stream bet. The payoff for a trio bet is eleven to one. For example, to bet $4 on the trio 10, 11, and 12, you would place $4 in chips on the line at either end of the 10-11-12 row, making sure your chips do not touch any other line. If 10, 11, or 12 hits on the next spin, you win $44.

Four-Number Bet

This is betting that one of four numbers will hit on the next spin. The numbers must all touch at one point on the layout. The payoff for a four-number bet (sometimes called a square bet) is eight to one. For example, to bet $1 on the four numbers 25, 26, 28, and 29, you would place $1 in chips on the point where the corners of the 25, 26, 28, and 29 boxes meet. If 25, 26, 28, or 29 hits on the next spin, you win $8.

Five-Number Bet

This is betting that one of the following five numbers will hit: 0, 00, 1, 2, and 3. No other five numbers can be played. The payoff for this bet is six to one. To bet $10, you would place $10 in chips on the side lines where either 0 and 1 or 00 and 3 touch. If 0, 00, 1, 2, or 3 hits on the next spin, you win $60.

Six-Number Bet

This is betting that one of six numbers in two consecutive rows on the layout will hit on the next spin. The payoff for this bet is five to one. For example, to bet $15 on 10, 11, 12, 13, 14, and 15, you would place your $15 in chips on either side line at the point intersected by the line dividing the 10-11-12 row and the

13-14-15 row (that is, on the outside edge between 10 and 13 or the outside edge between 12 and 15). If 10, 11, 12, 13, 14, or 15 hits on the next spin, you win $75.

The Outside Bets

Red

This is betting that on the next spin a red-colored number will come up. The payoff for this bet is one to one, or even money. For example, to bet $5 on the red numbers, you place your $5 in chips on the box marked "Red" on the outside of the layout. If a red number comes up, you win $5.

Black

This is betting that on the next spin a black-colored number will come up. The payoff for this bet, as for a red bet, is one to one. For example, to bet $10 on the black numbers, you place your $10 in chips on the box marked "Black" on the outside of the roulette layout. If a black number comes up, you win $10.

Even

This is betting that on the next spin an even number will come up. (This doesn't include 0 or 00.) The payoff for this bet is even money, one to one. For example, to bet $25 on the even numbers, you place your $25 in chips on the box marked "Even" on the outside of the layout. If an even number comes up, you win $25.

Odd

This is betting that on the next spin an odd number will come up. The payoff for this bet, as for an even bet, is one to one. For example, to bet $15 on the odd numbers, you place your $15 in chips on the box marked "Odd" on the outside of the layout. If an odd number comes up, you win $15.

Low Bet

This is betting that on the next spin a number from 1–18 will come up. The payoff for this bet is even money. For example, to bet $4 on numbers 1–18, you place $4 in chips on the box marked "Low" on the outside of the layout. If a number from 1–18 comes up on the next spin, you win $4.

High Bet

This is betting that on the next spin a number from 19–36 will come up. The payoff for this bet, as for low, is one to one. For example, to bet $7 on numbers 19–36, you place $7 in chips on the box marked "High" on the outside of the layout. If a number from 19–36 comes up on the next spin, you win $7.

Column Bet

This is betting that on the next spin a number from a particular column of twelve numbers will come up. The payoff for this bet is two to one, or twice your bet. A column bet is placed at the end of the layout below the column of your choice, where it says "2 to 1" (making it easy to remember the payoff odds for this bet). For example, to bet $5 on numbers 2 through 35 (the middle column), you put your $5 in chips in the "2 to 1" box below 35. If a number from 2–35 comes up on the next spin, you win $10.

Dozen Bet

This is betting that on the next spin a number from a particular group of twelve numbers will come up. You have three choices: 1–12 (1st dozen), 13–24 (2nd dozen), and 25–36 (3rd dozen). A dozen bet is placed in the appropriate box located alongside the thirty-eight numbered boxes. The payoff for a dozen bet, as for a column bet, is two to one. For example, to bet $15 on numbers 25–36, you place your $15 in chips in the "3rd 12" box. If a number from 25–36 comes up on the next spin, you win $30.

Calculating the Odds

Here's a simple way to calculate how much a winning straight bet will pay off (thirty-five to one odds). If the bet is an even number of chips, divide the number of chips by two, multiply by seven, and add a zero to your answer. So, for 8 chips, you calculate 4 x 7 = 28, then add a zero for 280 chips in winnings. If the bet is an odd number of chips, subtract one, then divide by two, multiply by seven, add the zero, and add thirty-five to your answer. (It's easier if you bet even numbers!) So, for 15 chips, you calculate 15 - 1 = 14, 14 / 2 = 7, 7 x 7 = 49, add a zero, then 490 + 35 = 525 chips in winnings. Why not just carry around a pocket calculator? You might attract unwanted attention in Nevada. It's a felony to use computers to beat casino games. Calculating odds is legal, of course.

There are a lot of ways of betting on roulette. The following table is a quick summary of the bets and their payoffs. Understanding the layout makes it much easier to understand how the betting works, and the color coding of the chips certainly helps.

Bet	Payoff
Straight (any single number)	35 to 1
Split (two adjacent numbers)	17 to 1
Trio (row of numbers)	11 to 1
Four-Number (square of numbers)	8 to 1
Five-Number (0, 00, 1, 2, 3)	6 to 1
Six-Number (two consecutive rows)	5 to 1
Red (eighteen red numbers)	1 to 1
Black (eighteen black numbers)	1 to 1
Even (eighteen even numbers)	1 to 1
Odd (eighteen odd numbers)	1 to 1
Low (1 through 18)	1 to 1
High (19 through 36)	1 to 1
Column (twelve numbers in a column)	2 to 1
Dozen (1–12, 13–24, 25–36)	2 to 1

BASIC ROULETTE STRATEGY

Before understanding roulette strategy, you must first understand what the house advantage is in roulette. The house advantage for all roulette bets is 5.26 percent, with the exception of the five-number bet, where the house edge is 7.29 percent. What that means is that for every $100 you wager, you'll get back $94.74 on average—and only $92.71 if you stick to five-number bets. Look at this as the casino's tax.

The house advantage comes from the use of the 0 and 00 (both being green numbers, the color of money). If these two numbers weren't on the roulette wheel, there would be no house advantage. All bets would be paid off at their true odds, that is, based on the ratio of the number of times one event will occur to the number of times another event will occur. For example, if there were no 0 or 00, players betting on red or black or odd or even numbers would have a 50 percent chance of winning. But with the 0 and 00, the actual chance of a red or a black or an odd or an even number is reduced to 47.37 percent.

So by paying one to one, when your odds of winning are 47.37 percent rather than 50 percent, the casino is making 2.63 percent off your wagers over time by not paying on true odds. Since the casinos are in business to make a profit, they need this house advantage. In other words, every once in a while, 0 or 00 will come up and all bets except the ones that include these numbers will be losers. If you want to improve your chances of winning, it's better to play games and make wagers that have the least house advantage. Roulette is not one of them, but it's easy and fun to play.

It's important to remember that the house advantage is an average over a long period of time. Sometimes you'll win more than you wager and other times you'll walk away with less. As mentioned, there's one bet where the house advantage is not 5.26 percent: the five-number bet, which gives the house a whopping 7.29 percent advantage, is the worst bet in roulette.

Charting the Wheel Strategy

One of the most popular strategies for roulette is *charting the roulette wheel.* Charting the wheel means checking the wheel for any bias. (A bias means a mechanical flaw that makes a particular number more likely to come up more often than statistical laws would predict.) To do this, scout out roulette wheels and find one that's coming up with certain numbers more often than others. In a perfectly balanced roulette wheel, a number should come up on average once in every thirty-eight spins.

Since we don't live in a perfect world and since roulette wheels are material objects, there can be flaws in them. Of course, casino operators inspect wheels for bias, so the house advantage isn't affected. Some casinos help chart their roulette wheels by adding an electronic chart board that displays the results of the last twenty spins.

This is very helpful when you first walk up to a roulette table. You can quickly identify any numbers that have been hitting frequently.

Why would a casino help a player chart a roulette wheel? Because it helps them more than it helps the players. The casinos are charting only the last twenty spins, a relatively short period of time. To properly chart a roulette wheel, a player should chart at least five hundred or more spins. The electronic chart board helps players by providing them with the results of the last twenty spins. This saves players time who are using the charting strategy and allows them to get into the game more quickly. Of course, this help increases the action and attracts more bettors, so casinos that use a chart board are getting more roulette players than the casinos without boards.

When you find a roulette wheel that has a bias, start playing the same number that keeps hitting. Sometimes you'll notice a certain sector of the wheel that's hot, a sequence of three or four numbers that keep hitting more often than others. In this case bet each number, every spin. Play them for thirty-eight spins. If you are winning money after thirty-eight spins, pocket your initial gambling money plus fifty percent of the winnings, and start over with the other fifty percent of your winnings. This charting strategy is fine for people who have the time and patience (and money) to chart a roulette wheel. For impatient gamblers there is another strategy.

Column Strategy

The column strategy lets you step right up to the table and immediately get into the game without having to chart a wheel. The column strategy consists of betting two of the three columns on the roulette layout. The payoff is at two to one. So if a $5 bet on both the first and third columns and a number in the third column comes up, you win $5 ($10 for the $5 third-column bet minus the $5 lost on the first-column bet). On the next spin, add $5 to the third-column bet and then bet $5 on the second column. This is playing on the assumption that the same column will come up two times in a row. A win again in the third column will win $15 ($20 for the $10 third-column bet minus the $5 second-column bet).

On the next bet, add $5 to the third-column bet, making it $15. Then make a $5 bet on the first column again. Always increase the bet on the winning column and rotate the second bet between the losing columns. If you win two times in a row on the same column, you are then gambling with the casino's money. This means you aren't risking any of your money for the next spin; you're gambling with your winnings.

If you get on a hot streak and have won at least a quarter of your starting money, try playing a couple of numbers straight up for the betting minimum on the inside. This way you are still gambling with the casino's money (your winnings) and you might get lucky and hit one straight up. This will quickly turn your little winnings into big winnings. You can play this same strategy on the dozen boxes (1st dozen, 2nd dozen, and 3rd dozen) because they too pay off at two to one.

The general principle in the columns or dozens strategy of betting is to be able to cover a maximum of possibilities with a minimum of money. When hitting one of your two bets, you will still come out ahead even though your other bet lost. By covering twenty-four numbers with two column bets, you're betting on almost two-thirds of the numbers on the layout, leaving only twelve numbers and the zeros uncovered. You can use this same principle with the split bet, trio bet, four-number bet, five-number bet (the worst odds), and six-number bet. However, to bet these with the same amount of coverage, you'd be risking too much money. That is why betting the columns or dozens is a good strategy. If you feel tempted to try any of the other bets, bet just one of them in addition to the columns or dozens bets.

In general, roulette is a poor table game to play. The house advantage is too large for a player to consistently win. This doesn't mean you won't win at roulette, but the longer you play the better the chance that the casino will take your money.

Roulette can be a very social game and exciting when a player hits for a number straight up. The best thing to do next time you're in a casino is to find a low-limit roulette table and play for a half-hour. It's fun and a good break from some of the other table games where the house advantage isn't so high but that require more concentration.

Roulette Wheels

The roulette wheels used in most reputable casinos are built to very close tolerances and balance. They are also checked every twenty-four hours. In those casinos with several wheels, the usual practice is to move the wheels from table to table to foil any player who may have found a pattern in the wheel at a particular table.

Human Bias

Professional roulette players try to find any way of beating the odds and upsetting the house advantage. One way is through the mechanical device of checking for a bias. Another way is through human bias, that is, checking for predictable characteristics in the way a particular dealer spins the wheel and drops the ball. It's natural. In repeating the same motions over and over for hours and days and weeks, a dealer is likely to develop a certain style, which may mean that he tends to spin the wheel and drop the ball in the same way and at about the same speed. If a player studies a particular dealer long enough, he or she may detect predictable styles. Then, when the ball is dropped, if the player can calculate quickly enough where it's most likely to land, based on that dealer's style, and place bets on the several most likely numbers, he or she can perhaps beat the odds. The edge may be small, but it could pay off.

ETIQUETTE

The most important aspect of roulette etiquette is knowing when to place your bets and when to wait. Between spins, the dealer gives all the players about a minute or so to place their bets on the layout. Then, the dealer will pick up the white ball and start it spinning in the direction opposite the spin of the wheel. While the ball is spinning fast, players can continue to place bets. But when the ball slows down enough to start to drop into one of the thirty-eight slots, the dealer will wave his hand over the layout and say, "No more bets." This means all players must stop making bets and can no longer touch any chips on the layout.

After a few seconds, when the ball has stopped in a slot, the dealer marks the number of that slot on the layout with a marker of some sort. He will then remove all losing bets before he begins to pay any winning bets. Players are not allowed to touch their winning bets until the dealer has finished paying each player and has removed the marker.

The other point of etiquette is simply a matter of common sense and courtesy. With all the players around a table and all the possible bets, things can get confusing. Be careful not to move chips placed by other players. Accidentally moving a chip slightly could make a big difference. For example, moving a chip off the 15 to the borderline means the difference between a straight bet on 15 and a three-number bet on 13, 14, and 15. If 13 or 14 comes up, you're making that player a surprise winner, which would be nice. But if 15 comes up as that player hoped, the three-number payoff of eleven to one would be disappointing when the player was expecting a straight bet payoff of thirty-five to one. So, a word to the wise: Be careful around the roulette layout.

Chapter Six
CASINO POKER

Many people have played poker at one time or another. All types of people play poker: kids, professionals, senior citizens, men, women, college students, mothers, fathers, and anyone else you can think of. Poker is a game that was developed in the United States by the 1830s. Historians are unsure of how the game came into existence. In its relatively short history, poker has become the most popular card game in the world in terms of the number of people playing and the amount of money won and lost. There are many different types of poker games. This chapter will cover the two most popular poker games played in casinos—seven-card stud and Texas hold'em—leaving Caribbean stud, Let It Ride, and pai gow for the following chapters.

POKER BASICS

The object of poker is to win the *pot*—the collection of chips or other bets made by the players during a hand of poker. There are two ways you can win the pot:

1. Have the highest-ranking hand.
2. Bluff other players into thinking you have the highest hand and dropping out. (This is why a face without an expression is called a "poker face.")

The strength of a poker hand is determined according to a hierarchy based on the odds of getting a particular hand in the first five cards from a fifty-two-card deck: 1 in 649,740 for a royal flush, 1 in 72,193 for a straight flush, 1 in 4,165 for four of a kind, 1 in 694 for a full house, 1 in 509 for a flush, 1 in 255 for a straight, 1 in 47 for three of a kind, 1 in 21 for two pairs, and 1 in 2 for a pair. The stronger your hand, the better your chances of winning the pot. To become a poker player you must know the hierarchy and how hands are ranked. (The cards are valued in the usual order from ace down to 2, except that an ace may also be counted as 1 to fill out the low end of a 5-4-3-2 straight. The suits are of equal rank.)

■■■■■■■■■■■■■■■■■■■■■■■■■■■■■■■■

POKER HAND RANKINGS (FROM LOWEST TO HIGHEST)

1. **High Card**   A hand without a pair, straight, or flush, valued only by its highest card
2. **One Pair**   Two cards of the same rank
3. **Two Pair**   Two cards of one rank and another two cards of another rank
4. **Three of a Kind** Three cards of the same rank
5. **Straight**   All five cards in a sequence but not in a single suit
6. **Flush**   All five cards are in the same suit but not in a sequence
7. **Full House**   Three cards of the same rank and two cards of another rank
8. **Four of a Kind**   Four cards of the same rank
9. **Straight Flush**   All five cards in sequence and in the same suit
10. **Royal Flush**   A, K, Q, J, and 10 all of the same suit

■■■■■■■■■■■■■■■■■■■■■■■■■■■■■■■■

In all games of poker, the dealer distributes the cards to the players, clockwise from his or her left (with the number and manner depending on the particular variant of poker). The players then take turns in rounds. There are four choices. You may *check* the bet (bet nothing but still remain in the game), *call* the previous bet (bet the same amount as the previous bet), *raise* the previous bet (increase the amount of the previous bet), or *fold* (giving up a chance to win the pot by not matching a bet).

You can check only when no other player has bet any money before it gets to your turn in that round. In casino poker there are only three raises permitted per round of betting. Once one player has bet money, the next players can call, raise, or fold. To stay in the game, you must bet equal to or higher than the previous bet. If you want to fold, because you don't think you can win, you forfeit whatever you've bet in that game.

In casino poker there is a betting structure. For example, if you're playing at a $2–$4 table, you may only bet or raise in $2 increments until a player has a pair showing or until the betting has gone around the table once or twice (different casinos have different rules). At that point, the amount of increments increases to $4. Because players in poker play against one another, the casino makes its money by *raking* 10 percent of the pot for each hand of poker. The maximum rake is generally set at $3, although that maximum can vary by casino and by table, depending on the betting increments.

When the players have finished their betting, they show their cards and the dealer declares the winner based on the hierarchy of hands as listed above. If the best hands are of the same rank, such as when two players are each holding a pair or a straight, the tie is determined in the following manner:

1. **High Card**—The highest card wins, then the next highest, and so on.
2. **One Pair**—The highest pair wins. If the pairs are of equal rank, the hand with the highest single card wins. If those singletons are of the same rank, the second-highest singletons are compared, and so on.
3. **Two Pair**—The highest pair wins. If the pairs are of equal rank, the hand with the highest second pair wins. If both pairs are identical in both hands, the game goes to the hand with the higher singleton.
4. **Three of a Kind**—The highest three wins. If the threes are of equal rank, the higher singletons are compared. If they're the same rank, the hand with the highest fifth card wins.
5. **Straight**—The high end of the straight determines the winner. If the straights are equal, card for card, the pot is split evenly between the two hands.
6. **Flush**—The highest card in the flush determines the winner. If the highest cards are the same, the next highest cards are compared, and so on.
7. **Full House**—The hand with the highest three of a kind wins.
8. **Four of a Kind**—The higher of the four-of-a-kind hands wins.

9. **Straight Flush**—The hand with the higher card wins. If the higher cards are the same, the hands are tied and the players split the pot.
10. **Royal Flush**—Players with a hand this great tie and split the pot.

That's it for the basics of poker. It's a relatively simple game, combining luck, strategy, and the ability to fool others about the value of your cards. If you understand these basics of the game, then you're ready for some of the variations.

Poker variations can be divided into two basic lines: draw and stud. The primary difference is that in draw poker the players hide all their cards from the other players, while in stud some cards from each hand are revealed. In draw poker, the players are allowed to discard as many as three cards from the hand dealt to them, in the hopes of getting new cards to make a better hand. There are at least two dozen versions of draw poker and a similar number of variations of stud poker. Draw poker is generally more popular, but big-money gamblers prefer stud poker.

STUD POKER

Stud poker is played in a series of rounds. After each round of betting, players get additional cards that can change the rank of their hand. After players receive new cards, they have another chance to bet. After the players have received all their cards and have made their final bets, there's the *showdown*. That's when all the remaining players (those who have not folded) show their cards to determine the winner.

The showdown begins with the player who made the first bet of the last dollar amount bet in the game. Consider the following round of betting. Player A bets $4. Player B raises Player A by betting $8 total ($4 for Player A's bet plus the $4 raise). Player C folds (drops out of the game). Player D calls by betting $8. Player A calls by betting $4. (Player A has already bet $4 in the round, so to call the bet of $8, he needs to throw in another $4.) Player B would have to reveal his hand first. Then, in a clockwise motion in turn, any player who can beat Player B's hand reveals their hand. If they can't beat Player B, they put their cards on the table face down.

Each poker game is different, so the number of rounds of betting may vary. In casino seven-card stud there are five betting rounds, while in casino Texas hold'em there are only four betting rounds.

In casino poker the game is run by a casino dealer, who deals every round, lets the players know whose turn it is to bet, what the player bet, and what rank of hand the players are showing, and then takes the casino's rake out of each pot. You must bet with chips—no cash. You're also not allowed to go into your purse, wallet, or pocket to get extra money. Extra cash may be kept on the table under your chips, and can be exchanged for chips, if necessary.

It's very important to wait until your turn to bet in casino poker. Betting out of turn can influence other people's bets—and get on their nerves. When playing casino poker, place your bets right in front of you. Do not throw your chips into the main pot as you might during a private poker game at a friend's house. Instead, let the dealer take the bets and put them into the main pot. Throwing chips into the main pot can cause confusion. When betting or raising in casino poker, place your chips in front of you in a single motion. In other words, you can't place chips to call the bet and then place more chips to raise.

SEVEN-CARD STUD: THE RULES

Seven-card stud is one of the original poker games. A standard fifty-two-card deck is used. Each player receives a total of seven cards, hence the name of the game. (Only five of those seven will be used to determine the value of the hand in the showdown.)

The game begins with the dealer dealing each player three cards, two face down (these are called "hole cards") and one face up. In casino seven-card stud, the player with the lowest up card must open the betting by betting $1. Every bet after that must be the minimum table bet. If it's a $2–$4 table, then every bet in the first betting round after the player who opens must be $2.

After the first round of betting ends, the dealer gives all remaining players (those who didn't fold) another card face up. (Players who fold don't reveal their hands. This would give the other players some idea about the cards the players who remain might have in their hands.) The second round of betting begins with the player with the highest-ranked poker hand showing. This will either be a high card (an ace or king, for example) or a pair. Again, all bets and raises must be in $2 increments, unless at least one player has a pair showing. In that case, the betting can be raised to the table maximum, $4. If a $4 bet is made in this round, then all bets and raises in this round must be in $4 increments.

After the betting in round two has been completed, the dealer gives each remaining player a fifth card, face up. Once again, the player with the highest hand showing begins the betting. If there is a tie for the highest hand showing, then the tying player who's closer to the dealer's left starts the betting.

At the end of the betting in round three, the dealer gives each remaining player a sixth card face up. Again, the player with the highest hand showing begins betting round four. If no player has a pair showing, then in this round players are still allowed to bet the table maximum, in this case $4. The betting doesn't have to be raised to the maximum; it's just an option.

After round four, the dealer gives all remaining players their last card face down. Now all players who are still in the game will have seven cards, three face down and four face up. The fifth and final betting round begins with the same player who started the fourth betting round. This is because the face-up cards remain the

How to Win by Losing

In poker rooms they've invented something called a "Bad Beat Jackpot." In order to win a Bad Beat Jackpot, you need to lose a game of poker with what would usually be a winning hand. The minimum hand needed to receive the Bad Beat Jackpot varies by casino. A usual minimum hand is four of a kind. Ironically, you're usually better off losing with a good hand and winning the Bad Beat Jackpot than you are winning the hand. Las Vegas Station casinos have taken the bad-beat jackpots to a new level, introducing Station's Super Bad Beat

same, since the seventh card was dealt face down. After all players have had a chance to bet or fold, then the showdown begins.

The players take turns revealing their hands, clockwise starting with the player who first made the last betting increment. Then it's basic poker: the player with the best hand wins.

All of this probably sounds more confusing than it really is. Let's take a look at an example of game of seven-card stud. In this example, there will be seven players. (That's the maximum number of players in seven-card stud, because there are only fifty-two cards used.) The players are Randy, Dan, Beth, Keith, Linda, Tracey, and Tom, seated in that order around the table from the dealer's left. The table limit game is $2–$4.

The Deal

The dealer deals everyone three cards, two face down and one face up.

(X = face-down card, C = clubs, D = diamonds, H = hearts, S = spades)

Randy: X, X, king S
Dan: X, X, 6 H
Beth: X, X, 8 D
Tom: X, X, 3 H
Keith: X, X, ace S
Linda: X, X, king H
Tracey: X, X, 5 D

After the deal, Tom starts the betting because his 3 is the lowest face-up card. Tom bets one dollar. The betting now continues in a clockwise motion. Keith now has a choice to call, raise, or fold. He decides to call (match Tom's bet and stay in the hand), so he bets $1. Next is Linda, who decides to raise the bet, putting in $2. (Two dollars is the table maximum until there's a pair showing.) Then Randy must call (bet $2), raise, or fold. Randy doesn't like his hand, so he folds and is out of the rest of this hand. He puts his cards face down, to hide them from the other players. He doesn't lose any

money on this hand because he didn't bet anything. Next is Dan, who decides to raise the bet. He puts in $4: $2 to match Linda plus another $2, which is his raise. Keep in mind he can only raise $2—no more, no less. The last of our seven players, Beth, decides to fold, so she's out of the hand but doesn't lose any money.

Now we're back to Tom, who started the betting at $1. If Tom wants to remain in the hand, then he must call Dan's raise, by adding $3 to the pot. Tom figures that his hand may be worth the minimum bet of $1, but it's not worth $4, so he decides to fold and is out of the hand, losing his $1. Now Keith, who called Tom's $1, needs to bet $3 in order to call and stay in the hand, which he does. Linda bet $2 last time, so she'll need to bet $2 to call or she can fold. Linda calls and bets $2. It's the same for Tracey: to remain in the hand, she must call by betting $2. When she puts in her $2, the first round of betting is finished because we're back to Dan and everyone has called his $4 bet: the four remaining players—Keith, Linda, Tracey, and Dan—each have $4 invested in the hand.

The dealer gives the four remaining players one card each. Their hands now look like the following:

Keith: X, X, ace S, 4 S
Linda: X, X, king H, 6 C
Tracey: X, X, 5 D, 10 D
Dan: X, X, 6 H, 2 D

The betting in round two begins with Keith, because his face-up cards give him the best hand at this stage. (Note: straights and flushes must consist of five cards, so even though Keith has two spades up and Tracey has two diamonds up, which means both could be on their way to a straight, it's just two cards at this point—an ace and a 4 for Keith and a 5 and a 10 for Tracey.) Since no player has a pair showing, the highest card face up is Keith's ace. Keith decides to bet $2, the table maximum when no one hand has a pair showing. Next Linda decides to call and bets $2. Tracey raises, betting $4 ($2 for Keith's bet and $2 for the raise). The other players can't tell from her raise if Tracey has just a good hand or a great hand, because any raise in this round must be $2—no more

How to Win by Losing
(continued)

Progressive, which links the company's three Las Vegas casino resorts. Beginning with an initial jackpot of $50,000, poker players will have a shot at the jackpot. Not only will the person losing the hand with a qualified "bad beat" get paid, but everyone playing poker in any of the three casinos will also get a cut: 40 percent goes to the losing hand, 20 percent to the winning hand, 10 percent to the other players at the table, and 30 percent to the rest of the players in the three casinos.

and no less. Next comes Dan, who needs to bet $4 to call and remain in the hand. Dan decides to fold and turns over his cards face down, losing the $4 he bet in round one. Now it's back to Keith, who must call with $2, fold, or raise. Keith decides to call and bets $2. Back to Linda, who faces the same decision as Keith. She too decides to call, adding $2 to the pot. This ends the second betting round.

The players remaining in the hand—Keith, Linda, and Tracey—each receive another card face up. The hands are then as follows:

Keith: X, X, ace S, 4 S, 3 S
Linda: X, X, king H, 6 C, king D
Tracey: X, X, 5 D, 10 D, ace C

Now the third round of betting begins. Linda has the highest hand showing, with a pair of kings, so she begins this round. She can either check (bet nothing but remain in the hand) or bet $2 or $4. (The higher increment is possible, now that a pair is showing.) Linda decides to check. Next comes Tracey. She thinks both Keith with his three spades and Linda with her pair of kings have potentially better hands than she does, so she also checks. Next is Keith. Keith may now bet or check. Keith decides to check. This ends this round of betting. No additional money was bet this round and no players were eliminated.

Now the three players receive another card face up. This is the last card they'll get face up. After this round of betting, they will get one more card face down. The hands look like the following:

Keith: X, X, ace S, 4 S, 3 S, 2 S
Linda: X, X, king H, 6 C, king D, 9 D
Tracey: X, X, 5 D, 10 D, ace C, ace H

Tracey has the highest hand showing, with a pair of aces, so she begins the betting. She can bet ($2 or $4), check, or fold. (It's never smart to fold when you can check, because it doesn't cost anything to check and you can always fold on your next turn to bet.) Tracey thinks her hand is good enough to beat Keith and

Linda, so she bets $4. Next is Keith. The cards showing give him a chance at a flush, even a straight flush (since the ace can be counted as the low end of a 5-4-3-2 sequence). Keith is holding a very good hand, so he wants to raise the stakes a little, but not so much as to scare Linda and Tracey into folding. Since the goal is not just to win the hand, of course, but to win as much money as possible, it's important to sense just how far you can push the other players without forcing them to fold. So Keith raises Tracey's bet by $4, putting in $8 ($4 for Tracey's bet and a $4 raise). Next is Linda. It will cost her $8 to call, $12 to raise, and nothing but all her bets to this point to fold. She decides to call and bets $8. If she had raised, then the other two players would have had to put in an additional $4 to stay in the hand. That would have been fine for Keith, but Tracey may have only the pair of aces showing and she might have dropped out. So, Keith and Tracey can wonder about what Linda's holding. It's good, but how good?

The last card for each remaining player is dealt face down. Each remaining player's hand looks like the following:

Keith: X, X, ace S, 4 S, 3 S, 2 S, X
Linda: X, X, king H, 6 C, king D, 9 D, X
Tracey: X, X, 5 D, 10 D, ace C, ace H, X

Now each player has received seven cards total, three face down and four face up. Tracey is once again the first to bet, since the final card dealt is face down, so the betting order is the same as for the previous round. Tracey believes she still has the best hand and bets $4. Keith once again raises Tracey's $4 bet, to $8. Linda didn't get the card she needed to help her hand and she knows Tracey has her beat with just the face-up cards, so she folds and is out of the hand, at a loss of $12.

The betting returns to Tracey, who has the option of putting $4 in the pot to call, raising again, or folding and letting Keith win the pot. She decides to raise, betting $8 ($4 for Keith's raise plus $4 for her raise). Keith then decides to raise again, and bets $8. That's the third raise, so there'll be no more raises. It's back to Tracey. Now she can call and bet $4 or fold and let Keith have the pot. Tracey decides to call and bets $4. Now it's time for the showdown.

Since Tracey called Keith's last bet, Keith must put down his five-card hand first. His seven cards are the following:

Keith: 7 S (X), jack C (X), ace S, 4 S, 3 S, 2 S, 10 H (X)

The best five-card poker hand Keith can make out of his seven cards is a flush—ace S, 7 S, 4 S, 3 S, and 2 S. Keith was one card (5 S) away from a straight flush, because he would have used the ace to complete the straight to the five (ace, two, three, four, and five).

Tracey must now beat a flush in order to win the pot. Her hand looks like the following:

Tracey: 7 D (X), 5 H (X), 5 D, 10 D, ace C, ace H, and jack S (X)

The best hand Tracey can make out of her cards is two pair, aces and fives. A flush is higher than two pair, so Tracey tells Keith he wins the pot and Tracey turns over her cards face down. Tracey lost $28 on that hand. The amount in the pot was $73. The casino rakes its share—$3, the maximum, since 10 percent would be greater than the maximum. Keith wins a total of $70, but since he put $28 in bets into the pot, his profit is $42.

That's an example of how a hand of seven-card stud is played. There's a little bit of luck, skill, and psychology in seven-card stud, so you have to become proficient at reading people and their hand potential in order to be a good seven-card stud player.

SEVEN-CARD STUD STRATEGY

To become a good seven-card stud poker player, you'll need to be able to recognize when to stay and when to fold after your first three cards are dealt to you. Below is a list of hands you should continue playing if you receive them on the opening deal:

1. Any three of a kind.
2. Any high pair (tens, jacks, queens, kings, or aces).
3. Any three cards to a straight flush.

4. Any three high cards to a flush.
5. Three cards in a sequence.
6. Any pair in the hole (that is, both cards in the pair are face down).

You must be patient to be a good poker player. You may go through long spells where you don't get dealt any of the above three-card hands, so you're better off folding as soon as possible, rather than betting and then hoping you'll draw a card to help you out. Since you can't count on luck to be with you all the time and since it's unwise to bet on every hand, you must learn to maximize your profits when you get dealt a good hand. You do this by learning to read the other players. Reading a player is learning how they bet, what hands they stay in on, and whether they can read you correctly.

From this reading comes the skill of poker playing. It'll take you a while to become proficient at reading players. A good method to use is to fold on the first ten or so hands, regardless of what you are dealt. This will give you time to concentrate and get a read on each player before you start gambling with your money. Because poker strategy is based on psychology and experience as much as on any formula, you need to play a lot to become a good player. There are also many books on this subject. If you become intrigued by this game, you should find and read some of these books. But the most important lessons to be learned come through experience: at poker, a good psychologist will generally beat a good mathematician.

TEXAS HOLD'EM: THE RULES

Texas hold'em and seven-card stud are somewhat similar. The main difference is that in Texas hold'em everyone has only two cards each (face down) for personal use and five cards face up in the middle of the table, to be shared by all the players. (Those are called "community cards.") So each player has seven cards from which to make the best five-card poker hand—except that five of those cards are used by all the other players as well. Texas hold'em can be played by up to nine players. Another difference is there are only four betting rounds in Texas hold'em as opposed to five in seven-card stud.

Texas hold'em is played with a standard fifty-two-card deck. Before any cards are dealt, there are two initial bets called *blinds* (because there are no cards yet on which to bet). This is the equivalent of an ante in other card games. The players that put in the two initial bets are determined by the button, a marker that rotates clockwise around the table, so that betting begins with a different player every game. The player to the left of the button puts into the pot a *small blind*. The player to the left of that player puts into the pot a *big blind*. Usually the big blind is the amount of the low spread and the small blind is usually half the big blind. (The spread is the table limit.) For example, in a $2–$4 game, the big blind would $2 and the small blind would be $1.

The casino dealer then deals each player two cards face down. Then, the player to the left of the big blind must call, raise, or fold. To call, that player would have to bet the same amount as the big blind. To raise, that player would bet the amount of the big blind plus the small amount in the betting spread. For example if you're playing at a $2–$4 table, the small amount is the $2 bet. Betting moves clockwise until either a player has folded or has called the last bet. There may be only three raises per round of betting.

After the first round of betting, the casino dealer deals each player three cards, face up in the middle of the table. These first three community cards are called the *flop*. Now all players remaining in the game have two cards for themselves face down and three cards face up that are shared by all players.

Next is another round of betting, starting with the player to the left of the button and moving clockwise. Each player has a choice to check (stay in but bet nothing, if no one else has bet any money), bet, raise (only if another player has previously bet), or fold (drop out and forfeit the pot). A bet may consist of the small spread or the large spread. (The large spread is an option only after the flop.) Betting continues until each player has called the last bet or folded. Again, there's a limit of three raises per round.

After the second betting round, the casino dealer reveals the fourth community card. Then comes a third round of betting. Once again, betting begins left of the button. This round of betting is identical to the previous round. Each player has a choice to check, bet, raise, or fold. The round ends when all players have either called the last bet or folded.

Next, the casino dealer reveals the final community card. Now the players each have two cards face down in their hands, plus the five community cards face up in the middle of the table. From these seven cards, each player remaining in the game must make the best five-card poker hand. The remaining players make their final bets. Once again, just as in the two previous betting rounds, the first player to the left of the button begins this round of betting. The choices are still to check, to bet, to raise, or to fold. After each player has either called the last bet or folded, the showdown begins.

The showdown starts with the player who made the last bet, not the last player who called. This player reveals his or her best five-card poker hand. Going clockwise around the table, the remaining players show their hands, if they can beat the previous high hand. If they can't beat the high hand, they're out. The player with the highest hand wins the pot. In the event of a tie, the players involved in the tie split the pot.

Take a look at a sample hand of Texas hold'em. In this example, there will be nine players: Mark, Jennifer, Kurt, Rob, Mike, Joe, Pam, Debbie, and George. Nine is usually the maximum number of players in Texas hold'em, but some casinos allow more players. The table betting limit is $2–$4.

The Deal

Everyone is dealt two cards face down.

(* = button, X = face down card, C = clubs, D = diamonds, H = hearts, S = spades)

*Mark: X (10 C), X (7 C)
Jennifer: X (6 C), X (10 S)
Kurt: X (8 S), X (ace S)
Rob: X (2 H), X (queen C)
Mike: X (9 D), X (6 H)
Joe: X (3 S), X (2 C)
Pam: X (4 S), X (4 C)
Debbie: X (ace D), X (king C)
George: X (3 H), X (6 S)

Mark has the button in front of him, so the two players to his left—Jennifer and Kurt—must pay the blinds. Since the betting spread is $2–$4, Jennifer pays the small blind ($1, half of the lower amount) and Kurt pays the big blind ($2, the lower amount).

After the blinds are paid, the dealer gives each player two cards, one at a time in a clockwise motion, starting with Jennifer because she is the first person to the left of Mark, who has the button. Then the first round of betting begins.

Rob begins the betting, because he's the player to the left of the player who paid the big blind (Kurt). Rob's choices are to call, raise, or fold. If Rob wants to call, he has to pay $2, the amount of the big blind. If Rob wants to raise the bet, he can raise it $2, no more, no less. (The betting increments in our example are $2 or $4. Players can bet the $4 increment only after the fourth community card is revealed.) Rob's two cards—a two of hearts and a queen of clubs—are pretty weak, so he decides to fold. He doesn't lose any money on this hand.

The next player to go is Mike, to the left of Rob. He's holding a six of hearts and a nine of diamonds, another weak hand. Mike's choices are the same as Rob's: call, raise or fold. Mike decides to fold, so he doesn't lose any money on this hand either.

The next player is Joe. He has a two of clubs and a three of spades. He can call, raise, or fold. Since he has two cards to a straight and wants to see the flop (the first three community cards), he calls the big blind bet of $2.

The next player is Pam, who has a pair of fours. Her choices are to call (bet $2), raise (bet $4, $2 for the call and a $2 raise), or fold. Pam has a start to an OK hand, so she's going to drive out some players by raising the bet. Pam raises and bets $4.

The next player is Debbie. She's holding an ace of diamonds and king of diamonds, very good cards with a lot of potential to develop into a strong hand. Debbie's choices are to call (bet $4), raise (bet $6, $4 to call and a $2 raise), or fold. Since her hand is not much right now, but with a good possibility of developing into a strong hand, she calls and bets $4.

Next is George. His two cards are six of spades and three of hearts, a very weak hand. His options are to call (bet $4 to call Pam's bet), raise (bet $6, $4 to call plus the $2 raise), or fold. George decides to fold and is out of the hand without losing any money.

Next comes Mark, and his two cards are the ten of clubs and seven of clubs. A good start to a possible straight, flush, or straight flush. Mark's choices are to call (bet $4 to call Pam's bet), raise (bet $6, $4 to call plus the $2 raise), or fold. Mark decides to call and bets $4.

Now we are back to Jennifer. Jennifer first bet the small blind, which is $1. To remain in the hand, she must now either call, raise, or fold. To call would cost $3. Why only $3? Since Jennifer already bet $1 for the small blind, she'd now have to put into the pot the difference between the small blind ($1) and the last bet ($4). With only a six of clubs and a ten of spades, Jennifer decides to fold and is out of the hand with a loss of $1.

Now it's Kurt's turn again. Kurt initially bet the big blind, $2. If he wants to stay in the hand, he must either call (bet $2 to make up the difference between the last bet and the big blind bet) or raise (bet $4, $2 to call to make up the difference between the big blind and current bet plus a $2 raise). Kurt can also fold and be out of the hand. Since he has two spades, he decides to call and bets $2.

Now it's Joe's turn again. The first time around he called the big blind bet of $2. Now he can call (bet $2 more to call Pam's bet), raise (bet $4, $2 to call plus $2 to raise), or fold. Joe decides his chances of getting a straight and beating the four other players are slim, so he decides to fold. Joe's loss on this hand is $2.

Now we are back to Pam. Since everyone called her bet of $4, it's time to reveal the flop or the first three community cards. The casino dealer deals three cards to the center of the table face up, so all remaining players can see the cards. The cards are seven of diamonds, ten of diamonds, and king of hearts. Each player mentally adds these three community cards to his or her hand. The table now looks like the following:

Want to be the Best Poker Player in the World?

Every spring Binions Horseshoe Casino, in downtown Las Vegas, hosts the World Series of Poker. It attracts professional and amateur poker players from around the world who each pay a $10,000 entry fee. The poker game is Texas hold'em and lasts for three or four days. The winner walks away with over a million dollars. Throughout the month leading up to the World Series of Poker, from mid-April into mid-May, Binions hosts different types of poker tournaments, some of which award the winners an automatic entry into the World Series of Poker. If you have the nerve to ante up the $10,000 and face down the best players in the world, you could be crowned the World Series of Poker champion and walk away with a million dollars.

Community Cards: 7 D, 10 D, king D
*Mark: X (10 C), X (7 C)
Kurt: X (8 S), X (ace S)
Pam: X (4 S), X (4 C)
Debbie: X (king C), X (ace D)

Now the second round of betting begins. Pam is the first player still in the hand to the left of Kurt, who paid the big blind, so she begins the second round of betting.

Pam still holds just a pair of fours: the community 7 D, 10 D, and king D are of no good to her at this point. Her choices are to check (bet nothing but remain in the hand), to bet $2, or fold. She decides to check and see what happens.

In Debbie's hand, the community king D teams with the king C in her hand to give her a pair or four diamonds, for a possible flush. She can check (bet nothing and stay in the hand), bet $2, or fold. Debbie decides to bet $2 on the possibility of getting her flush.

Mark benefits from the community's 7 D and 10 D to pair up with the 10 C and 7 C in his hand, for two pair. His choices are to call (bet $2 to call Debbie's bet), raise (bet $4, $2 to call Debbie's bet and $2 to raise), or fold. On the strength of the two pair, Mark decides to raise and bets $4.

Kurt's best poker hand right now is ace high. The community cards don't help him at all. His choices are to call (bet $4 to call Mark's bet), raise (bet $6, $4 to call Mark's bet plus $2 to raise), or fold. Since he didn't get good cards on the flop, Kurt decides to fold. His loss on this hand is $4.

We're back to Pam. Pam checked the first time around, so she now needs to call (bet $4 to call Mark's $4 bet), raise (bet $6, $4 to call and $2 to raise), or fold. (Note: Only in casinos in Nevada can you check and raise in the same round.) Pam reevaluates her hand and decides to fold, losing $4 on this hand.

Now we're back to Debbie. Debbie bet $2 the first time around this round, on her pair of kings. Her choices now are to call (bet $2 to call Mark's bet), raise (bet $4, $2 to call and $2 to raise the bet), or fold. Debbie decides to call and bets $2. This ends the second round of betting.

Now we're down to two players, Mark and Debbie. The casino dealer deals the fourth community card face up in the center of the table: a king of spades. Now the table looks like the following:

Community Cards = 7 D, 10 D, king H, king S
*Mark's hand = X (10 C), X (7 C)
Debbie's hand = X (king D), X (ace D)

Now the third round of betting begins with Debbie, the first remaining player to the left of the player who bet the big blind. The fourth community card makes her pair of kings into three kings. She also has the possibility of getting a flush if the last community card is a diamond. Debbie's betting choices are check, bet (bet either $2, or $4, the higher increment now that there are four community cards), or fold. Debbie decides to bet $4, since she feels she has a stronger hand than Mark.

Mark's best hand is still two pairs, kings and tens. Actually, he could also have a pair of sevens, but poker hands can consist of only five cards, so he goes with the two higher pairs. Mark didn't improve his hand this round. His choices are to call (bet $4 to call Debbie's bet), to raise (bet $8, $4 to call Debbie's bet plus $4 to raise), or to fold. He decides to call and bets $4. This ends the third round of betting.

Now the casino dealer deals the final community card face up in the middle of the table. That fifth community card is the king of clubs. Now the table looks like the following:

Community Cards: 7 D, 10 D, king H, king S, king C
*Mark: X (10 C), X (7 C)
Debbie: X (king C), X (ace D)

Debbie begins the final round of betting because she is the first remaining player to the left of the player who paid the big blind. Debbie's poker hand is very strong: four kings. Debbie's choices are check (bet nothing but remain in the hand), bet ($2 or $4), or fold. Debbie decides to bet $4.

Mark's hand has improved to a full house, three kings and two tens. Mark's choices are call (bet $4 to call Debbie's bet), raise (bet $8, $4 to call Debbie's bet plus $4 to raise), or fold. Mark decides to call and bets $4. Now the hand is over, except for the showdown.

Mark called Debbie's final bet, so Debbie must form her best poker hand. She turns over her two hole cards and says "four kings." Mark would now reveal his cards if he could beat Debbie's hand. Since he can't, he concedes the hand and the money in the pot goes to Debbie.

The total amount in the pot is $43. The 10 percent casino rake would be $4.30, but the maximum is $3, so the pot is reduced to $40. Debbie makes a profit of $24 and Mark loses $16 on this hand. This completes a hand of Texas hold'em.

TEXAS HOLD'EM STRATEGY

Like seven-card stud, you'll need to know when to continue your hand by judging the value of your first two cards. To play Texas hold'em well, you'll need to be patient, be able to read players, and have a little bit of luck. If you want to cut your losses and maximize your profits, you should stay only on these two-card hands:

1. Any high pair (ten, jack, queen, king, ace).
2. Any ace and king of any suit.
3. Any ace and queen of any suit.
4. Any ace and jack of any suit.
5. Any king and queen of any suit.
6. Any queen and jack of any suit.
7. Any jack and ten of the *same* suit.
8. Any king and ten of the *same* suit.
9. Any king and jack of any suit.
10. Any ten and nine of the *same* suit.
11. A pair of nines.
12. Any queen and ten in the *same* suit.
13. Any nine and eight in the *same* suit.
14. Any eight and seven of the *same* suit.

By playing only when your first two cards are in the list above, you'll minimize your losses. By keeping to the above list, you'll play only when you have a reasonable chance to win the hand. You'll still need to get lucky and get some good community cards to go with your first two cards, but at least you'll be off to a good start.

Learn to read the other players and their betting styles. Someone's betting style might be to stay in every hand in the hopes of drawing a good hand. Knowing this when you're still in can be very profitable to you. As in seven-card stud, it'll take some time to learn how to read players, but once you develop that skill, you'll be a much better Texas hold'em player.

POKER ETIQUETTE

In casino poker games you are up against other players at your table. That's different from every other casino game, where it's you against the dealer. Using proper etiquette in casino poker can make it a fun game. However, one breach of etiquette can turn a whole table of players against you.

The first thing to make sure of when playing casino poker is to verify the type of poker game being played and its table limits. It can be very embarrassing if you sit down to play seven-card stud and they're playing Texas hold'em. The same is true if you think you're playing at a $2–$4 table and it's actually $5–$10.

After you verify the type of poker and the table limit, be sure to bet, raise, check, or fold on your turn. It's not good etiquette to bet out of turn. Making bets when it's not your turn can change the way other players bet. For example, if the player to your right (who bets before you) isn't sure whether or not he's going to call the bet, and then you raise the bet before he makes his decision, this could very well cause that player to fold instead of call. That means less money in the pot for the eventual winner and makes the game less interesting.

Understand how the game is played, pay attention, and avoid making mistakes. Then you and your fellow poker players will have an enjoyable time—and you may walk away from the table with some chips in your hands.

Chapter Seven
CARIBBEAN STUD POKER

I f you enjoy playing poker, then Caribbean stud poker can be a fun table game to play with a lure of winning a large jackpot. Caribbean stud poker is played on a table that's similar to a blackjack table. As in blackjack, it's you against the dealer.

This game became popular in the Caribbean and on cruise ships. Both have been notorious for not offering the players the best odds in casino games. This is partly due to the lack of competition. After all, what are you going to do, leave the cruise ship and gamble elsewhere? In general, Caribbean stud poker is not a good game to play because of the large house advantage, 5.3 percent. Bearing that in mind, it can still be a fun game to play that offers the chance to win a lot of money quickly.

THE RULES

The game is played with a standard fifty-two-card deck. As many as six can play. In front of each player is an ante square, a betting circle, and a $1 slot for the chance at the progressive jackpot. The object of the game is to beat the dealer's hand. In the ante square,

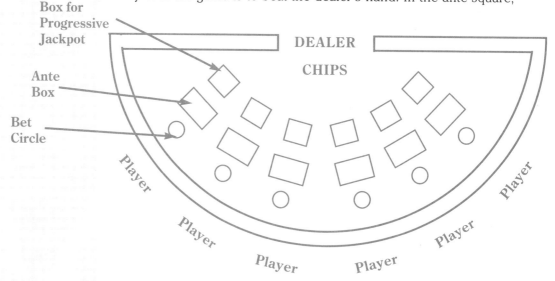

Figure 7-1
A typical Caribbean stud layout.

each player puts a wager of at least the table minimum and no more than the table maximum. The dealer then deals each player five cards face down and five to himself, with the last card for players and dealer turned face up. Figure 7-1 shows the Caribbean stud table.

You now have to decide to play your hand or fold. If you decide to fold, you lose your ante wager. If you think you can beat the dealer's hand, then play. If you decide to play, you must place double your ante in the betting circle. The amount you can bet must be exactly double your ante wager. After all the players have decided to play or fold, the dealer then reveals his hand to everyone. The dealer then turns over each player's cards one person at a time. If you have a higher hand than the dealer, you win.

What do you win? If the dealer has a hand of ace-king or higher, he's considered to be "qualified," which means he pays both your wagers (ante and bet). If the dealer does not qualify, then you get paid only for your ante wager. Here's a surprise: even if your hand can't beat what the dealer is holding, you still get your ante back if his hand fails to qualify. If the dealer qualifies and you beat his hand, you get paid on your bet wager according to the payout schedule:

■ ■

CARIBBEAN STUD POKER PAYOUT SCHEDULE

One Pair	even money or 1 to 1
Two Pairs	2 to 1
Three of a Kind	3 to 1
Straight	4 to 1
Flush	5 to 1
Full House	7 to 1
Four of a Kind	20 to 1
Straight Flush	50 to 1
Royal Flush	100 to 1

■ ■

Caribbean Stud Software

If you have a PC, are connected to the Internet, and want to practice Caribbean stud before going to a casino, you can download free Caribbean stud game software at this Web site: http://www.mcp.com/softlib/win dows-utilities/games.html.

Keep in mind that the payouts can only be up to the table's maximum payout. Before you sit down to play, ask your dealer what the maximum payout is for the table.

A big lure of Caribbean stud poker is the large progressive jackpot. However, this is a not a good bet, because the odds are highly in the casino's favor. Still, if you wish to play the progressive jackpot, place a dollar chip in the slot in front of your player position, usually in front of the betting circle. Just before the dealer gives each player their cards, the dollar chips will drop in the box below the table automatically and turn on the red light next to each player who is playing the progressive jackpot.

To win the entire progressive jackpot, you must play a dollar for the jackpot and you must get a royal flush. Good luck! A royal flush is dealt only once in 649,740 hands, on average. There are four other hands that get you a portion of the progressive jackpot: a straight flush, a four of a kind, a full house, and a flush. Now take a look at the payout schedule for the progressive jackpot hands:

PROGRESSIVE JACKPOT PAYOUT SCHEDULE

Flush	$50.00
Full House	$75.00
Four of a Kind	$100.00
Straight Flush	10% of Jackpot
Royal Flush	100% of Jackpot

CARIBBEAN STUD STRATEGY

There's not much to Caribbean stud poker. The basic strategy is to stay on any hand in which you have a pair or higher. Another good tactic is if you have a pair that is higher than the dealer's up card, then stay; otherwise, fold your hand. The idea is that if the dealer's up card is higher than your pair card, than it's a good chance he could beat you if he has a match to the up card in his hand. However, if you have a match of the dealer's up card, than you can stay with your hand as long as you have at least a pair. If you have an ace-king and a match of the dealer's up card, then it's a good idea to stay as well.

The strategy to follow for playing the jackpot is to play the extra dollar only if the jackpot is $150,000 or greater. Just keep in mind that every time you play the dollar for the jackpot, you're going to go through your betting money more quickly. Waiting until the $150,000 mark before playing the jackpot will cut your time being played for the jackpot considerably. Also, if it's been a while since the jackpot has been hit and it reaches the $150,000 mark, there's a better (though still not likely) chance over time of actually hitting the jackpot.

ETIQUETTE

There are only a few concerns with etiquette regarding Caribbean stud poker. First, watch the table minimum-maximum sign to make sure you're playing on a table suited to your betting style. Second, watch to make sure you don't touch your cards until the dealer gives all players their cards and accounts for all the remaining cards. Wait until the dealer gives you the OK to look at your cards.

Chapter Eight
LET IT RIDE POKER

et It Ride poker is a game where you try to obtain a high-ranking poker hand without playing against an opponent. You win if you get a minimum hand of a pair of tens. Let It Ride is played at a table similar to a blackjack table. There can be up to six players. The atmosphere at a Let It Ride table is very friendly because the players aren't competing against each other. Figure 8-1 shows the Let It Ride table setup.

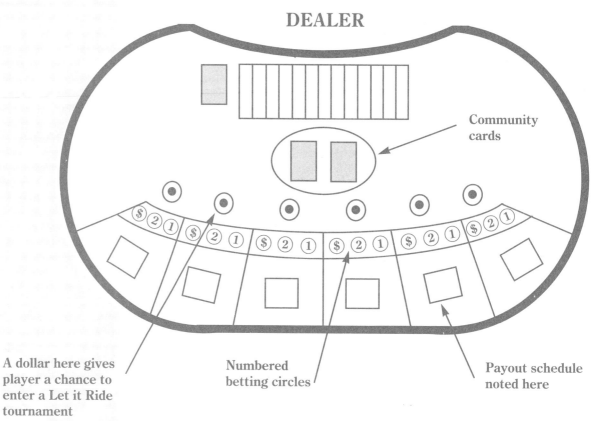

Figure 8-1
A typical Let It Ride table setup.

THE RULES

Let It Ride is played with one standard fifty-two-card playing deck. The players are required to make three wagers of the same amount. The players make all three wagers while the dealer is shuffling the cards. The wagers can range from the table minimum (usually $5) to the table maximum, but the three wagers *must* be the same. Each player places his or her three wagers on the table in the three numbered betting circles (1, 2, $) directly in front of his or her place, as shown in Figure 8-1.

Why three wagers? The rules of Let It Ride are designed to let the player make two choices on whether or not to let his or her bets ride. You can pull back your first two wagers, but the last wager *must* remain in the last betting circle. If you were allowed to pull back all three wagers, then the casino would lose money on Let It Ride because people would pull back any bet that was not a winner.

The dealer deals each player three cards, then places two cards face down. These are the community cards—cards that each player uses in their hand. Each player forms a five-card hand composed of his three cards and two community cards. After receiving their three cards, the players each must decide to either pull back his or her first wager or "let it ride." Now you see how the game got its name. Pulling back a wager is simply telling the dealer to remove your bet from the betting circle, so it's no longer considered a bet. At the end of the game, you can take the chips back.

After each player has made a decision on the first wager, the dealer turns the first community card face up. Each player now has to decide on the second wager. Once again, a player can pull it back or let it ride.

After each player has made a decision about wager two, the dealer turns the second community card face up. The three cards in your hand and the two community cards make up your five-card poker hand. If a player has decided to let it ride and makes a final bet, there is no pulling back the first or second bets. In other words, the last and final bet for each player has to remain on the table and can't be removed. Players lose their last wager if they don't have at least a pair of tens or higher. Players are paid according to the value of their five-cards hand. The payout is as follows:

LET IT RIDE PAYOUT SCHEDULE
(HIGH HAND TO LOW HAND)

Royal Flush	1,000 to 1
Straight Flush	200 to 1
Four of a Kind	50 to 1
Full House	11 to 1
Flush	8 to 1
Straight	5 to 1
Three of a Kind	3 to 1
Two Pair	2 to 1
Pair of Tens or better	1 to 1

The minimum needed to win is a pair of tens. If you have less than a pair of tens, you lose all your wagers remaining on the betting circles. If you have three wagers remaining on the betting circles, you get paid the appropriate payoff for each wager according to the payoff schedule.

It's a simple game. The only decisions you have to make are whether or not to let your first two wagers ride or pull them back out of the betting. After the dealer turns over the final community card, he pays off all winning bets, takes all losing bets, and returns first and second wagers that were pulled back.

Let's take an example. You approach the Let It Ride table and check the table minimum-maximum sign. The table minimum is $5. So you decide to buy in for $50, meaning you exchange $50 cash for $50 in chips. Now you make your three equal wagers. You decide to bet $5 on this hand. You place a $5 chip in each of the three betting circles in front of you.

Now the dealer gives the players their three cards and places two cards face down as the community cards. You look at your hand: ace of hearts, ten of diamonds, and seven of spades. You have to decide whether to pull back your first wager or let it ride. Since you don't have a pair of tens or better (the minimum to win your bet) and no chance for a flush or straight, you should pull back your first wager.

Now the dealer turns over the first community card, which is a jack of clubs. You have to decide about your second wager. It makes sense to pull it back once again, because you still don't have a winning hand and you have no chance for a straight or flush. So you now have only $5 remaining as a bet.

You place your three cards under your last remaining bet and wait for the dealer to turn over the last community card. The dealer flips over the ace of diamonds. Now the dealer looks at each player's hand and either pays them or removes all their remaining wagers. The community ace of diamonds gave you a winning hand, a pair of aces, for your remaining third wager of $5. The dealer would pay you $5 for your hand (one to one for a pair). If you had left the first two wagers on their betting circles instead of pulling them back, the one-to-one payoff would have won you $15.

LET IT RIDE STRATEGY

There's one main part to a good Let It Ride strategy. You must know when a hand is a winner. You already know the minimum winning hand is a pair of tens. The rest comes from knowing when to leave your first two wagers on the table.

A player can accumulate large sums of money very quickly in Let It Ride. However, in order to win a lot of money, you have to be lucky to get very good hands. The table below shows you the odds of each hand being dealt on five cards, with no draw (rounded to the nearest fifty):

ODDS OF POKER HANDS AFTER FIVE CARDS AND NO DRAW

High Card	1 to 1
One Pair	1 1/2 to 1
Two Pair	20 to 1
Three of a Kind	46 to 1
Straight	250 to 1
Flush	500 to 1
Full House	700 to 1
Four of a Kind	4,150 to 1
Straight Flush	65,000 to 1
Royal Flush	649,750 to 1

As you can see, the chances of getting a four of a kind or better hand are pretty slim. Now take a look at the Let It Ride payout table. See how the true odds of obtaining a certain poker hand are much greater than the odds in the payout table.

For example, let's say you got a four of a kind. The true odds of getting this hand are 4,150 to 1. So for every 4,150 hands dealt, you're going to get, on average, only one four of a kind. If you were paid true odds on this four of a kind, you'd get $4,150 for every dollar wagered. The casino, however, will pay you only fifty to one. Paying less than true odds is how the casino makes its money. That is their house advantage in this game. So if you had a $5 wager remaining on the Let It Ride table and hit four of a kind, your payoff would be only $250—far less than a true-odds payoff of $20,750.

Here's a note worth remembering if you're ever lucky enough to get a royal flush in Let It Ride. Most casinos have a maximum payout of $25,000. This means if you have three wagers of $100 each and you get a royal flush, the casino is only going to pay you $25,000, not the $300,000 ($100,000 for each $100 bet) that you'd expect according to the payout table. So if you're going to bet those amounts, make sure you ask the dealer what the casino maximum payout is for a royal flush—just in case.

Keeping in mind all of the above, here's a short table to guide you on when to let your first and second wagers ride:

After 3 Cards / Decision #1	After 4 Cards / Decision #2
Stay if you have:	*Stay if you have:*
A winning hand (pair of tens or better).	A winning hand (pair of tens or better).
Three consecutive cards to a straight of the same suit. *Don't* stay with A-2-3 suited or 2-3-4.	Four cards of the same suit, regardless of rank. A possible flush.
Three almost consecutive cards in the same suit and one being a high card (10 or higher). For example 8-10-J of the same suit.	Four consecutive cards with at least one high card (10 or higher). *Don't* stay if you have four cards to a straight with no high card.
Three almost consecutive cards of the same suit with two holes and two high cards. For example, 9-Q-K suited.	

Many players believe you can't remove your second wager if you left your first wager. This is wrong. You may remove either wager. They're independent of each other. One wager has no effect on the other wager.

A popular feature that's being added to Let It Ride games in Las Vegas casinos is the chance to enter a quarterly tournament. For a dollar per hand, you can hope to catch at least a straight flush and maybe even a royal flush to qualify to participate in a quarterly $3 million tournament. To have a chance to qualify for the quarterly tournament, you must bet one dollar on the large circle (the tournament betting circle) in front of your three small betting circles before you're dealt your three cards. Each tournament is composed of the top qualifiers from each qualifying quarter of the year, usually around fifty players. The top player in the tournament walks away with the grand prize.

Even if you get lucky and qualify for the tournament, that one dollar bet is still a sucker's bet. Remember that the chances of being dealt a royal flush are almost six hundred fifty thousand to one. So on average you'll spend $650,000 just for a chance to be in the tournament. Not a good bet.

If you follow these basic strategy tips and play smart, you can enjoy Let It Ride. Maybe you'll get lucky, catch a royal flush, and take home $25,000.

ETIQUETTE

The most important thing to remember is to make three equal wagers. You can't always depend on the dealer to check that you're doing this correctly. After you make your three wagers, you are not allowed to touch them until after the hand is over. If you want to pull back a wager, scratch your cards on the table in a pull back motion. This will signal the dealer to remove your wager from the betting circle and place it back near you so it's no longer a wager. This is very important. The casino doesn't like you touching your chips once they're in action.

When the dealer places the cards on the table, he will put them on his side of the betting circles in front of each player. The dealer must first make sure all the cards are accounted for before you are allowed to look at your cards. You'll know it's OK to look at your cards when the dealer picks up your cards from in front of your wagers and places them closer to you. If you try to pick up your cards before the dealer moves them, the dealer may scold or at least remind you not to do that and your action may attract the attention of the pit boss. Attracting the pit boss causes unnecessary attention to your table and likely will make you and the other players nervous.

The only other miscue you can make is trying to make a wager that's below the table minimum or above the table maximum. It's pretty easy to avoid this mistake by locating the table minimum-maximum sign located on the table.

Chapter Nine
PAI GOW POKER

Pai gow (pronounced pie-gow) poker is believed to be a combination of American poker and the Chinese domino game pai gow. It's thought that the game originated in the late 1800s when the Chinese helped build the U.S. railroads.

Pai gow poker is played at a table very similar to a blackjack table. Figure 9-1 shows a typical pai gow poker layout. There's a great deal of interaction among the players at a pai gow poker table, so in that way it's very similar to blackjack. Each player tries to beat the dealer. Players often interact with each other, creating an atmosphere of "us versus them."

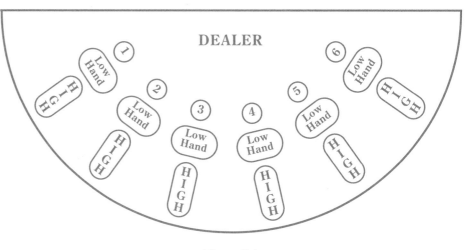

Figure 9-1
A typical pai gow poker layout.

Pai gow poker requires fewer decisions per hour than almost any other game in the casino. This means that over a long period of gambling you'll lose less playing pai gow poker than in most other casino games. In fact, the only table game that is slower is Caribbean stud. On the average, pai gow poker has about twenty-four hands played in an hour. For comparison, the average for blackjack is sixty hands per hour.

The house advantage for pai gow poker is 2.3 percent. By way of comparison, in blackjack the house advantage is 0.5 percent.

Remember that the house advantage is a percentage of each bet you make that the casino takes in, kind of like a tax the casino collects to let you play the game. The casino claims this tax by paying your winning bets at less than true odds. On average, in pai gow poker, for every $100 wagered the casino pays out $97.70 and takes in $2.30.

THE RULES

The object of pai gow poker is to beat the dealer in two poker hands that you create from seven cards you're dealt. The table can have up to six players and a dealer. Pai gow poker is played with a standard fifty-two-card deck plus one joker. The joker is used either as an ace or as any card needed to complete a straight or flush. It cannot be used as a wild card in other ways. The usual poker rankings are used in pai gow poker, with one exception—five aces (four aces plus the joker) is the highest hand possible.

When you approach the pai gow table, you should first be aware of the minimum-maximum betting limits for the table. After claiming a seat at the table, place your bet in what's called the betting circle. The dealer then shakes a container with three dice to determine which players will be dealt to first. Each player's position is assigned a number from one to seven, including the dealer's position. Position number one is located to the right of the dealer. When the total on the thrown dice exceeds seven, subtract seven from the total and the difference indicates the person who will be dealt first. For example, if the total on the dice is twelve, the player in position number five will receive the first hand.

The dealer then deals everyone seven cards face down, starting with the player whose number came up on the dice throw. Each player then sorts his or her cards from highest to lowest. Then players sort their cards into a five-card hand (high hand) and a two-card hand (low hand). This is called *setting* the cards.

The following is the rank of pai gow poker hands, which is the same as for regular poker with the exception on the highest hand:

■ ■

POKER RANKINGS (FROM LOWEST TO HIGHEST)

1.	**High Card**	A hand without a pair, straight, or flush, valued only by its highest card
2.	**One Pair**	Two cards of the same rank
3.	**Two Pair**	Two cards of one rank and another two cards of another rank
4.	**Three of a Kind**	Three cards of the same rank
5.	**Straight**	All five cards in a sequence but not in a single suit
6.	**Flush**	All five cards are in the same suit but not in a sequence
7.	**Full House**	Three cards of the same rank and two cards of another rank
8.	**Four of a Kind**	Four cards of the same rank
9.	**Straight Flush**	All five cards in sequence and in the same suit
10.	**Royal Flush**	A, K, Q, J, and 10 all of the same suit
11.	**Five Aces**	All four aces plus the joker (this rank is used only in pai gow poker)

■ ■

When you sort your seven cards into two hands, the five-card hand must rank higher than the two-card hand. This means, for example, that if you are dealt two pairs, you must put the higher of the two pairs in your five-card hand. If a player has a higher-ranking two-card hand than his five-card hand, then the player automatically loses his or her wager. (This is known as a *foul* hand.) For example, if you sort your seven cards into J-J for the low hand and A-K-Q-8-5 for the high hand, you lose. After creating your two hands, place them face down in their correct spots on the layout: the two-card hand in the box marked "low hand" and the five-card hand in the box marked "high hand."

Remember that your five-card hand (high hand) must rank higher than your two-card (low hand) according to the poker hands chart above. You want each to be as good as your seven cards allow. The best possible low hand would be a pair of aces. Below are some examples of pai gow hands and how you should set them:

Example 1   You're dealt 2, 7, 7, 9, 10, jack, ace (of different suits). First, look at what would be your highest-ranking poker hand with all seven cards. The best hand you could create with these seven cards would be a pair of sevens. The pair must go into the high hand. This leaves the 2, 9, 10, jack, and ace. Take the two highest-ranking cards remaining—ace and jack—to create your low hand. The remaining 2, 9, and 10 are used to complete the high hand. So, you set your hand like this: high hand = 2, 7, 7, 9, 10 and low hand = ace, jack.

Example 2   You're dealt 5, 6, 7, 8, 9, 9, king (of different suits). First look at what could be your highest-ranking poker hand with all seven cards. Here, the best hand you could create with all seven cards would be a straight. You put the straight into the high hand. The remaining two cards—9 and king—make up your low hand. Set your hand like this: high hand = 5, 6, 7, 8, 9 and low hand = 9, king.

Example 3   You're dealt 3, 3, 6, 8, 8, 9, 10 (of different suits). Your highest-ranking poker hand with all seven cards would be two pair, threes and eights. You would split the pairs, putting the lower-ranking pair (threes) into the low hand and the eights into the high hand, along with the six, nine, and ten. Set your hand like this: high hand = 6, 8, 8, 9, 10 and low hand = 3, 3.

These three examples should help you understand the basics of splitting the seven cards into a high hand and a low hand. Remember that the joker can be used as an ace or as any card needed to complete a straight or flush. To show how a joker can affect a hand, let's change example three above by dealing a joker instead of one of the threes.

Example 4   You're dealt 3, 6, 8, 8, 9, 10, joker (of different suits). Your highest-ranking poker hand with all seven cards would be a straight, using the joker: 6, joker, 8, 9, 10.

That straight would make your high hand. Then your low hand would be the remaining 3 and 8. If you chose to put the pair of 8s into your low hand, your high hand would be 3, 6, 9, 10, joker. Even if you used the joker as an ace, your high hand would still be only a high card hand, which would rank lower than low hand, so you'd automatically lose your wager. Set your hand like this: high hand = 6, joker (=7), 8, 9, 10 and low hand = 3, 8.

How do you win at pai gow poker? To win your bet, you must beat the dealer on both the high hand and the low hand. You lose if the dealer wins both hands. If you and the dealer have hands of the same ranking (which usually only happens in the two-card low hand), it's called a *copy*. The dealer or banker wins all copies. Most hands in pai gow poker are pushes (ties): you win one hand and the dealer wins the other hand. In those cases, neither player nor dealer wins and the bet remains on the table. The player can pick it up, leave it for the next hand, or add to it.

In determining who wins the five-card hand, the standard poker hierarchy prevails with the addition of the unique pai gow hand of five aces (four aces plus the joker). In terms of the low hand, the hierarchy also prevails, although with only two cards it's impossible to have anything other than the lowest two ranks of hands: a pair or a high card. It doesn't take much to win the low hand. Many times the low hand will be won by whoever has the higher card. For example, if you have in your low hand a seven and a Jack and the dealer has a five and an eight, you win. Since neither hand holds a pair, it's a battle of high cards and your Jack beats his eight.

Each player plays against the dealer or banker. After each player has set his or her high hand and low hand, the dealer or banker sets his hand. Dealers have strict rules on how they set their hands: they have no choices. If a player is banking a game instead of the casino, the player banking the game is free to set the hand any way he or she wishes, just like the other players, as long as the two-card hand is lower than the five-card hand.

While the players are setting their cards, the dealer's cards remain face down on the table. If the casino dealer is banking the game, then the dealer can help set your hand. So if you get confused, be sure to ask the casino dealer what would be the right play. The dealer is allowed to help you because he has no idea what cards he has at this point, since he doesn't look at his cards until all the players have sorted their hands into high hand and low hand. Because the dealer must follow strict rules in setting his hand and because he doesn't know what's in his hand, he can help players who request assistance without the possibility of bias.

All bets in pai gow poker are paid off at even money minus a 5 percent commission. Even money means simply that the amount you wager is the amount you'll be paid if your hand wins. For example, if you bet $25 and both your hands beat both the dealer's hands, you'll win $23.75 ($25 minus 5 percent commission, or $1.25), plus, your $25 bet will remain in the betting circle. It's important to make your bets in increments of $5. When bets aren't in $5 increments, the casinos will round up the commission to the nearest $0.25, so you lose a little more of your winnings. This 5 percent commission is how the house makes its 2.3 percent advantage—along with the fact that dealer wins all ties or copy hands.

Banking a Game

A player may choose to deal or bank a pai gow poker game. To bank a game, a player must have enough chips on the table to cover all the other players' wagers if they were all to win their bets. How often a player is allowed to bank a game varies from casino to casino. It's to the player's advantage to bank as often as possible, since the rules are in favor of the house or dealer. The disadvantage to banking a game is it may require a large amount of money to start banking a game.

When a player banks a game, that reduces the house advantage because that player pockets wagers in the case of ties or copy hands. However, the casino takes a 5 percent commission on every winning wager. This is how the casino still makes money when a

player chooses to bank a hand. The casino also limits the number of times a player may bank. Usually it's once every seven hands. This would give each player an opportunity to bank a hand every rotation on a full table, including the casino dealer.

BASIC PAI GOW POKER STRATEGY

The strategy of pai gow poker comes in setting your hand properly. To win your bet, you must win both your hands. So it's better to set your seven cards as two average hands rather than as one powerful hand and one low hand. (Remember that low hands are often won just on high cards.) The table below tells you what would be the proper play for each of the hands.

SETTING PAI GOW POKER HANDS

What's in Your Hand	Proper Setting
High Card (no pairs, straights, or flushes)	Use the second and third highest cards as the low hand. Use the high card plus the other four cards as the high hand.
One Pair (two cards of the same rank)	Use the highest two unpaired cards as the low hand. Use the pair plus the other three cards as the high hand.
Two Pair (two sets of pairs, of different ranks)	If you have a single ace, use the ace plus the next highest unpaired card as the low hand. If not, use the lower pair as the low hand and the higher pair as the high hand.
Three Pair (three sets of pairs, all of different ranks)	Use the highest pair as the low hand and the two other pairs in the high hand with the remaining single card.
Two Pair and a Straight	Set the hand as two pair (*above*), ignoring the straight.
Three of a Kind	Use the three of a kind in the high hand and the next two highest cards as the low hand. Exception: if your three of a kind is aces, then use a pair of aces for the high hand and the third ace plus the next highest card as the low hand.

What's in Your Hand	Proper Setting
Two Threes-of-a-Kind	Use the lower three of a kind in the high hand. Use a pair from the remaining three of a kind as the low hand.
Straight	Use the straight as the high hand and the remaining two cards in the low hand.
Six-Card Straight (six cards in sequence but not of the same suit)	Use the two highest cards without breaking a straight as the low hand. Use the straight as the high hand.
Flush (five cards of the same suit but not in sequence)	Use the flush in the high hand and the two remaining cards as the low hand.
Flush and Two Pair	Ignore the flush. Use the lower of the two pairs as the low hand. Put the higher of the two pairs into the high hand.
Full House (a pair and a three-of-a-kind)	Use the pair as the low hand. Use the three of a kind in the high hand.
Four of a Kind	If aces, kings, or queens, split them into a pair for each hand. If jacks, tens, or nines with an ace or king, use the four-of-a-kind in the high hand. If jacks, tens, or nines without ace or king, split the four into a pair for each hand. Any other four of a kind: put into the high hand.
Straight Flush (five cards in sequence and of the same suit)	Use the straight flush as the high hand. Use the two remaining cards as the low hand.
Five Aces (all four aces plus the joker)	Use two aces as the low hand and the three remaining aces in the high hand.

Counting cards in pai gow poker has no benefit, since the cards are shuffled after each deal. The best betting strategy is to play the streaks. In other words, increase your bets when you're winning and play the table minimum when losing. A betting strategy that is good for beginners is to place a bet equal to the table minimum and then, if that bet wins, let your original bet stay plus all the winnings. If the next hand wins, increase your bet by one unit (the table minimum) and keep the remainder of your winnings from the second bet. Now you are gambling entirely with the casino's money. Continue this until you win five hands without losing or when you lose a bet. Once you win five in a row or lose a hand, start over at the table minimum.

Let's take an example. You start by betting the table minimum, $5. On the first hand you win, so you get to keep your $5 bet plus you win $5. On the second hand, you bet a total of $10 (your original $5 bet plus the $5 you won in hand one). You push hand two; since you neither win nor lose, you still have $10 out to bet. On hand three you bet the same $10 as hand two. You win hand three. Your $10 remains out there for the bet, plus the dealer gives you $10. This time you increase your bet $5 to $15 and keep the remaining $5 (which is what you initially bet in hand one). Now you're gambling entirely with the casino's money after just three wins without a loss. If you win five hands without a loss, cut back your bet to $5 and start over. If you bet at the $5 minimum table and reach the start-over point, five wins, you'll have profited $40 plus a chance to win $5 more on the next hand. Keep in mind if you lose hand two you'll have lost $10, $5 of your original bet plus $5 you won in hand one. You go to casinos to win money, not to break even. That's why you let your bet and winnings ride after winning one hand.

ETIQUETTE

There are three concerns with etiquette when playing pai gow poker. The first relates to any casino table game. Be aware of the table minimum-maximum bet limits, which will always be indicated by a sign. Making a incorrect wager is embarrassing. The second concern is making sure you always set the cards correctly. You must set the five-card hand higher than the two-card hand. It can be very costly, plus embarrassing, to set the two-card hand higher than the five-card hand. The third concern is to never let other players see your cards. The casino doesn't want players to show their hands because if players knew what cards were held by the other players, they would have an edge.

Chapter Ten
BACCARAT AND MINI-BACCARAT

Baccarat

While baccarat has the aura of elegance, some of the casinos want to dispel that. Check out this comment from the World Wide Web site for Harrah's Las Vegas (http://harrahs.lv.com): "Baccarat: It's as simple as ABC. You can pick it up just by watching the play for a few minutes. So forget the image this game projects of celebrities and high rollers. Forget the tuxedos and evening gowns. Be bold! Next time you're strolling by our Baccarat pit (strange name for such an elegant place), don't just keep walking. Step inside. Our dealers will greet you like a long-lost cousin and be delighted to answer any questions you might have."

Baccarat (pronounced bah-ca-rah) is the most glamorous game in the casino. The game was invented in the 1500s by the French aristocrats who didn't have anything better to do. In some European countries, the game is called chemin de fer. When you think of a baccarat player, you often think of James Bond, along with wealth, class, and prestige. Baccarat is played with high betting minimums and limits in specially designed betting areas of the casino called high-limit areas. The usual betting minimum is $20 a hand.

From this high-limit game, casinos developed a game for lower-limit players called mini-baccarat. Mini-baccarat is the same game as baccarat, with the same rules, but it's played at a different type of table for lower limits. The usual minimum wager for mini-baccarat is $5 a hand.

Baccarat and mini-baccarat have a low house advantage at 1.17 percent to 1.36 percent. The difference between the two house advantages is whether you bet on the bank hand (1.17 percent advantage) or on the player hand (1.36 percent advantage). So for every $100 you bet, you'll win $98.64 or $98.83 back on average over the long haul. Contrary to what many people may think, baccarat is a very simple game to learn. You don't have to learn any special strategy, count cards, or have a difficult betting system to play baccarat or mini-baccarat correctly.

THE RULES

In baccarat and mini-baccarat, the object is for the players to bet on the winning hand. Baccarat tables can fit up to fifteen players, but mini-baccarat tables usually have room for only six or seven. No matter how many players are at the table, however, there are only two hands dealt—one to the dealer and one to the "player." Both hands are dealt next to each other, face up, by the dealer or the person holding the shoe in baccarat. In both games usually six or eight standard decks are used to play. The casino decides on the number of decks to use.

There are three choices in making a bet in baccarat or mini-baccarat. You can bet on the "player" hand, the banker hand, or a tie. Make these bets by placing your chips in the appropriate space in

front of you, clearly marked "player" and "banker" or numbered (for a tie). You make your bets before any of the cards are dealt. (Since all the cards are dealt face up, it wouldn't be much of a challenge if you made your bet after the cards are dealt!)

Whichever of the two hands totals nine or comes closer to nine wins. All cards count their value, aces count as one, and all tens and face cards count as zero. To total up a hand, add the values of the cards. It's just simple math—almost. If the total of a hand exceeds ten, drop the tens digit. For example, if the hand consisted of an eight and a nine, the total would be seventeen, which would be reduced to seven.

A little confusing, perhaps. But don't worry: there's no need to understand all the rules of baccarat or mini-baccarat perfectly, since the dealer or croupier plays both hands and does it all by the book. So, you're betting on a game of chance played by an expert. Relax and enjoy!

Although the rules are the same for baccarat and mini-baccarat, there's a slight difference in the mechanics of play. In baccarat, the shoe (a holder for the cards) is passed around the table and the players take turns dealing the cards. Players feel more involved in the outcome of the game when they deal the cards from the shoe. It also adds to the glamour of playing baccarat. A player holds the shoe until the player hand beats the dealer hand (also known as the bank hand). Then the shoe is passed to the next player counter-clockwise around the table. In mini-baccarat, the mechanics of the game are simpler: the dealer handles all the cards.

The dealer begins by dealing two cards each to the player and to the banker, face up. If either hand is dealt a total of eight or nine on those first two cards, it's called a natural. The eight is called *le petit* natural and the nine is called *le grand* natural. A natural wins the hand. A grand natural beats a petit natural because nine is greater than eight. If both hands are naturals, the game ends in a tie. If not, a third card is dealt.

In baccarat, after the initial two cards are dealt to both the player and the bank, a casino employee, the *call man*, will indicate to the player with the shoe that it's time to deal the next card and who gets it. In the higher-limit baccarat, the casino uses two dealers who handle all the chips, whether it's collecting losing bets, paying winning bets, or making change. Each dealer

The Twelfth Week

One of the best stories to come out of the baccarat rooms in the last decade involved a group of dealers. In late 1991, a group of eight baccarat dealers from the Las Vegas Hilton turned an initial $80 stake ($10 per person) into $103,000 by betting one NFL football game per week, par-laying their winnings and winning eleven consecutive bets. The dealers' goal was to continue their parlay until they either lost or reached fifteen straight wins. Had they been successful, the group would have cashed in on a $1.3 million profit. The odds against winning fifteen straight are about 33,000 to 1. When they reached their eleven cor-rect bets, the odds against win-ning the remaining four games were only fifteen to one. Alas, they lost in week twelve.

is located in the middle of the table across from the call man and is responsible for one side of the table. In the simpler game of mini-baccarat, the casino dealer handles deals all the cards and all the chips.

As mentioned above, if either hand is a natural, the hand ends. If neither the player nor the banker has a natural, the dealer or call man then determines whether either hand gets a third card according to the following rules. The dealer must always play the player hand first, then the banker hand.

Player's Two-Card Total	Player Must
Zero through five	Draw another card
Six or seven	Stand
Eight or nine	Stand (it's a natural!)

The banker hand is always played according to how the player hand was played. If the player had a natural, the banker does not draw a card. If the player hand stands with a six or seven, the banker hand must always do the following:

Banker's Two-Card Total	Banker Must
Zero through five	Draw a card
Six or more	Stand

When the player hand draws a third card, the banker hand must always do the following:

Banker Two-Card Total	Banker Draws Only When the Player's Third Card Is
Two or less	(always draws)
Three	ace, two, three, four, five, six, seven, nine, or ten
Four	two, three, four, five, six, or seven
Five	four, five, six, or seven
Six	six or seven
Seven	(always stands)

When both hands have been played out, the hand closer to nine wins. The dealer then pays those who bet on the winning hand. If the hand ends in a tie, the dealer pays those who bet on a tie. In that case, all bets on the player or the banker are pushes. In other words, they don't get paid but they don't lose their wagers.

The payoffs for each of the three bets are as follows. A wager on the player hand winning is paid off at even money (one to one). So if you bet $5 and the player hand wins, you'll win $5. A wager on the banker hand is paid off at even money minus a 5 percent commission. So if you bet $5 and the bank hand wins, you'll win $4.75 ($5 minus a 5 percent commission). Since the bank hand has a very slight edge over the player hand, the casino charges a commission when you take advantage of this edge by betting the bank hand. A wager on a tie is paid off at nine to one or eight to one, depending on the casino. A tie is the worst wager you can make in baccarat or mini-baccarat. The house advantage is 9.5 percent at nine to one and 18.5 percent at eight to one. Since the casino uses six or eight decks, the likelihood of a tie happening is ten to one. By not paying the true odds, the casino is making money every time you bet a tie.

BACCARAT STRATEGY

Baccarat and mini-baccarat are games that require almost no skill. There aren't any complicated strategies to foul up, nor do you have to count cards. All you have to do is pick the player hand or the banker hand to

Get Paid for Looking Good

Sometimes the casino will employ *shills* to play in baccarat games. A shill is a person paid by the casino to play table games. Usually this person is very pretty or handsome and dressed elegantly. By employing shills, the casino adds glamour and class to the game. Since many baccarat games involve very high stakes, there are usually very few players. Therefore, the shills make it more fun and glamorous for the high-stakes players. You'll never see a shill on a mini-baccarat game.

win or bet on a tie. Your decision will mainly be a guess. With the low house advantage of baccarat and mini-baccarat, players can play for hours, winning sometimes and losing sometimes, almost at random.

As a kind of strategy, some people like to track the winner of each hand in baccarat and mini-baccarat. They think that this will help them determine the winner of the next hand. Sometimes the game lends itself to trends. For example, the bank hand might win four in a row, then the player hand wins four in a row. If you're tracking the winners, you might very well bet on the banker's hand next because of this pattern.

Tracking the winners shows only who's won in the past; it doesn't show who'll win the next hand. So this strategy is questionable. If you are successful picking the next winning hand by tracking the past winners, by all means continue your tracking.

Sometimes players get sucked into betting large amounts on a hand that hasn't won in a long time. Don't let this happen to you. For example, if the player hand has won ten times in a row, a lot of people tend to think the bank hand has to win in the next couple of hands, so they bet large amounts on the bank hand. This is a very bad method of gambling. While the law of probability would be in favor of the bank winning, it doesn't mean that will happen.

A good strategy is to bet only the amount you can afford to lose on each hand and to have fun while you make these bets. There really is no effective strategy here that will allow you to beat the house. The game is mainly played for fun and with the expectation of not losing or winning too much. Anyone who does win big at this game is just lucky.

ETIQUETTE

There aren't too many etiquette problems when playing baccarat or mini-baccarat. The main point is to place your bets inside the correct betting box. Don't set it on the line: this will only cause confusion. Make your bets before any of the cards are dealt. Once the cards are dealt, don't touch your money. Let the dealer handle your chips if need be.

The only other caution is to make sure you sit at a table that's within your betting budget. Sometimes that $100 minimum table can look like a $10 minimum table. It can be quite embarrassing if you sit down and pull out your $10 chips only to be told your bet is a little low.

Chapter Eleven
BINGO

You're probably familiar with the game of bingo. Little kids play it around the house, while their parents or grandparents play it in the church social hall. But there's probably a lot you don't know about this game.

For instance, you probably don't know how bingo originated. Well, don't feel bad, because nobody really knows for sure. The most likely story is that bingo evolved from the Italian lottery, which dates back to 1530 and is still popular today, known as lotto. It spread throughout Europe and then crossed the Atlantic Ocean. The current form of the game dates back to around 1880. In the early twentieth century, it was known as beano and played at county fairs around the United States. A caller would take numbered disks from a cigar box and players would use dried beans to mark their cards, until somebody yelled, "Beano!"

Among the visitors at one of those fairs in the 1930s, according to the story, was a toy salesman from New York, Edwin S. Lowe. While he was hanging around the beano area at a carnival in Florida, he was struck by the popularity and simplicity of the game. He introduced the game in New York. It's reported that one game was won by a woman who called out, in flustered excitement, "Bingo!" Lowe put two and two together—the great popularity of that simple game and the unusual accidental name—and won when he developed and marketed the game.

Bingo became even more popular as community organizations would sponsor games to raise money. Legalized first in New York and New Jersey in the 1950s, it has spread beyond churches and social halls into casinos. It's been estimated that about $10 billion is wagered annually in some 50,000 bingo halls across North America. In a recent national survey on gambling, 75 percent of the 1,200 Americans questioned stated that they approve of bingo, while only 69 percent expressed approval of state lotteries and 62 percent approved of legalized gaming in general.

THE RULES

Bingo is a game of numbers, not unlike Keno or other lottery games. The game is run by a caller, who draws numbers at random, from 1 through 75 (each accompanied by one of the five letters in the word "bingo"), and calls them out to the players. Each player pays for one or more game cards. This is known as a *buy-in*. Each of the cards consists of a five-by-five grid of numbered squares, with the center square marked as a free space. (See Figure 4-1.) In the traditional game, you are supposed to get five numbers in a row, column, or diagonal covered to win. Now the object is to fill in squares in any of a number of patterns identified by the caller before the game begins. (More on those patterns shortly.)

As the caller announces each number drawn, the players check their game cards for that number. Whoever has that number marks the square. The caller continues to announce numbers until someone fills in a pattern and shouts, "Bingo!" At that point an employee (called a *floorperson,* or a *checker*) will inspect the winning card for two things: to make sure that the numbers marked form the correct pattern for that particular game and that the numbers marked have been called. If the pattern and the numbers are right, the game is over, and the winner receives the prize. If more than one card wins, the prize is distributed among the players with winning cards.

B	I	N	G	O
14	23	41	59	65
9	17	32	48	69
10	29	Free	57	73
12	20	38	49	66
2	22	44	51	70

Figure 4-1
A typical bingo card.

It's just that simple, at least for the basics. That's how Edwin Lowe knew he had a winner when he discovered bingo. Now, on to some details that Lowe probably never imagined.

If you played bingo as a kid, you probably used tokens to mark your cards. Well, that's impractical when the players are elbow to elbow, and the excitement is building. That's why bingo parlors generally use crayons or felt-tip markers (called *daubers, dabbers,* or *dobbers*) to mark the squares on paper cards known as *throw-aways*. But you may also find games using plastic cards with sliding covers to mark the squares (*shutter cards* or *fingertip cards*) or disposable cardboard cards with fold-down tabs in addition to the simple cards and tokens just as you used years ago.

But whether you use tokens on cardboard or felt pens on paper, this aspect of the game is basically the same as when Edwin Lowe made his mark in gambling history. In the "B" column, the numbers go from 1 to 15. In the "I" column, from 16 to 30. Under "N", from 31 to 45 (and the free center spot, of course!). The numbers from 46 to 60 are under "G". In the "O" column are the remaining numbers, 61-75.

When the game was known as beano, those numbers were drawn from a cigar box. Now, they're usually printed on balls that are spun around in a cage or a glass blower, to ensure that each number is chosen at random. The caller then places each ball in a *masterboard* or *rack*. Many bingo parlors also have electronic boards to post numbers as they're drawn and called, which makes it easier for the players to note and mark the numbers on their cards.

Some bingo operations also use an extra ball, distinctively colored and without any numbers. If this ball is drawn, the players can cover any one square on their cards as they like at any time during that game.

There may be differences in the type of cards, the means of drawing the numbers, and in the use of a wild ball, but the only real complication in bingo games is the patterns.

As mentioned earlier, before each game the caller announces the pattern for that game. A simple game pattern might consist of filling in a single row, perhaps the top or bottom, or completing two rows (double bingo) or getting all four corners of the card. Other patterns might be to form letters, such as T or X or Z, or even short words, such as HI.

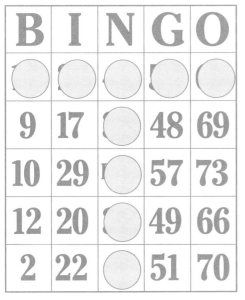

Figure 4-2
T Pattern.

Figure 4-3
Z Pattern.

Some of these patterns are easy for a bingo novice to understand, such as letters, a picture frame (the outside 16 squares), or inside square (the eight squares and the free squares that form the center of the game card). Other patterns may seem a little more unusual, such as bowtie, happy face, Mutt and Jeff, tic-tac-toe, hang the caller, and love letter.

Figure 4-4
HI Pattern.

Figure 4-5
Bowtie Pattern.

Figure 4-6
Happy Face Pattern.

Figure 4-7
Mutt & Jeff Pattern.

Other patterns include six pack (a 2 x 3 cluster anywhere on the game card) and double postage stamps (two 2 x 2 clusters in any two corners of the card or in designated corners), also known as double Dutch or double Pennsylvania. It may be unnecessary to point out here that many of the patterns are known under several names, further confusing bingo beginners. Rest assured that the game operators or the aficionados around you will be more than happy to explain the patterns being used in a particular session—if you ask before the game begins.

The hardest pattern is usually saved for the final game of a session, when the stakes are highest, the *coverall* (also known as *blackout* or *jackpot* bingo). Usually only 48, 49, or 50 balls are drawn. The first player to fill all twenty-four squares on his or her card wins. If there is no winner (which is very likely, considering the odds, which we'll discuss shortly), the caller may keep drawing numbers to produce a winner, although the prize is generally reduced. (The laws in some jurisdictions require a payout, so in those states, coverall games must continue until somebody wins—even if the prize is modest.)

You may also encounter the opposite pattern, *no-number*, where numbers are drawn and called until only one game card remains totally unmarked. This is a game where the person who is usually the loser wins!

There are also variations on coverall. For example, in Texas blackout, all even or odd numbers are covered at the start of the game: if the first ball drawn is an even number, all evens are covered; if odd, all odds are covered. Then the game continues as usual for coverall.

The basics of the game are simple, but virtually every bingo hall and parlor is likely to try something a little different, to add a little variety to life. We can't cover all the possibilities, but you won't have any trouble adapting to them as you go and enjoying the local differences.

A few terms might help you feel at home wherever you play. When a player needs only one number to win, that's called a *wait*, logically enough. If you need two numbers to win, that's called a *wait for a wait*. And a player who suddenly realizes he had a bingo on a number called previously is known as a *sleeper*. Finally, games played before the regular session begins are known as *early bird* games, while games played after the regular session are called *late bird*, of course!

PLAYING THE ODDS

So, what are your chances of winning at bingo? That depends, of course, on the game. We need to distinguish between coverall and games using any other patterns, because in coverall the numbers drawn are limited.

When fifty numbers—the maximum for a full payout—are drawn, the odds are 1 in 212,086 for a player with a single card. Those are the best odds that you can expect for coverall. You might not even do that well.

If you're playing a game in which only forty-nine numbers are drawn, those winning odds drop to 1 in 407,857. And what about a game in which forty-eight numbers are drawn? For suckers only: you're facing odds of 1 in 799,399! If nobody wins, and they continue the game for a reduced jackpot, your odds improve, of course, as the prize money decreases. With every ball drawn, the odds are about twice as good, an optimist would point out. But a pessimist would argue that the odds are still heavily against you: 1 in 112,284 for fifty-one balls, 1 in 60,458 for fifty-two balls, 1 in 33,081 for fifty-three balls. Even if the caller draws five more numbers, your odds are only 1 in 10,359. By ball sixty, you're at about 1 in 5,000 or so. Maybe you're starting to feel luckier, but you're still fighting considerable odds. That's why coverall winners are rare, unless the caller continues to draw numbers.

As you might imagine, the odds of winning are better when the game pattern uses fewer squares—and the caller draws numbers until somebody wins. But what are the odds that's you?

Whether the pattern is simple or complex, you have to figure in the number of cards being played in that game. Many players use a half-dozen or a dozen cards, especially in games with higher payouts. If there are 200 cards in play, any single card has a 1 in 200 chance of winning. If you play five cards, your odds improve, but only slightly, to 1 in 40—but so does your financial investment. And what if the other 199 players each have five cards as well? (By the way, you may find people in casinos using the word *on*, as in 3-on or 6-on. *Face* is another name for a card, as well. A 3-on or a 6-on would be a sheet or a strip with three or six game cards or faces.)

Some people believe that their chances of winning increase proportionately with the number of cards they play. Although that's true, the advantage is less than most people expect—or hope. Take our example of 200 cards in play. Your odds go from 1 in 200 to 1 in 40 if you're playing five of those cards rather than a single card. But consider your odds from another angle: by paying five times as much to play, you're only decreasing your odds of *losing* from 199 out of 200 to 195 out of 200. And you're also losing your money five times as fast.

In short, it pays to check out a game and mentally calculate your odds before laying down your cash and picking up your cards. The more cards you play, the more interesting the game. But the key is to play where there are fewer cards competing for that prize.

WINNING AT BINGO

So, how do you increase your chances of winning? Well, since bingo is basically a game of chance, like the lottery from which it evolved over the centuries, perhaps the best way to win (or at least lose the minimum) is by avoiding the games that offer the worst odds. Consider what it costs to play, the amount of the prize, the number of cards being played, and the number of squares to be filled in the game pattern.

Compare, for example, a game that costs $1 a card and pays $50, with about 100 cards in play, and a game that costs the same $1 a card and pays $100, with 200 cards in play. Your odds of winning are better in the first game, of course: 1 in 100 vs. 1 in 200. But the payout (50 to 1 vs. 100 to 1) makes the two games about even, if you're in bingo for the money, rather than just the thrill of victory.

Keep in mind that few games of chance return such a low percentage of the proceeds as bingo. Bingo operations may keep between 25 percent and 40 percent of the buy-in money. The best payout that you can find is 80 percent at most. If you hope to win at bingo, understanding the payout is an important consideration.

Your best chance to win is to find bingo games that have the worst atmosphere: anything that might reduce the number of players—or, more precisely, the number of cards being played—will improve your odds. If you can do without cozy surroundings and great lighting and free drinks or whatever else might attract players, then you can avoid the bigger crowds and seek out better odds. Of course, such parlors may not be very much fun to visit. On the other hand, if you're just playing for fun and the off-chance of winning, then pick the parlor you find most inviting.

We've also mentioned that many players try to increase their chances of winning by playing more cards. That strategy seems statistically sound: players who play more cards are more likely to win, but they're also investing more money in the game and—according to at least one gambling expert—their chances of losing are about the same. Of course, if you can get a deal by buying several cards, so that you're not paying the full price, then you've got a little advantage in terms of your investment.

Some experts advise players to purchase and get as many numbers as they can on a maximum of four cards, to balance numerical coverage and financial investment. But there's nothing magical about having four cards. Many bingo players believe in choosing cards that contain certain numbers in strategic locations on the cards, such as in diagonals and corners or "high-win" squares in straight bingo. (The 16 high-win squares are the squares in any rows of five that include the center, free square.) They swear by "lucky" numbers, digits that have a special significance to them, for whatever reason. Do people who play by "special numbers" win more often? No—but they probably get more passionately involved in the game than other players. Unless you're in it just for the money, that emotional excitement can be a big part of playing bingo.

Along similar lines, many players trust in their good luck charms: trinkets, photographs, rabbit's feet, four-leaf clovers, religious objects, and other items. Some keep them in their pockets, while others place them around their game cards. Some people play according to their astrological signs and the horoscope. Again, there doesn't seem to be any charm that's definitely advantageous, but the curious assortment of things certainly makes bingo games more colorful.

Speaking of color, we should probably add here that many bingo players believe in the power of colors, and their clothes reflect this. For example, red is associated with energy, exerting a vital magnetism. Some players prefer green, the color of money, in hopes that it will attract more of the same. Add a lucky hat or a magical scarf to an outfit of a chosen color, and they believe the ensemble will ensure they win!

Some players like to choose a lucky seat, a particular location in the room that seems auspicious, perhaps facing a certain direction. (That's not unlike people who will choose a particular table in a restaurant. Does that location actually improve the food? Not likely. Does it make the food seem to taste better? Some would swear by it.) Others like to have a lot of elbow room, or room to stretch out their legs and be more comfortable. Do such preferences improve their chances of winning? Yes, but only to the extent that the players can concentrate better on the numbers called.

One published guide to winning consistently at bingo provides some recommendations for gaining a numerical advantage through the laws of probability. It advises players to study the patterns of numbers drawn as each game progresses, then to try choosing game cards that fit those patterns. This guide also suggests trying to choose cards with a lot of numbers in "the median range"—although what that term means isn't really clear!

One suggestion is that you should select cards that cover a wide range of numbers. Someone has calculated that in three cards chosen at random, the combined 72 squares will average 22 duplicate numbers and 25 missing numbers. So, it's reasoned, you should choose cards that cover as many of the seventy-five numbers as possible. That makes sense in terms of hitting on more numbers as they're drawn, which is good for a psychological boost, but some players might argue that a single number that shows up on three cards is as helpful as three numbers that show up on one card each.

Also, this strategy doesn't work for coverall or blackout games. In fact, the opposite strategy is recommended: you should choose cards that have as many duplicated numbers as possible (the locations of the duplicated numbers are of no importance). This is the number concentration method. To maximize on this strategy, try to choose about six numbers (odds and evens, high and low) to be heavily duplicated. The reasoning behind this strategy is to fill up as many squares as quickly as you can, since only forty-eight to fifty numbers will be drawn. You should also buy as many cards as possible if playing coverall or blackout.

At the risk of confusing you, it should be mentioned that some players recommend another strategy for coverall games, the even distribution method. This strategy consists of choosing cards that cover as many of the seventy-five numbers as possible.

So, there are two opposite approaches to winning at coverall. Which one makes more sense? That's up to you. You may want to experiment a little with both approaches. There certainly must be reasons for bingo experts to disagree so fundamentally!

Some players advocate a system of tracking numbers. To use this system, according to one expert, you need to play four cards at most for each game. You bring along to each bingo session a sheet of paper listing the numbers from 1 to 75, then check off each number as it's called, for the entire session of games. Do this for at least five sessions. (It seems to be assumed that you play in the same parlor and that the same mechanism is used for dispensing the numbers at each game.) Then, you gather your tracking sheets and count the number of times that each of the 75 numbers was called. Divide that tally by 75 to determine the relative probability of each number. Then, the next time you play bingo, select your cards to take maximum advantage of the numbers that you've tracked as most likely to be drawn.

One essential point to bear in mind when a friend or a book recommends a certain mathematical system: so much depends on the type of game. The guide that advises players to focus on the "high-win" squares may give you an advantage, but only in straight bingo. That system may not do you any good if you're playing an H pattern, for instance.

Also, you may not be free to choose the game cards. In that case, of course, no mathematical system would help you win. We should add that it could be very frustrating if you have your heart set on a certain configuration of certain numbers. It's been calculated that there are 111,007,923,832,370,565 possible configurations of those twenty-four numbered squares!

All in all, whatever may be said about bingo, it remains basically a lottery. Consider the following definition:

A lottery is any scheme for the disposal or distribution of property, by chance, among persons who have paid or promised to pay any valuable consideration for the chance of obtaining such property, or a portion of it, or for any such property upon any agreement, understanding, or expectation that it is to be distributed or disposed of by lot or chance, by whatever name the same shall be known.

A lot of legal mumbo-jumbo, but that description certainly applies to bingo: a game of chance. (If you're curious, that passage is from the gaming laws for Nevada—where millions play bingo for money every year. Go figure!)

MANAGING YOUR MONEY

In bingo, as in almost any form of gambling, the true secret to winning may be in controlling your losses. This advice may be even more valid for bingo because of its obvious attractions as a game: it's simple to play, and there's always a winner—except in coverall, where the big prize is likely to cause players to forget about the odds that nobody will win.

The first rule, then, would be not to gamble more than you can afford to lose. That's a good basic guideline for any type of gambling, but experience shows that gamblers tend to forget the basics when they start getting into the game. Set a limit—and keep to it.

Another guideline is to pace your spending according to the potential winnings. For example, if the prize for a regular game is $50, you should not spend more than $50 playing for the whole session. If you do, even if you win, you've lost.

With many casinos in stiff competition for the bingo buck, it pays to check out what they have to offer. There are bingo newsletters and general gambling magazines that keep up on casino action. So you might find, for example, that *Casino Player* might rate the Palace Station Casino as the best bingo operation in Las Vegas, with Binion's Horseshoe and Sam's Town getting honorable mention. You should always understand the reasons behind any ratings, of course. The hours of operation, for example, might not matter to you as much as the minimum buy-in or the payout—the higher the payout the better.

(Note: although "buy-in" can refer to the purchase of a single game card, the word can have a different meaning in some casinos. For example, one casino uses the word to mean "the single purchase of a predetermined set of bingo cards, which usually includes two 6-ons (12 cards) for each of the 15 regular games, a Super Jackpot 3-on (3 cards on a strip), a Late Game Jackpot 3-on, and a single chance at the Do-It-Yourself Jackpot." Whew! And we won't even mention what's in that casino's Double Buy-In!)

Finally you should also keep in mind that bingo can be addictive. Some players are hooked on playing the game no matter what the prizes and the odds. Some players automatically buy their usual half-dozen or dozen cards every game. As we've said before, if you like bingo for the social atmosphere and the action, that's great. But if you want to win more than you lose, then you should avoid getting hooked on any aspect of the game. Play smart.

CYBER BINGO

In the nineteenth century, bingo was popular at county fairs. In the twentieth century, it spread to community organizations of all sorts and to casinos big and small. As we approach the beginning of the twenty-first century, bingo is continuing to expand. Thousands of bingo enthusiasts are enjoying versions of their game on the World Wide Web.

The nature of the Web is such that we cannot possibly provide addresses for all the sites that feature bingo, nor could we guarantee that all or any of the sites we might list will be around a month from now. We just want to mention a few sites as representative of the cyber spread of bingo:

Planet Earth's Bingo and Gaming Newspaper
URL: http://www.binglebugle.com
This site includes links to other bingo sites, a hot list for finding local games, and Aunt Bingo's Advice Column.

CyberBingo
URL: http://www.precyse.com/CyBingo.html
An online site for playing Bingo. You register and then can play games for "generous cash prizes."

Bingo Online
URL: http://www.angelfire.com/ma/bingoonline
A good site for bingo enthusiasts, with information, news, chat, and links to sites where you can play bingo online.

From these sites you can link to others dedicated to bingo. You can also use any of the various search engines: just enter "bingo" and click on the search key. Then, bingo! You've got enough bingo for anyone. You can play bingo on-line, download bingo software, talk bingo with other fans, buy bingo accessories such as seat cushions and travel bags, and keep up on bingo news from around the world.

Also, if you're new to casino bingo, you can become a little more familiar with it before you even set foot in a casino, by visiting any of the many Web sites maintained by casinos. Since they want you to come and have fun playing in their establishments, they hope that their sites will provide you with the information you need to feel comfortable with the game as they play it. So, use a search engine to explore sites in whatever area of the country interests you. That way you'll be ready to have a great time.

ETIQUETTE

When you sit down for a session of bingo, you're meeting neighbors that you'll have to live with for a while. Whether you personally enjoy the social dimensions of bingo or are in it primarily to win, you should respect the players around you and allow them to enjoy the atmosphere and camaraderie. So, think of a bingo game as a cultural microcosm and play by the unwritten rules.

Some players have favorite spots or like to have a lot of room. Don't insist on taking over your "territory" or on asserting your rights to "territory" staked by someone else. The same goes for good luck charms, power colors, lucky rituals, and all other such beliefs: consideration and tolerance are the most important virtues around the tables. You may not take stock in such things, but you shouldn't be discourteous toward those who do believe. And if you're one of those believers, don't let your beliefs infringe on the rights of others.

Finally, if you should happen to win a game, congratulations! And please show proper consideration for all those around you. Nobody likes to lose, but we all feel better if we lose to someone who's gracious about winning.

Remember that bingo is a waiting game. As expectations build and stress levels rise, people can be easily distracted, even annoyed, by otherwise trivial things—especially players trying to keep track of as many as twenty cards! If you tend to hum, to drum your fingers on the table, to chew gum noisily, or to fidget, remember that the key to being a good neighbor is respect.

BINGO GLOSSARY

blackout—Another name for coverall, the highest-paying bingo game, in which the caller draws only 48, 49, or 50 balls and the first player to fill all twenty-four squares wins. (Also known as jackpot bingo.)

buy-in—When a person buys one or more game cards to play bingo.

checker—A member of a bingo staff who verifies winning game cards (also called a floor person).

coverall—The highest-paying bingo game, in which the caller draws only 48, 49, or 50 balls and the first player to fill all twenty-four squares wins. (Also known as blackout or jackpot bingo.)

dauber—An ink marker used to check off called numbers on bingo cards.

early bird—Bingo games played before the regular session begins. If there are games after the regular session ends, those are late bird games.

face—A bingo card on a strip or a sheet. (Also known as an *on*.)

floor person—A member of a bingo staff who verifies winning game cards (also called a checker).

jackpot—The highest-paying bingo game, in which the caller draws only 48, 49, or 50 balls and the first player to fill all twenty-four squares wins. (Also known as coverall or blackout bingo.)

masterboard—Apparatus in which the bingo operator places each ball drawn, after calling out the number (also called a rack).

no-number—A bingo game in which numbers are drawn and called until only one game card remains totally unmarked and wins the prize.

on—The number of bingo cards (also known as *faces*) on a sheet or a strip, e.g., a 3-on or a 6-on.

rack—Apparatus in which the bingo operator places each ball drawn, after calling out the number (also called a masterboard).

shutter card—A permanent, hard plastic bingo game card on which each square can be covered by a shutter that the player slides to mark each number as it is called.

sleeper—A bingo player who suddenly realizes a number drawn earlier made him or her a winner.

throwaway—A disposable paper bingo card.

wait—A number that a player needs to complete the winning pattern in bingo. When a player needs two numbers to win, it's called a wait for a wait.

Chapter Twelve
KENO

The game of keno comes from China, where it was a lottery-type game of long ago. The game involved Chinese characters that told a story. Fortunately, the modern game is far easier to understand and to play.

A popular casino game, keno is essentially a lottery that takes place every five or ten minutes, depending upon the casino. In each game the casino randomly selects twenty numbers from one to eighty. The games are short, taking about thirty seconds to call. The appeal of keno is that it offers large payoffs for a relatively small wager. However, the casino edge in keno is quite large—30 percent. Compare that with blackjack, where the house edge is only a half percent.

In Las Vegas, you can play keno in the keno lounges located in the casino or at most bars and restaurants in the hotels. You're likely to find keno tickets or cards or sheets, crayons, and instruction booklets available almost everywhere that generally explain how to play the game and make the most basic bets—which give the house its best advantage.

In the keno lounges you can sit in comfortable chairs and relax while you mark your keno sheet with the crayons. It's a good place to play keno and at the same time read the paper. With only ten to twenty decisions per hour, it's one of the cheapest places to gamble in the casino. Keep in mind you won't win very often, but at least you're reducing the amount of money in play per hour to a minimum.

THE RULES

The object of keno is to correctly guess a certain amount of numbers that are pulled from the eighty keno numbers, kind of like in a bingo game. The amount you need to guess correctly depends upon the amount of numbers you choose and the casino in which you're playing. Casinos vary the amount of numbers you need to guess correctly from the amount of numbers you've chosen. Payoffs vary from casino to casino, so you might want to shop around for a good casino with higher payoffs for keno.

How many numbers can you select? You may generally select anywhere from one to ten numbers. (Some casinos let you select twenty numbers, but ten is the most common maximum.) For example, you can select one of the eighty numbers, and if that number comes up in the next game, you're a winner. If you bet $1, then you'll get back $3 or triple your money. Let's take another example. You bet $1, you select ten numbers, and all ten numbers come up in the twenty that are pulled in the next game. Congratulations! You win $25,000—the big jackpot! You'd also win if you got five, six, seven, eight, or nine numbers correct. The more numbers you correctly guess, the more money you win. However, the odds that you'll correctly pick ten of the twenty numbers pulled is one in over 8.9 million. So it hardly seems fair that they only pay you $25,000 on your $1 bet.

What the odds are telling you is that *on average* you'll correctly guess all ten numbers only once in over 8.9 million games. You do the math. At a $1 per game, you'd be spending over $8.9 million and getting back only $25,000. Now you know why this is a bad game for the players.

How many numbers should you play? Most people play six or seven numbers. The most common bets are straight bets. A straight bet is when a player marks X numbers on a keno sheet for Y number of games at Z price per game.

There are four parts to filling out a keno ticket or card. First, select your numbers, and using the crayon provided by the keno lounge put an X through those numbers on the card. (Those numbers are called "spots.") Second, decide on the amount you wish to wager on this keno game. Most people play the minimum bet, usually a dollar. Put the amount in the "price per game" box on the card. Then you decide how many games you wish to play these numbers at this wager and put your choice in the "number of games" box. Finally, indicate how many numbers you've selected in the right-hand column, in the space labeled "#Spots/Ways Rate." Your card will look something like the typical keno card shown in Figure 12-1.

Take your keno ticket to the keno writer at the counter or give it to a keno runner. In return, this person will give you a ticket showing the numbers you marked and the amount you bet on those numbers. Check that ticket to make sure that it correctly shows your selections. If not, get it corrected before the game begins. The ticket returned to you is what determines your entry in the game, not the card you filled out with the crayon.

Now watch the keno board light up with the numbers that are selected for your keno game. If you're enjoying the atmosphere or reading the newspaper and you happen to miss your keno game numbers, just take your ticket to the counter and the keno writer will

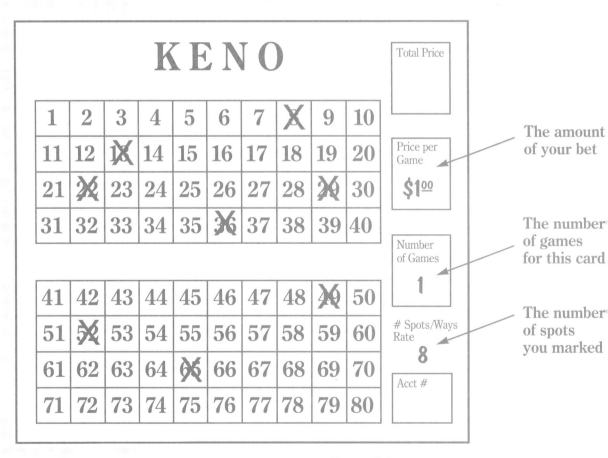

Figure 12-1
A typical keno card for one game with eight spots marked and with a $1 bet.

check your ticket to see if you won money on that game. The numbers are marked on ping pong balls and put into a clear hopper with a mixing bar in the middle. You may recognize this as the same way that state lotteries select their numbers.

There's another way to play keno numbers, called "way" tickets. It's the same process as a straight bet or straight ticket, but you can group numbers together to make additional wagers. What's the advantage to a way ticket? Usually, the ticket minimum bet is lower than the usual straight ticket minimum wager. This saves you time and money instead of making out three keno sheets for each group of three bets.

To mark your way ticket, mark each number with an X and indicate the amount of your bet under "Total Price" as explained above. Then draw a circle around all of the numbers in each group. The key to a way ticket is that you are making the same bet for each group.

Let's say you mark a total of nine numbers and circle three groups of three. Now you write 3/3 in the right margin, under "#Spots/Ways Rate," meaning you're making three separate wagers on each one of the groups of three numbers. That's easy enough.

But you can make a few more bets with that one way ticket. For example, you could easily add three bets, based on the same numbers, as shown in Figure 12-2. This ticket indicates your three straight bets plus bets on the three possible combinations of two groups of three—Group A with Group B, Group A with Group C, and Group B with Group C. That gives you six bets, a six spot ticket that you indicate by putting 3/6 under "#Spots/Ways Rate." (This is known, quite logically, as a "combination way" bet.)

Now if you happen to hit six numbers (three numbers in one group and three numbers in another group), your ticket would cover you. You get these extra chances for no additional cost than the 3/3 way ticket.

Keno is very simple to learn. If you have any questions, don't be shy about asking someone at the keno lounge. The runners are there to help you enjoy playing the game. Just remember that keno is one of the worst games in the casino to play if you want to win because of its high house advantage—25 percent or higher. But the playing atmosphere can be relaxing, especially if you're taking a break between more active games.

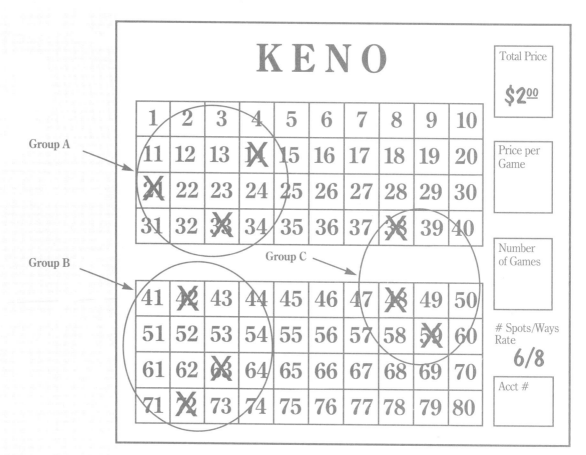

Figure 12-2
A typical keno card marked for a "way" bet. In this case, there are
three bets of six numbers each (3/6), A with B, A with C, and B with C.

KENO STRATEGY

There's only one sure-fire strategy to use in keno—don't play. Keno's large house advantage makes it impossible for players to win over the long haul and unlikely over a short haul. You might better consider it more like a form of entertainment than as gambling: you pay a little money to have a little fun without expecting to win anything in return. If you want to play keno, play for only a short period of time. Then take your winnings, if you have any, and play another game where the odds are better.

Let's say you decide to take your chances and play keno. Watch a couple of games first. Notice how certain numbers and patterns tend to come up more often then others. When you see a number or pattern appearing frequently, then play that number or pattern. Numbers and patterns tend to repeat themselves. There is no logical reasoning for this because each game is independent of others. The numbers that come up in one game have no impact on the numbers that will come up in the next game. It's strange, but you'll sometimes find that a certain number will repeat for ten games in a row.

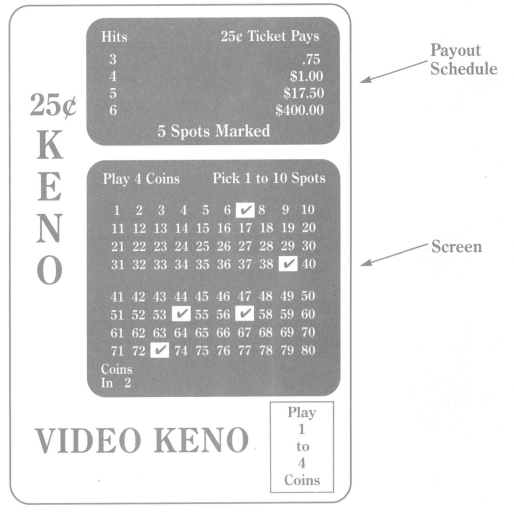

Figure 12-3
A typical video keno machine.

One pattern could be that all the numbers turning up are multiples of ten (10, 20, 30, 40, 50, 60, 70, and 80). Maybe it could be a square—four spots whose corners meet on a keno ticket, such as 1, 2, 11, and 12, or 4, 5, 14, and 15, or 23, 24, 33, and 34. Whatever pattern you note, play it.

Another suggestion is to play as few numbers as possible. You'll have a better chance of winning and win more frequently. Try playing with just three numbers. That way you will win if two or three numbers are correct. Of course, you are not going to win the $25,000 that would be possible by trying to guess all ten numbers, but then it's rare that any player wins the big jackpot. Remember those odds: one in over 8.9 million. The jackpot is just a sucker's bet.

VIDEO KENO

Video keno is the same game as regular keno, but it's played at a slot machine with a video screen. There are eighty numbers to select, and you select your numbers using a wand that's attached to the screen. You can play video keno for as little as a nickel a game, but most video keno games are a quarter. Figure 12-3 shows a video keno setup.

After you've selected your numbers, push the play or start button. The machine randomly selects ten winning numbers that it highlights on the screen. The area on the screen above your playing card tells you how many numbers you'll need to win anything and the dollar amount you'll win if you hit that many.

The big difference between regular keno and video keno—besides the mechanical difference—is how often you can play each game. With regular keno you've got only between ten and twenty games per hour. With video keno, it's up to you how many games per hour you play. Video keno costs you less per game than regular keno, so you can afford to play more games per hour in video keno.

ETIQUETTE

There's not much to get you in trouble when playing keno. The booklets provided in keno lounges are very helpful in explaining minimum bets, the number of hits you need to win anything, and the payouts. Before playing keno, please consult these booklets.

Chapter Thirteen
WHEEL OF FORTUNE

The wheel of fortune, or big six wheel, is a form of the popular carnival game by the same name. In casino wheel of fortune, you gamble on the outcome of the next spin of the wheel. The wheel is six feet in diameter and stands upright. There are fifty-four slots the wheel can stop on when it's spun. Each of the slots has one of six symbols. Usually the wheel's symbols are $1, $2, $5, $10, $20, and joker. In front of the dealer there's a table with each symbol on it.

THE RULES

Learning how to play the wheel of fortune is very simple. You bet on the symbol you think is going to appear on the next spin of the wheel. To bet on that symbol, place your chips on that symbol on the table in front of the dealer. After all players have made their bets, the dealer spins the wheel and the slot at the top when the wheel stops is the winning symbol. The dealer then takes all the losing bets and pays the winners. The amount of the payoff varies depending on the symbol of the winning slot. Below is a list of the payoffs:

Symbol	Payoff
$1	even money or 1 to 1
$2	2 to 1
$5	5 to 1
$10	1 to 1
$20	20 to 1
Joker	40 to 1

As noted above, the wheel has fifty-four slots. There are twenty-four slots with the $1 symbol, fifteen with the $2 symbol, seven with the $5 symbol, four with the $10 symbol, and two each for the $20 symbol and the joker.

You may make as many bets as you want per spin. Just remember that only one of the symbols is going to hit. Unfortunately for players, the wheel of fortune has a very large house advantage, ranging from 11.1 percent to 24 percent. What that means is for every $100 you bet on the wheel of fortune, you are only going to get paid back on average between $76 and $88.90. Comparatively, slot machines have an average house advantage of 10 percent or lower.

Keep in mind the wheel of fortune can be a lot of fun. There's usually no crowd around a wheel of fortune game, probably because the casino enjoys such a great advantage. It takes no skill whatsoever, so anyone can play, and it requires no thought, so it can provide a nice break from more demanding games. To succeed, you just need to get lucky.

WHEEL OF FORTUNE STRATEGY

There really isn't much strategy to playing the wheel of fortune. It's really a game of luck. As in all casino games, however, there are some bets that are better than others. You're better off putting your money on the $1 symbol where the house advantage is the lowest—11.1 percent. The worst symbols you can bet on are the $20 symbol and the joker. The house advantage of these bets is 24 percent. In other words, the higher the payoff, the larger the house advantage.

Because of the large casino advantage, limit your investment in the wheel of fortune to just a few spins. Predicting where the wheel is going to stop can be very tough. It can be entertaining as players rejoice when they win or groan when they lose, but you can enjoy the entertainment without placing any bets. In terms of smart gambling, you're better off saving your money for another game.

ETIQUETTE

There is no special etiquette involved in the wheel of fortune. Simply place your bet on the number you want and watch the spin.

Chapter Fourteen
SPORTS BETTING

The most popular form of gambling in the United States is on sporting events. At the time of this writing, the only state that legally accepts sports wagers is Nevada. The sports books in Nevada are averaging between $40 and $50 million in bets on the Super Bowl alone. (A sports book is a sports wagering facility that functions as a business on its own or as part of a casino.) That's only the amount of legal gambling done on that one single game. If we include the gambling done through bookies, friends, relatives, and co-workers, the estimated amount of money gambled on the Super Bowl alone would be around $200 million.

The federal government believes that sports wagering is a business of between $40 billion and $200 billion annually. This includes legal sports books and all illegal sports bets. Estimates vary widely because it's impossible to track illegal betting. But if you consider that in 1995 sports wagers in Nevada exceeded $2.1 billion, with more than half of that on football, you realize that sports betting— legal or otherwise—is big business.

This chapter covers legal sports betting in Nevada casinos. You'll learn how to read the big board in casino sports books plus cover betting on baseball, basketball, boxing, football, hockey, and horse racing.

THE RULES

The Line

The Nevada sports books are kept busy year-round setting a *line* for a variety of wagering activities. The object of sports books is to set a line between two teams, a method of handicapping one or the other, equalizing the risk of the wager so that the amounts bet on each team are more likely to be comparable. Sports books don't make their money by betting against the bettors as they do in most other casino games. They make their money on a vigorish (or commission) on every bet made, so the best way to make money is by promoting betting activity. Setting a line can make betting on any event a more attractive proposition for gamblers.

Sports books set a line by either penalizing the favored team or assisting the underdog team. The betting line will fluctuate right up till the start of the game according to two main consideration:

conditions and bets. If there's any change in any factor of any potential significance for the outcome of the event—such as an injury to a player, or a suspension, or predictions of weather that might favor one team over the other—the sports books might adjust the line to reflect that change in conditions. If one of the teams is attracting more betting money than the other, the sports books will change the line to encourage more balanced betting. The sports book wants to get an equal amount bet on each team and to attract as much betting money as possible. Of course, if an event isn't stimulating enough gambling activity, sports books can change the line to draw more bets.

There are two different types of betting lines in sports, the point spread and the money line. The difference is in the amount and the odds.

In a point spread bet, the underdog is given extra points so that the bet is won or lost not simply on the outcome of the game but on an "adjusted" outcome. The two sports that use this form of betting the most are football and basketball. A bet on the favorite will win if the favorite beats the underdog by a total greater than the point spread. A bet on the underdog will win if the underdog wins the game or loses by less than the point spread.

For example, if the Oakland Raiders are favored by ten points over the New York Jets, if you bet on the Raiders you have to accept the point spread of ten. That means that the Raiders must beat the Jets by more than ten points in order for you to win your bet. If they win by a closer score, you lose. If you bet on the underdog Jets and they win the game, then you win the bet. But you'd also win if the Jets lose by fewer than ten points. If the Raiders were to defeat the Jets by exactly ten points, then no bettor would win and all money would be returned.

Let's say the outcome of the game was Oakland 42, New York 17. To figure out who wins if the point spread is ten, add ten points to the final score for the Jets. So the score to the sports books is then Oakland 42 New York 27. Any person who bet the Raiders would win because they won by more than ten points. In sports parlance, they beat the spread—as, by extension, did all the people who bet on them.

How does a sports book make its money on a point spread? For the sports book to make money, they charge a vigorish (commission). To make a sports bet with a point spread, you have to bet $11 to win $10. So, in the above example, if you wanted to bet the Raiders, you'd bet $11 and would have received $21 ($11 for your original bet plus the $10 you won) when you cashed in your winning betting slip. Even though the casino paid every winning bet on the Raiders, it would still make money because there was likely an equal amount of money bet on the New York Jets. Anyone who bet the Jets would have lost the $11. The sports book is really making only $1 on every $11 bet on the Jets, because the other $10 is going to be paid as the winnings to people who bet the Raiders.

That's the reason the sports books want an equal amount bet on each team. When there's an equal amount bet on each team, the sports books are guaranteed to make money unless calculating the final score and the point spread results in a tie. When that happens, no bettors make any money but they still have to cash in their tickets to get back their bets.

You may bet the point spread with any amount of money as long as you don't go over the casino's betting limit. To find out the betting limit, ask one of the workers at the sports book counter. It's smarter to bet in $11 increments, because the sports books will round down on bets not divisible by eleven, thus charging you a higher vigorish.

For example, let's say two people bet the same team to win but different amounts. Person A bet $220 (an amount divisible by eleven evenly) and Person B bet $200 (not divisible by eleven evenly). Let's say their team wins and covers the point spread. Person A will get his $220 back plus $200 for his winning bet, a total of $420. Person A was paid off at eleven to ten. Person B will get back his $200 plus $180 for winning his bet, a total of $380. Person B was paid off at ten to nine. Because the $200 bet is not divisible by eleven evenly, the sports book rounds it down and takes a greater commission. Person B would have been paid $181.81 if the sports book paid him eleven to ten, so he loses $1.81 for not betting in increments of $11.

The house advantage when making football point spread bets is 4.54 percent. For you to come out ahead when betting football with the point spread, you have to win your bets 52.38 percent of the time. If you can do this, you'll come out a winner.

The point spread is the most popular form of betting when it comes to college and professional football and basketball games. It's simple— once you understand how you can lose betting on the winning team.

The other type of line is called the money line or just the line. When you bet the money line, there is no point spread. Instead, the difference is reflected in odds. The money line penalizes the people who bet the favorite by making them bet a lot to win a little. The people who bet the underdog bet a little to win a lot. When you bet the money line, the final outcome of the event is what determines the winners and losers. You'll see the money line listed on a sports book's big board as in the following example:

Cincinnati −175
Tampa Bay +150

Let's look at what the -175 and +150 mean. If you want to bet Tampa Bay, the underdog, you'll win $150 for every $100 bet if the Buccaneers win. This doesn't mean you have to bet $100. It's just an easy number to work with. You can bet any amount you wish and you'll get three to two odds. (For every $2 you bet, you'll win $3.) If you want to bet Cincinnati, the favorite, you'll win $100 for every $175 bet. That means that for whatever amount you bet, you'll get paid four to seven odds. (For every $7 you bet, you'll win $4.) When you risk more money than you'll win, this is called a *lay bet*. A lay bet occurs in sports bets when you bet the favorite on the money line.

Even though the point spread is listed on the board with the money line, the point spread is not added to the final score of the game. It's there to let you know by how much the oddsmakers favor one team to beat the other team. The house advantage with the money line is about the same as with the point spread, 4.54 percent.

Over/Under

Another type of bet you can make on most sporting events is an over/under bet. This bet is on the total number of points scored by both teams during the game. What you want to decide is if the total final score will be over or under the amount the oddsmaker has set. The over/under bet has nothing to do with which team wins the game or the point spread on the game. An over/under on a betting board might look like the following example:

Baltimore   O/U
Houston   45

An over/under bet is just like a point spread bet in that it's paid off at ten to eleven: for every $11 bet you'll win $10. As with point spread bets, you should make over/under bets in increments of $11 to keep the house advantage at its minimum. If the final score of the above game is Houston 31, Baltimore 17, then anyone who bet the over would have won the bet, because the scores combined equal 48, three points over the over/under figure.

Football Bets

The most popular sport for betting is football, both college and pro. There are several options when betting football games. You can bet the point spread, the money line, and the over/under. In addition to those bets, you can bet *parlays*.

A parlay card is when you bet on the outcome of at least three games. There's no advantage to betting a parlay card. It only lessens your chances of winning because you have to choose three winners instead of just one. Of course, if you manage to win your bet, you'll get paid at higher odds than if you bet it straight on single games. Some parlay cards lose if the game ends in a tie. Make sure you read the parlay card so you understand the rules.

Here's what a parlay might look like. Let's say you pick Team 1, Team 2, and Team 3 and you bet $11 to win $10. That means that you first have an $11 bet on Team 1. If you win that bet, your payoff goes to wager at eleven to ten that Team 2 will win. If that bet also wins, the payoff goes on to bet on Team

3, again at eleven to ten. In a parlay bet, each bet is dependent upon the previous bets.

In other words, you bet games in a sequence. If you win the first game, it sets up your bet on game two. This continues until either you lose a bet or you win all your bets. The games don't have to be played in the same sequence. For example, if you make a parlay bet with college football games and NFL games, you can have the first bet be a NFL game on Sunday and the second bet on a college game played the day before. However, you must make your bet before any of the games have started.

Here's what will happen to your money:

Bet #1: $11 that Team 1 wins   Result of Team 1 winning, get paid $21

Bet #2: $21 that Team 2 wins   Result of Team 2 winning, get paid $40

Bet #3: $40 that Team 3 wins   Result of Team 3 winning, get paid $69

So your $11 investment gets you almost $69. The true odds of getting each of the three picks correct are seven to one, which would result in a payoff of $77. The house advantage on three team parlays is 12.5 percent. This is not a particularly good bet.

Another parlay type bet is called a *teaser*. A teaser is when you select three or more teams and each team has to beat an enhanced point spread. Teaser bets are different because sports books give additional points over the regular point spreads. For example, if Denver is favored by seven points over Seattle, a teaser card might offer Denver –4 or Seattle +10. This means that you take off four points from Denver's final score or add ten points to Seattle's final score. The more attractive point spread teases you into making these bets. However, there is a down side. Teaser cards pay off at lower odds than other parlay cards. What about ties? Some teaser cards state that ties win, others state that ties lose, while some prevent ties by making their special point spread ending with a half point. Since a team can never beat another by a half point, point spread ties are impossible.

You're better off just making straight bets on each individual game rather than betting on parlay or teaser cards. You're also better off betting the money line over the point spread and over/under. The oddsmakers are very skilled at selecting the initial point spread of a game, so you're better off betting the game's outcome without points. This may require betting more money and winning less money by betting the favorite. And finally, bet with your head and not your heart. Don't bet your favorite team every week. Do some research to make a smart bet.

Basketball

Basketball bets can be made on both college and pro games. In basketball bets, a sports book will offer a point spread and an over/under as well as parlay and teaser cards. Basketball bets are based on the point spread, so when you bet the favorite, you give points to the underdog team. Along with a point spread there will be an over/under on the total of the final score. On a sports book's board, you might find it looking like this:

		O/U
Indiana		
MICHIGAN STATE	+5	146

The team listed first will be the favorite. The team listed in capital letters will be the home team. The line in the above game is Michigan State plus five, so five points will be added to the final score of Michigan State to decide point spread bets on this game. If you bet on Indiana, you win the bet if they win by six points or more. If you bet on Michigan State, you win if they win the game or if they lose by four points or less. If the final score is Indiana winning by five points, then the game is considered a tie for bettors. When a tie occurs you'll get all your money back. If you bet the over/under, you'll win or lose depending on whether the points scored by both teams total over or under 146.

A teaser bet is usually offered in addition to the point spread and total. As in football, a teaser bet in which additional points are given or taken will pay off at lower odds, and that's only if you win all your teaser bets. The parlay works the same way as for football.

Baseball

Baseball betting in sports books isn't nearly as popular as football and basketball. Part of that reason is that baseball has been slipping in popularity with the public. Baseball sports bets are only on professional teams. Baseball odds are shown as a money line. For example, the board in a sports book might look like this:

LOS ANGELES DODGERS   –7 ½
St. Louis Cardinals 6 ½

The home team will be listed in capital letters and the favorite will be listed first. What's different about this money line and the one used for football games is it's based on a $5 bet instead of football's $100 bet. In the above example, the Dodgers are favored over the Cardinals. If you bet the Dodgers to win, you win $5 for every $7.50 bet. If you bet the Cardinals to win, then for every $5 bet, you'll win $6.50. Remember that no points are added to the final score when you bet a money line bet. You can tell the favorite by the minus sign in front of the Dodgers' money line odds. That's how you know you'll have to lay $7.50 to win $5.

In addition to the money line in baseball, some sports books will offer an over/under. It works the same as a football over/under. The oddsmaker selects an amount he thinks the combined score of both teams will be. What you have to determine is whether the score of the game will be over that number or under that number. All over/under bets are paid off at eleven to ten: for every $11 bet you'll win $10.

Hockey

Hockey is America's fastest-growing sport. The amount of money bet on hockey games in sports books is rising. Sports books offer bets only on NHL games. The odds in hockey are listed as a point spread. For example, the board in a sports book would list a hockey game like the following:

Toronto Maple Leafs   1 ½
OTTAWA SENATORS

Toronto is listed first so they're the favorite over Ottawa by 1 ½ goals. Ottawa is the home team because they're listed in capital letters. Since Ottawa is the underdog team, you'll add 1 ½ goals to their final score to determine who wins the bets. If you bet Toronto, you need to win by two or more goals in order to win your bet. If you bet Ottawa, you'll win if Ottawa wins the game or if they lose by only one goal. Point spread bets are paid off at eleven to ten odds: for every $11 bet you'll win $10.

In addition to a point spread bet, some sports books will offer an over/under bet. It works the same as all other over/under bets. The oddsmaker will select an amount he thinks the combined score of both teams will be. You have to determine if the combined score of both teams will be over or under that amount. Over/under bets are paid off at $10 for every $11 bet.

Boxing

Boxing prize fights are listed in terms of a money line. Like all other money line bets, the favorite will be listed first and the underdog second. Here's an example of a prize fight on the big board in a sports book:

Tyson	11
Holyfield	8

The money line in boxing is based on $5 bets. If you bet Tyson in the above fight, you'd have to bet $11 to win $5. If you bet Holyfield to win, you'd bet $5 to win $8. Unless you follow boxing on a regular basis, you are better off avoiding boxing sports bets. The house advantage can be considerably higher than for other sports bets.

In addition to the money line bet offered on boxing prize fights, you can make special bets. These special bets are bad bets to make because of their high house advantage. Some of these special bets might be for Tyson to knock out Holyfield, for Tyson to win in three rounds or less, or for Tyson to knock Holyfield down three times. These bets are usually sucker bets and should be avoided.

Horse Racing

Besides the large board of sports bets, you'll find a board devoted to horse racing. Horse races are shown live via satellite every day in a sports book. There are three basic horse racing bets you can make: a win bet, a place bet, and a show bet. If you bet a horse to win, then that horse must win the race for you to win the bet. If you bet it to place, then it must finish first or second. If you bet a horse to show, then a first, second, or third will win your bet.

The minimum amount you can bet on horses is $2. The odds can be reflected as X amount to one. Sometimes you'll see them listed as X to two. The odds will fluctuate right up until the race begins. They change due to the amount that bettors are putting on each horse. To make a good, sensible bet on horse races, you'll need to get the *Daily Racing Form*. This is a publication that lists each horse for each race. For each horse you'll find a detailed history of the horse's past performances, trainer, owner, jockey, etc. You should read the *Daily Racing Form's* "How to Read the Racing Form" section before betting on the horses.

The *Daily Racing Form* provides bettors with the most comprehensive coverage of any horse's past performance, important information for handicapping a race. Listed for each horse are the races (in reverse chronological order, with distance and track conditions), and details about the performances—split times for each quarter, speed, jockey's name and weight, the first three horses and their finishing times, as well as a brief comment, such as "bobbled start" or "closed well."

A smart bettor compares this information against information in the track's official program and knowledge about the conditions of the track. There's no sure thing, of course, but there are definitely some bets that are smarter than others.

In addition to the win, place, and show bets, horse racing offers some exotic bets: an exacta, a daily double, a trifecta, and a pick six.

With the exacta you need to pick the horses that finish first and second in the race and the exact order of their finish. When you bet the daily double, you need to pick the winning horses of the first two races. The trifecta is similar to the exacta, except you need to pick the correct order of finish for the first three horses in the race. With the pick six, you need to pick the winner of each race for the first six races. Needless to say, these bets are bad bets to make, but if you get lucky and get them right, the payoff will be much higher than the normal win, place, and show bets.

Future Bets

A future bet is a bet on a team winning a championship. To take professional football as an example, at the beginning of each NFL season, the oddsmakers will put odds on each team winning the Super Bowl. As the season progresses, these odds are changed according to how well their season is going. You may also make a future bet on the NBA, NHL, MLB, and some college championships. You can bet any amount you wish, and you'll receive the odds as they stand on that particular day. Let's say that in July you bet the New England Patriots to win the Super Bowl. The odds you received were twenty to one. As the NFL season progressed and the playoffs started, the odds on New England might have dropped to eight to one. If New England won the Super Bowl, you'd get paid at twenty to one, which is what the odds were when you made your bet.

A future bet can provide some added excitement throughout the season, but it's a bad bet. If you want to make a bet on your favorite team, then make a minimal bet on your team to win the championship. This should make the games a little more interesting, especially if they have a good season and make it to the playoffs, but it won't cost you a lot if they don't go all the way.

SPORTS BETTING STRATEGY

When making sports bets, make sure you research the teams. A sure way to lose is to always bet your favorite team. Injuries can be a big factor in sports bets. Another factor can be whether the team is playing at home or on the road. These and many other factors can help you determine a smart sports bet.

The best bet to make when betting sports is the money line. All you have to do is determine the winner of the game. There are no point spreads to affect the outcome. When a good team is playing a bad team you'll have to bet more money than you'll win, but it's probably worth it. Also, you can bet the underdog for a little money on the hope of winning a lot. Stick with the sports you follow. Don't make a sports bet just to bet the game or make the game more interesting.

If you're really interested in making sports bets, shop around at the sports books at various casinos. The odds each sports book offers will be a little different. Remember: the sports books change their odds to balance out the amount of money bet on each team. If you were going to bet the Knicks plus five against the Heat, then why wouldn't you take the Knicks plus six against the Heat? The sports book right next door might offer that additional point. It pays to shop around.

ETIQUETTE

Watching a game in a sports book can be a lot of fun. It can be crowded and noisy and sometimes make you feel like you're actually there at the game. But you probably don't want to be in a pack of people who bet the other team and then start cheering really loud when your team scores. This can anger the people you're around, and lead to excitement that may make your experience less pleasant. Instead, find a group of people who bet the same team you did, and it will be more fun for everybody.

The only other etiquette to watch when making sports bets is when you make the bet itself. On the big board next to the team and type of bet you want to make there will be a number. You must use this number when making your bet. For example, if you wanted to bet the Washington Redskins over the Detroit Lions, then you need to find that game on the board.

```
136. WASHINGTON  –3 –140          O/U
137. Detroit          150   48
```

When you want to bet the Washington Redskins on the money line, then you'll need to say "136, Washington Redskins for $140 on the money line over the Detroit Lions." The number you give tells the sports book clerk which team you're picking. State the amount, the type of bet, and the opposing team. Since there are so many sports teams and types of bets, this helps the clerks set up your bet quickly and correctly. In the example above, the bet was that the Washington Redskins would beat the Detroit Lions. Since Washington is the favorite (we know this because it's listed first for that game) and the bet is the money line, you have to bet $140 to win $100, because posted next to Washington is "–140". Remember: with the money line, there is no point spread. If you were betting on Detroit, then you would win $150 for every $100 bet. In this case, if you put your $140 on Detroit, you would win $210.

By following the guidelines and rules of the game, you should have a fun and enjoyable time making sports bets in casinos.

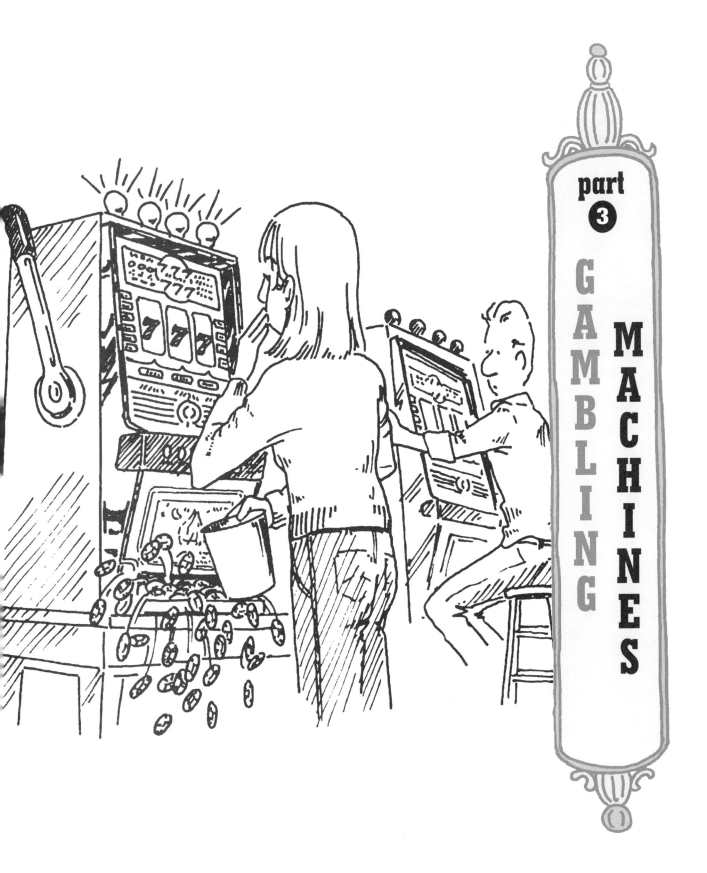

part **3**

GAMBLING MACHINES

Chapter Fifteen
SLOT MACHINES

S lot machines are the most popular game in the casino. Why do you think the casinos have so many slot machines? Two reasons: it's the most popular casino game, and it brings in a high house advantage for the casino. Why do so many people play the slot machines? Maybe because there are so many of those one-armed bandits! It's also because they are easy to use and provide results quickly.

The average casino advantage for slot machines is around 15 percent. That means for every $100 you play on the slots, you'll get back around $85, on average. That's a big chunk of the action, especially when compared with the 0.5 percent advantage for blackjack. Think of the house advantage as a casino tax. You're paying a 15 percent tax to play the slots.

Slot machines were invented in the late 1800's by Charles Fey. The slot machines back then were mechanical. Today's slot machines are computers. Despite the changes in their design, slot machines have a universal appeal. You play them at your own pace and without any skill at all. There are frequent payoffs, with the jingling of coins and a sense of excitement. Every one-armed bandit beckons with the possibility of winning the jackpot on your next pull.

HOW THEY WORK

Let's look how a slot machine works today compared with the machines of the early days. Slot machines in the early days were driven by mechanical devices. Each machine had reels and levers that were the guts of the machine. The reels had symbols on them which, depending on how they lined up across the payline (the line across the middle of the slot machine), determined whether or not you got paid and, if so, how much.

These have now given way to computer-driven slot machines. Today's machines each contain a single microchip called a random number generator (RNG). This single microchip is the most important technology in today's slot machines. The RNG runs quickly through numbers that are assigned certain combinations on the reels of the slot machine. As soon as you drop your first coin into the

slot machine, the random number generator stops and sends its current number to the reels, determining what combination of symbols will appear on the payline after you pull the handle.

For example, say you decide to play a $1 Red, White, and Blue slot machine. After obtaining change from the change clerk, find what you think is a lucky machine. You decide to play three coins a pull. As soon as the first coin is dropped into the machine, the RNG stops and waits for the handle on the side of the machine to be pulled or the spin button to be pressed. As you insert the other two coins, the RNG stays on the same number. Now you are ready to pull the handle. As soon as you pull the handle, the reels on the Red, White, and Blue machine begin spinning. The RNG sends the combination to the reels that are assigned to the number it's stopped on. Let's say the RNG stopped on 1,234. Whatever combination of symbols the programmer assigned to 1,234 will now appear on the payline. If the programmer assigned red seven, white seven, and blue seven to number 1,234, then that exact combination will appear on the payline. You'd be very happy if that red seven, white seven, and blue seven appeared, because that would be the jackpot on the Red, White, and Blue slot machines.

The RNG is continuously selecting random numbers when no one is playing the machine, generating numbers from one to the maximum number of different combinations that particular machine can create. The maximum possible of combinations on a slot machine is determined by the number of reels and the number of symbols on each reel.

If a machine has three reels with twenty-five symbols on each reel, then the possible number of combinations is 25 x 25 x 25 = 15,625. So a three-reel machine with twenty-five symbols each has 15,625 different combinations. Only one of those will be the jackpot combination. It's very difficult to find out how many symbols each reel has on a slot machine. Each reel may have anywhere from twenty to 150 symbols. The slot machines with a lower number of symbols and a lower number of reels provide a better chance of hitting the jackpot.

In the last example, the Red, White, and Blue slot machine with three twenty-five-symbol reels had a possible 15,625 different combinations. Now if the machine next to it had three reels and

Slot Machine Timing

A comment often heard in the slot machine area is "He hit my jackpot!" This comes from players who gave up on a machine only to have someone else sit down at that machine and immediately win big. This comment is based on frustration rather than fact. On most slot machines, the reel positions are the result of the random number generator, which is stopped at the time a coin is inserted. It's nearly impossible, therefore, that if the other person had continued to play that machine, he or she would have won that jackpot. That would have required inserting the coin at the precise time the winning player did. Very unlikely!

only twenty symbols on each reel, there would be only 8,000 different combinations (20 x 20 x 20). Wouldn't you rather play the machine with only 8,000 combinations than a machine with 15,625? The chance of hitting the jackpot would be almost twice as good. Unfortunately, you can't tell which machine has the lower number of symbols on each reel.

However, you can see that a machine with fewer reels is more likely to hit the jackpot. A machine with three reels and twenty symbols on each reel has 8,000 different combinations. Now if that machine had four reels with twenty symbols each, it would have 160,000 combinations. Which machine would you rather play?

FLAT TOPS VS. PROGRESSIVES

Slot machines come in two types—flat top and progressive. A flat top slot machine is a machine where the jackpot is fixed, no matter how many coins you feed it. Flat tops operate independently from any other slot machine. Usually the flat top slot machines have a smaller jackpot than the progressive slot machines.

Progressive slot machines have a jackpot that grows with the number of coins you insert. Usually progressive slot machines are linked to a group of other slot machines; the jackpot grows within that group. A sign above the group of progressive slot machines shows what the jackpot is worth. You can even watch it grow as players keep feeding coin after coin into the machines. Some progressive slot machines are linked to other progressive slot machines in other casinos. For example, the MegaBucks progressive slot machines are linked to all other MegaBucks slot machines in the state of Nevada. The MegaBucks slot machines offer jackpots in the millions of dollars.

Which machine is right for you? If you're hoping to win one of the jackpots that could change your life, then play the progressive slot machines. Keep in mind you'll most likely be throwing your money away. If you want to win smaller amounts more frequently, then play the flat tops machines.

The Smell of Money

The next time you walk through a casino take a look at the layout and design of the casino. Everything from the design of the carpet to the way the casino is laid out is planned to keep the players playing longer. The latest innovation in casino design is appealing to the players' sense of smell. The casinos and slot machine manufacturers are experimenting with different scents that emanate from slot machines to enhance your gaming pleasure and perhaps lull you into a false sense of security.

STRATEGY

The old cliché "I'd rather be lucky than good" is the best advice for a slot player. However, there are some simple strategies you can use when playing slot machines.

The first thing is don't bet over your head. Just take enough money to have a good time and make sure that if you lose it all you won't be in a financial pinch. Once you determine your bankroll for gambling, determine what denomination slot machine would be right for you. Here's what you can expect to spend on average for an hour's worth of play on different denomination slot machines:

NUMBER OF COINS BET

	One Coin	Two Coins	Three Coins
Nickel slot machine	$30	$60	$90
Quarter slot machine	$150	$300	$450
Dollar slot machine	$600	$1,200	$1,800

This is the amount of money you'll insert into a slot machine in an hour. This doesn't take into account any money you may win from that slot machine.

Play the maximum number of coins allowed when playing slot machines. This allows you to take advantage of the extra money the machine pays out when you hit the jackpot. You get this bonus only when you have the maximum number of coins in play. For example, on a slot machine the jackpot payout could look like the following:

NUMBER OF COINS BET

	One Quarter	Two Quarters	Three Quarters
Jackpot Payout	1,000 coins	2,000 coins	5,000 coins

Notice that when you go from one quarter to two quarters, you get double the payout—exactly what you'd expect for risking twice as much money. However, when you go from two quarters to three quarters, you get 167 percent more. This is an extra 2,000 coins payout for hitting the jackpot with the maximum number of coins played.

Payoffs on slot machines are in the number of coins, not a dollar amount. The only time the payout is listed in dollar amounts is if the machine uses denominations of $5 or higher or it's a progressive jackpot payout machine.

Now that we know you'll always play the maximum number of coins allowed for a machine, we can look at the above table to see what denomination machine is right for you. Keep in mind the dollar amounts listed in the table are the amounts of money you'll insert into that denomination machine in an hour, but doesn't take into account any money you may win.

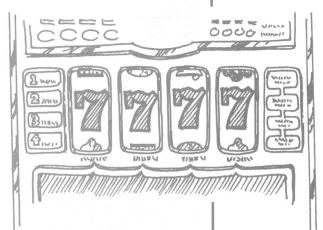

Figure what it will cost you to play a certain denomination on average for one hour, assuming the machine pays out at 85 percent. Let's say you can afford to play a quarter slot machine with three coins a play for one hour. If you play three coins every pull for one hour, your long-term average return would be $382.50. If you look at the table on the previous page, under three coins and a quarter machine, you'll see that you spend $450 an hour. Of that $450, you can expect, on average, to get back $382.50. Remember: in the short run, you could end up with a lot more than $450 or get back only $100. But if the machine is set to 85 percent return, then on average you can expect to get back 85 percent of the money you insert into the machine.

The best advice for playing slot machines is to play your session bankroll through a slot machine once. Then walk away, whether you win or lose. The longer you sit at a machine, the more likely you are to walk away a loser. Hit and run. Never chase your losses.

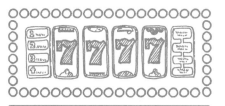

The Best Five Plays When Playing Slots

1. **The higher the denomination, the greater the return.** Thus, $5 machines pay back better than dollar machines, $1 machines pay back better than quarter machines, and quarter machines pay back better than nickel machines.
2. **Play the maximum number of coins.** For almost all multiple-pay and multiple-play machines, the maximum coin line tends to yield a better percentage payback.
3. **Sometimes the maximum number of coins in a lower-denomination machine do not pay back as much as a single coin in a higher-denomination machine.** You might find that you are in better shape playing a single dollar on a $1 machine than you are playing the maximum number of coins on a quarter machine.
4. **The bigger the progressive jackpots, the smaller the returns on the other winning combinations.** Giant linked progressives are withholding a much greater percentage of the average play in order to pay out the giant jackpots.
5. **Play within your comfort zone.** Establish a comfort zone you can afford to play within. This means to set limits for the amount of money and denomination of machine. You should also establish a time limit for your gambling.

Slot Clubs

Another good habit to get into when playing slot machines is to always use the casino's slot club card in the machine you're playing. Every coin you run through the machine yields points on your card. Once you reach a certain level, these points can be redeemed for various prizes. The prizes vary from casino to casino but usually include free rooms, free food, hats, show tickets, and sometimes cash back. Casino slot club cards are an added benefit to slot players. If you don't take advantage of casino's slot clubs cards, it's like throwing away money.

Hitting It Big!

On January 27, 1996, John Tippin of Honolulu, Hawaii, won the largest jackpot to date— $11,968,359. The previous record lasted only three months, which is very unusual, since the previous record had lasted at least a year. Mr. Tippin was on vacation at the Las Vegas Hilton when he lined up the four MegaBucks symbols across the payline to claim his new wealth. MegaBucks slot machines are a system of progressive slot machines linked throughout the state of Nevada to offer a large jackpot. In order to win the MegaBucks jackpot, you have to do like Mr. Tippin and line up four MegaBucks symbols across the payline. Most slot machines have three reels, but since the MegaBucks machines offer a chance at millions, they have four reels.

To use a slot club card you'll have to fill out a form at a customer service booth at the casino. Then they'll give you a card that looks like a credit card or ATM card with your name on it. When you play a slot machine, you insert this card into the slot that's marked for the casino slot card. When you want to redeem the points you've accumulated, take your card to the customer service booth and the person there will check to see how many points you've earned. The points are earned by the amount of money you play through the machines, not the amount of time spent on machines.

ETIQUETTE

You may think that playing slot machines is as simple as finding an open machine and playing at your own leisure. There are, however, a couple of things to keep in mind when selecting a machine. If you see a change bucket resting in a slot machine payout tray, then that machine is being used. If you see a stool leaning up against a slot machine, then that machine is being used.

The first time I was in a casino, I played a slot machine that had a change cup in the tray and promptly got an earful from the person who was playing that machine when he returned from the bathroom. I did not know someone was playing that machine nor did I know a person could "hold" machines. I didn't have the nerve to tell the person that I had just won $50 on his machine. I figured it would just add fuel to the fire.

When you find an unoccupied slot machine, ask the person playing nearest that machine whether anyone is using the machine you want to play. That person may know if the machine is in use. In fact, the person you ask might be using it. Some people like to play two machines at once. Using a reserved machine is the only breech of etiquette you can commit. Once you find a machine that's open, you can play at your own pace.

Using the tips outlined in this chapter will help you have fun playing slot machines, and you're likely to keep your losses to a minimum. You may even get lucky and come out ahead, and if you're really lucky, way ahead.

Chapter Sixteen
VIDEO POKER

V ideo poker is an electronic gaming machine much like a slot machine. There are several different variations of video poker machines. The most common are Jacks or Better, Jokers Wild, Deuces Wild, and Bonus Poker. Like slot machines, video poker machines are controlled by a microprocessor. Also like slot machines, the microprocessor chip is called a Random Number Generator (RNG). (See Chapter 14 to find out more on how the RNG works.) The RNG determines what hand you'll receive for each game.

That is where the similarities stop between the slot machines and video poker machines. Unlike a slot machine, video poker machines require some skill to be successful over the long run. To win at video poker, you must first understand the ranking of poker hands.

POKER HAND RANKINGS (FROM LOWEST TO HIGHEST)

1.	**High Card**	A hand without a pair, straight, or flush, valued by its highest card
2.	**One Pair**	A hand with two cards of the same rank
3.	**Two Pair**	A hand with two cards of one rank and another two cards of another rank
4.	**Three of a Kind**	A hand with three cards of the same rank
5.	**Straight**	A hand with all five cards in a sequence but not in a single suit
6.	**Flush**	A hand with all five cards in the same suit but not in a sequence
7.	**Full House**	A hand with three cards of the same rank and two cards of another rank
8.	**Four of a Kind**	A hand with four cards of the same rank
9.	**Straight Flush**	A hand with all five cards in sequence and in the same suit
10.	**Royal Flush**	A hand with A, K, Q, J, and 10 all of the same suit

Every video poker game is played with a standard fifty-two-card deck, except Jokers Wild, which adds at least one joker to the deck. In video poker there is no opponent, so the object is to get the highest-ranking hand possible. Payoffs are according to the ranking of your hand.

PICKING THE RIGHT VIDEO POKER MACHINE

When you're in a casino, you won't have to look to hard to find video poker machines. They're right alongside the slot machines. The first thing to do is find a *good* video poker machine, not one that's hot (paying a lot), but one that has a lower house advantage than other video poker machines. Once you find the ones with the lower house advantage, then you'll hopefully find one that's hot as well.

When looking for a video poker machine with a lower house advantage, look first at each machine's payout table posted above the video screen. Then look at how much a full house pays with one coin and how much a flush pays with one coin. The machines that you want to find will pay nine coins for a full house and six coins for a flush. A machine of this type is called a 9/6 (nine to six) machine.

A 9/6 machine tells you that if you inserted one coin in the machine you'd win nine coins if you got a full house and six coins if you got a flush. For Jacks or Better, this is the best machine to

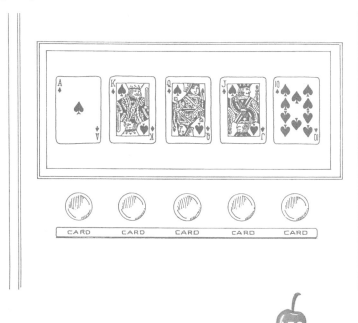

find. You may find machines that pay only 8/5 (eight coins for a full house and five coins for a flush).

Why would you want to play a machine that'll only pay you eight coins for a full house, when the machine right next you pays nine coins for a full house? By finding a 9/6 Jacks or Better video poker machine, you're taking the first step in increasing your chances of winning money playing video poker.

For some of the other video poker machines mentioned earlier (Jokers Wild, Deuces Wild, Bonus Poker), you'll have to look at their payout schedule and compare them with other machines of the same type to find the lower house advantage machines. Just as for the Jacks or Better machines, compare the full house/flush payouts between the two machines.

PLAYING VIDEO POKER

After you find a good video poker machine (one with a low house advantage), look at the payout schedule to find the minimum hand needed to win. With a Jacks or Better machine, you'll need a pair of Jacks or higher to win. (That's how the machine got the name Jacks or Better.) Remember that in video poker there is no opponent. You get paid by how high your hand ranks.

Here is the payout table for a Jacks or Better machine with one coin played:

Hand	Payout
pair of jacks or better	I coin
two pair	2 coins
three of a kind	3 coins
straight	4 coins
flush	6 coins
full house	9 coins
four of a kind	25 coins
straight flush	50 coins
royal flush	800 coins

After you've inserted coins, the machine deals you five cards. Now you look to see how high your hand is and what hand you could potentially get if you drew some more cards. This is where the skill comes into play. You now need to decide which cards to keep and which cards to discard for new cards.

If you want to keep a card, hit the hold button located just below the card. Do this for every card you want to keep. After you've selected your cards to hold and pushed their buttons, hit the draw button. Now the machine takes away the cards you didn't keep and replaces them with new cards. Then the game is over. If you have a winning hand (a pair of jacks or better), you get paid the amount for the rank of hand you obtained.

VIDEO POKER STRATEGIES

You have the option of playing from one to five coins per game. Play the maximum coins (five) per game, because the payout for a royal flush with five coins played is greater than just five times the payout for one coin. The casino adds a bonus of 1,000 coins for hitting a royal flush with the maximum number of coins played. Also, if you're playing a progressive video poker machine, then you win the amount in the jackpot. All other payouts are just the same as for one coin multiplied by the number of coins played. For example, if you played five coins and hit a flush, it would pay thirty coins (twenty-five coins plus the five you put in).

Some of the strategies used when playing video poker are different from the strategies used in regular poker. Because you're playing against yourself, there's no bluffing. Because there's no opponent, there's no possibility of a tie, so no reason to hold a kicker. (A kicker is a high card held, usually with a pair, to serve as a tie-breaker in case another player has a pair of the same rank.) Discard anything that you might keep as a kicker in regular poker, with the hope that you'll get a card to improve your hand. The table below should help you make decisions when playing a Jacks or Better poker machine.

JACKS OR BETTER DECISION TABLE

Your Hand (first 5 cards)	Decision
mixed low cards (2–10)	hold none; draw five
one high card (A, K, Q, or J)	hold high card; draw four
any two high cards	hold both high cards; draw three
any three high cards	hold three high cards; draw two (if two of the three high cards are of the same suit, then hold those two and draw three)
any three cards to a straight flush	hold those three cards; draw two
a four-card straight	hold four cards; draw one
a four-card flush	hold four cards; draw one (if you have a low pair (2–10) pair, then split it up (or keep the flush and get rid of the low pair)
a four-card straight and flush (not a straight flush)	hold four cards for the flush; draw one (if you have a low pair (2–10) then split it up)
three cards to a royal flush	hold three cards to a royal flush; draw two (split up pair)
four cards to a royal flush	hold four cards to a royal flush; draw one (split up everything except a straight flush)
four cards to a straight flush	hold four cards to a straight flush; draw one (split up any pair)
two pair	hold both pairs; draw one
three of a kind	hold the three of a kind; draw two
straight flush	hold all five cards
four of a kind	hold all five cards (no reason to draw the extra card: it only gives the machine a chance to malfunction)
full house	hold all five cards
flush	hold all five cards (if you have four to a royal flush, hold those four and draw one)
straight	hold all five cards

A Word About Progressive Jackpots

When you play a video poker machine that offers a progressive jackpot, then you better watch what the payouts are for a full house and a flush. A progressive jackpot for video poker machines is a jackpot where the player who gets the highest hand possible (usually a royal flush) gets paid a jackpot that's higher than usual for that particular hand. Progressive jackpot video poker machines take a small percentage of your bet and add it to the progressive jackpot. This is not taken from your winnings but from the amount of money you put into the machine. Some casinos lower the payout on machines that offer the progressive jackpots and take a portion of your bet to add to the progressive jackpot. In this case, make sure the progressive jackpot is large enough to make it worth your while to play these machines. It's been published in several video poker "how to" books (the main source seems to be Stanford Wong's *Professional Video Player*, LaJolla, CA: Pi Yee Press, 1993) that, for a Jacks or Better machine, the progressive jackpot should be at least the following for each denomination in order for you to benefit from playing these machines:

- ♠ on a quarter progressive Jacks or Better machine, the jackpot should be at least $2,200 before you should play
- ♠ on a fifty cent progressive Jacks or Better machine, the jackpot should be at least $4,400 before you should play
- ♠ on a $1 progressive Jacks or Better machine, the jackpot should be at least $8,750 before you should play
- ♠ on a $5 progressive Jacks or Better machine, the jackpot should be at least $44,000 before you should play

If the jackpot is above these listed amounts, then make sure you play the maximum number of coins. If not and you hit the royal flush, you won't win the progressive jackpot. Always play the maximum number of coins to get the highest return.

It's OK to try playing video poker with only one coin to see if you like it, but don't let it become the norm when you sit down to a video poker machine. When you're first trying video poker, play a low minimum (nickel) machine to see if you like it. Once you determine that video poker is for you, then start playing the maximum number of coins for that machine.

The house advantage in video poker is linked directly to the payoff chart, particularly the payoffs for a full house and flush. Below is a chart of the house advantage for the different payouts for video poker.

JACKS OR BETTER MACHINE

Machine Payoff for Full House/ Flush with maximum coins	House Advantage
6/5 machine	5.0%
8/5 machine	2.7%
9/6 machine	0.5%

To take full advantage of the low house percentage on 9/6 machines, you must play the maximum number of coins. The house advantage takes into account a player hitting all the possible payouts at all the different numbers of coins played. This includes a player hitting a royal flush with the maximum number of coins played. If you could be sure that you wouldn't hit a royal flush, you could play the minimum coins, since the payouts would be the same, as posted—6, 8, or 9 times your investment for a full house or 5 or 6 times your investment for a flush. But if you got lucky with a royal flush, you'd lose out on the bonus of 1,000 coins—and leave it for the house. So, if you aren't playing the maximum number of coins when you hit a royal flush, you create a much bigger house advantage. So, once you feel comfortable playing video poker, remember to go for the max!

part **4**

MONEY MANAGEMENT

Chapter Seventeen
MONEY MANAGEMENT

In this chapter you'll find out about the best way to manage your money in a casino. This is very important, because when you travel to a casino you're usually carrying a lot more cash than you normally would carry. Covered will be tips on protecting yourself and your money, comps (complimentary gifts) that the casinos offer and how you can obtain them, and gambling systems and why they don't work. All these tips will help you enjoy your vacation at a casino resort and leave for home without that terrible feeling that you've spent or lost more money than you intended.

MANAGING YOUR GAMBLING MONEY

Managing your gambling money while taking a vacation at a casino resort can make all the difference between having a great trip or coming home busted. It's very important to set aside an amount of money within your means for gambling on this vacation. Then dole the money out in even amounts over the number of days you will be there. For example, if you plan on being at a casino for three days and you've set aside $1,000 for gambling, allow yourself to gamble with $333.33 per day. This will stretch your gambling entertainment over three days, which certainly beats losing all your gambling money on the first day. It's easy enough to go through your entire allotment in one day, which can only mean trouble as you start spending more than you planned. Once you've used your daily allotment, find other alternatives for entertainment. (See Chapter 2 for some ideas.)

After you determine the daily dollar amount to allow yourself for gambling, find the games you want to play that day. Each game has a certain average number of decisions per hour. A decision constitutes an outcome on your bet. Some games have a higher number of decisions per hour than other games, which means more chances to lose your money or win something. Below is a list of games with their average number of decisions per hour of play. This list is based on playing at a full table for one hour of play. If you're playing in a less crowded casino, the number of hands per hour will increase.

Game	Decisions per Hour
Baccarat	80
Blackjack	60
Caribbean Stud	40
Craps (pass line bet)	30
Keno	7
Let It Ride	40
Mini-Baccarat	130
Pai Gow Poker	24
Poker	30
Roulette	50
Slot Machines	400
Video Keno	300
Video Poker	500

After you've determined what games you want to play that day, figure out how long you'd like to gamble. It might be a four-hour session or a couple of three-hour sessions. In either case, find how many decisions you're likely to be making per hour for the game you want to play and multiply that by the number of hours you're planning on playing to give you the total number of decisions for that game.

For example if you have $300 to spend for one day and you want to play blackjack for three hours, then you can expect about 180 decisions in that period for that game. Then you'll have to hunt around to find a table limit within your range. You wouldn't want to sit down at a table with a $25 minimum bet, because you probably won't last the three hours you've set aside for gambling on blackjack. Instead, you probably want to find a $5 or $10 minimum table, so you can withstand extended losing streaks. By dividing up your money and calculating the number of decisions per game per session, you're assuring yourself of getting the most gambling time out of your money. Keep in mind that regardless of the game you're playing, if you don't use good strategies, you probably won't last the entire session with your bank roll.

At the end of your session, take whatever money you have left over and set it aside for the rest of your trip. Just because you have $200 remaining from that session's bankroll doesn't mean you can add that to your next session's money. When you get home, you'll thank yourself for taking this approach. It doesn't matter whether you win or lose: don't use that money for the next day's gambling. If you don't feel you can control your urge to use this money, then mail it home in a secured envelope. Setting this money aside will help you limit the amount of money you lose.

Some sessions you'll win and other sessions you'll lose, but if you keep aside the session money you've already used for gambling, that will help prevent you from losing all the money you brought to gamble with. Limiting your gaming sessions to a set amount of money will help you have a good time while you're at the casino and not be sorry that you went to the casino when you get home and realize how much money you lost gambling.

Another thing you should do when taking a trip to a gambling casino is leave your credit and ATM cards at home. If you have to bring a credit card with you to pay for accommodations, then pay for the room and leave it in the hotel's safe deposit box. The casinos have cash advance machines all over the place, making it too easy for you to get access to more money. Even using these machines can get expensive: they usually charge from $10 to $20 per transaction.

You can easily gamble much more than you intended if you're not careful. Somehow, when you're at the gambling table, $50 or $100 no longer seems like that much money. Then suddenly it's gone and only later do you think about what you could have done with that money instead of giving it to the casino.

Try bringing travelers checks when going to these resorts. First, if you lose them or they get stolen, you can get your money replaced. In addition, it will be more difficult when you're at the tables to just dig into your wallet to get more money. You'll have to cash the checks at the cashier's cage. That extra step will help you realize how much money you've lost and, at the very least, will pull you away from the tables when you're losing. A general rule you should follow is to walk away when you're losing and increase your bets when you're winning.

Tipping the Dealer

Should you tip or bet for the dealer? That's a question players frequently ask. It's up to the individual. You must remember that every time you do this it becomes a percentage of your win or loss result. Let's assume that you are flat betting (not varying your bet) and your unit increment is $5. Let's also assume that you are playing multiple-deck blackjack. The table will usually have three or four players, because a low minimum table limit usually attracts more players. Therefore, you will get about sixty hands per hour. If you were to bet/tip only $1 per hand, you would be "giving away" $60 per hour. That's twenty percent of your bankroll.

Rather than tipping the dealers, make bets for them instead. You do this by placing a bet for him or her in front of your bet. Therefore, if you win the dealer pays you and wins something. Most dealers prefer this and many times will root for you to win, knowing that they will make money also. Also when you do this, they know immediately that they have a chance of getting money. If you wait to tip after the playing session, they don't know that they are getting any tips from you. That knowledge may result in some added benefits as you play the game. The dealer may give you better deck penetration and not selectively shuffle.

You must be careful never to collude with a dealer. There have been instances when players and dealers have been in collusion with each other, such as when a dealer pays a push or a bust hand. There have also been times when dealers have flashed their hole card to players in order to later get a payoff outside the casino. This can result in a large fine and jail sentence if a crooked dealer is caught.

To consider playing for the dealer, he or she must be friendly and courteous. Some players try to get other players to also make bets for the dealers. This usually ingratiates you with dealers.

PROTECTING YOURSELF

The casinos in the past have had suspect owners, operators, and patrons. Today's casinos are legal and closely monitored by the government. The owners and operators are legitimate business people who closely watch the casino's day-to-day operations. Many casinos are owned by large corporations, such as ITT Sheraton, Hilton, Mirage Resorts, Caesar's Entertainment Corporation, and Bally. All of these companies have stock traded on the major exchanges. The chances of a casino cheating you are very slim. A casino that gets caught cheating could lose its license and be subject to severe fines. So you don't have to worry about casinos cheating you. The house advantage allows them to make enough money.

However, casinos draw a diverse group of people. It's not an unlikely scenario that a fellow customer could rob you or cheat you out of your money. Casinos tend to attract professional people looking for a good time, but there are also people who view casinos as a place to swindle people out of their money.

How do you protect yourself from these people? Here are some ideas:

- ♠ Be aware of your surroundings.
- ♠ If you keep in pairs, it's a lot safer than wandering around by yourself.
- ♠ Carry with you only the money you've allotted yourself for that session of gambling.
- ♠ Leave all your remaining cash or travelers checks in the hotel safe deposit box. Don't trust leaving it in your hotel room. Sometimes the staff can be dishonest.
- ♠ Keep an eye on your chips when you're gambling. Crooks will sometimes try to distract you and slip a few chips away while you're not looking. The dealers will also help you keep an eye on your chips.
- ♠ Always count your chips before you leave the table to use the rest room. If you have a lot of chips, leave a few of them to hold your spot and take the rest with you to the rest room.
- ♠ Use the "buddy" system when going to the rest room. Most rest rooms don't have an attendant, so it's better to have a friend with you to reduce the possibility of being robbed.

Using common sense when carrying a large sum of money or chips will help you to have a safer time at the resort and casino.

GAMBLING SYSTEMS

Eventually all people will discover that someone is playing a gambling system at their table. A gambling system is a set way to bet or play a game. You must follow strict rules when following a system in order for it to work correctly. Even when it works correctly, however, it's still a poor way to gamble. Gambling systems are designed for you to follow rules. But following these rules doesn't change the fact that the casino still enjoys an advantage over the player.

Following are a couple of gambling systems that are popular— and I'll also show you why they don't work. Be skeptical when someone says they have a gambling system for you.

Martingale System

The first gambling system almost everyone encounters is the Martingale System or Double Up. The principle behind this system is that every time you lose a bet your next bet should be twice the amount of your lost bet. Keep doing this until you win and eventually you'll win the amount equal to your first lost bet. Let's look at an example:

Say you're playing blackjack at a $5–$500 limit table. Let's say you start by betting the minimum of $5. You lose that first bet. On your second bet you double the amount lost on the first hand. You bet $10. You lose this hand. Now you have to double the amount of your last bet, so you bet $20. This time you win. You lost a total of $15 on the first two hands and won a total of $20 on the last hand. You profited $5, which was the amount of your first bet.

This system works very well on paper. But what happens if you lose seven hands in a row? You would have lost $635 over seven hands and your next bet would have to be $640. That's over the maximum for this table. You could go to other tables to accommodate that bet, but do you really want to be risking $640 to only profit $5? Or look at it this way: if someone wanted to make a bet with you over a game, but you'd have to bet $640 and they would bet

only $5, you wouldn't make this bet. So remember that when you bet this way, you're chasing your losses, which is the worst way to gamble. When you're losing, you want to minimize your bets or not bet at all. Only press your bets when you're winning.

The Martingale system gets you in trouble by chasing your losses. You may be asking yourself, "How likely is it that I'll lose seven or more hands in a row?" It happens a lot more often than you think. If you don't believe, try it out by guessing the outcome of a coin flip, where there's no advantage to either side. (Remember: the casino has an advantage in all the games offered in a casino.) This experiment costs you nothing at all—far less than it would cost you to learn the same lesson using the Martingale system in a casino.

Cancellation System

The next system you might discover is the Cancellation system. In the Cancellation system, first determine your single unit bet (the minimum amount you bet). If you're playing at a blackjack table with a limit of $5-$500, then your one unit bet might be $5. This system is set up so that you make a series of bets until you eliminate the numbers of units bet. Let's take a look at an example.

Let's say you're playing blackjack at a $5-$500 limit table and your one unit bet is $5. Start with a sheet of paper with 1 - 2 - 3 on it, representing the number of basic unit bets: one equals $5, two equals $10 (two times the basic unit), and three equals $15 (three times the basic unit). Add the two ends (1 and 3) to make your first bet of four units or $20. If you win, then the number remaining is two, so your next bet would be a two-unit bet or $10. If you win the second bet, you win the total number of units bet, six units (1 plus 3 plus 2). You can start with any three sequential numbers, such as 3, 4, 5.

With this system, the problem again arises that if you lose a bet you'll be chasing your losses. Let's say you lose the first bet of four units. To eliminate the number of units bet you have to add the number of units lost to the end of your sequence, so your string of numbers would be 1-2-3-4. Now you'd still have to bet the ends on bet two, which would then be five units ($25). This system, like the Martingale system, is very bad because you'll soon be risking a lot of money in order to make a very little profit. Try this system by guessing the outcome of a coin flip. You will soon find out that this system, like the Martingale, can quickly get you into trouble.

Betting systems are a poor way to gamble. A good strategy is finding an amount of money you are comfortable gambling with and sticking to it. Only after winning do you want to alter your bets. Then you want to increase them. Remember this rule: **Never increase your bets when you're losing.** This is a sure way to lose your money quickly and will prevent you from having an enjoyable time at the casino.

COMPS

When you start playing casino games, you'll hear other players ask the casino pit boss for comps. A comp is something complimentary. The casino pit bosses rate your level of play at the tables. They take notice of how long you play and calculate your average bet. If you qualify for a complimentary, the pit boss will gladly give it to you, but *only* if you ask. A comp might be a free ticket to the buffet, show tickets, your room, or any amenity the casino offers.

If you're interested in trying to get comped, the first thing you need to do is get a V.I.P. card at the guest services desk when you arrive at the casino. If you play the slot machines, insert this card in order to receive credit for the money you play. (The machine electronically keeps track of your play.) If you play table games, give the card to the pit boss at the table you're playing. It's very important to wait until the pit boss picks up your card before you start to gamble at the table. Any money gambled before he writes your information down won't be credited toward your comp.

If you want to check your status (how much you've played), take your card to guest services and they'll run your card through the computer to see how many points you've accumulated. It takes a certain number of points to qualify for various levels of comps. If you want to know what each level is, ask either a pit boss or a person at guest services.

Most people think comps are only for high rollers. That's not true. It may take lower-level players longer to reach comps, but they can indeed qualify. A typical level of play to get a free room would have to be an average bet of $25–$50 (depending on the casino you're playing) with at least four hours at this level. To receive a lower-level comp, such as food or a show, you could bet at a lower level for the four hours or at the higher level for less time.

Don't continue to gamble just to receive comps. Casino games are geared for the casino to win over the long haul. The longer you play, the more likely you are to lose. Why do casinos offer comps? They want you to play longer in their casino. They sacrifice a $20 meal to have a chance that you'll lose $100 at the table while you're trying to get a comp. Give them your card when you sit down and play as long as you like or for the set time you were going to gamble. When you leave, ask the pit boss for your card back and then ask him for a comp. It never hurts to ask, even if you've been gambling for only a short time. Stay within your gambling budget. If the comps come with your level of play, then you've earned a bonus.

part 5

GAMBLING DESTINATIONS

Chapter Eighteen
CASINO DESTINATIONS

This chapter offers a listing of casinos throughout the United States and Canada. You'll also find a few Web addresses to help you locate casinos in other parts of the world. Keep in mind that the world of casino gambling is constantly changing, so the phone numbers and addresses listed here along with the ones you may find on the Internet may not be current.

In general, the listings are by state or province and alphabetical by the name of the establishment. For Nevada, all the Las Vegas establishments are listed first, followed by those for the rest of the state.

Most of the casinos listed here have toll-free 800 phone numbers, not all of which are listed here. If you wish to reach them via their 800 number, call the toll-free 800 directory at 1-800-555-1212. This is a free phone call and the operator will be able to give you the 800 number of the casino you're looking for. If you're planning a gambling-oriented vacation, look for those places listed as hotel and/or resort. If you're taking your children, check with hotels as to their facilities for entertaining children. Several of the newer hotels, especially in Las Vegas, now have many attractions for kids as well as adults.

UNITED STATES CASINOS

Arizona

Apache Gold Casino
P.O. Box 1210
San Carlos, AZ 85550
(800) APACHE-8
(800) APACHE-3
Fax: (520) 425-7696

Bucky's Casino
Hwy. 69 and Hwy. 89
Prescott Resort & Conference
Center
1500 E. Hwy. 69
Prescott, AZ 86301
(520) 776-1666
Fax: (520) 778-7954

Casino of the Sun
7406 S. Camino De Oeste Rd.
Tucson, AZ 85746
(800) 344-9435
Fax: (520) 883-0983

Cliff Castle Casino
353 Middle Verde Rd.
P.O. Box 4677
Camp Verde, AZ 86322
(520) 567-9031
Fax: (520) 567-9711

Cocopah Bingo & Casino
15356 S. Ave. B
Summerton, AZ 85350
(520) 726-8066
(800) 23-SLOTS

Desert Diamond Casino
7350 S. Old Nogales Hwy.
P.O. Box 22230
Tucson, AZ 85734
(602) 294-7777
Fax: (602) 294-9955

Fort McDowell Casino
Hwy. 87 and Fort McDowell Rd.
P.O. Box 18359
Fountain Hills, AZ 85269
(602) 837-1424
(800) THE FORT

Gila River Casino (Firebird)
5512 Wildhorse Path
1201 S. 56th St. #C
Box 5074
Chandler, AZ 85226
(800) WIN-GILA
(602) 796-7712
Fax: (602) 796-7712

Harrah's Phoenix
Ak-Chin Casino
15406 Maricopa Rd.
Maricopa, AZ 85239
(602) 802 5000
(800) 427-7247
Fax: (602) 802-5050

Hon-Dah Casino
Hwy. 73 and 260
P.O. Box 3250
Pinetop, AZ 85935-3250
(602) 369-0299
Fax: (602) 369-0382

Hualapi Casino
Grand Canyon West
P.O. Box 761
Meadview, AZ 86444
(520) 699-4161
Fax: (520) 699-4163

Mazatzal Casino
Mile Post 251 Hwy. 87
P.O. Box 1820
Payson, AZ 85547
(520) 474-6044
(800) 552-0938
Fax: (520) 474-4238

Pipe Springs Resort & Casino
North Pike Springs Rd.
HC 65 Box 3
Fredonia, AZ 86022
(801) 559-6537
Fax: (602) 643-7260

Yavapai Gaming Center
Junction of Hwy. 69 and 89
1505 E. Hwy. 69
Prescott, AZ 86301
(520) 445-6219
(800) SLOTS-44
Fax: (520) 778-7954

California
Barona Casino
1000 Wildcat Canyon Rd.
Lakeside, CA 92040
(800) 227-U-BET
Fax: (619) 443-2856

Bicycle Club Casino
7301 Eastern Ave.
Bell Gardens, CA 90201
(800) 292-0015
Fax: (310) 806-3137

Cache Creek
Indian Bingo & Casino
14455 Hwy. 16
P.O. Box 65
Brooks, CA 95606
(916) 796-3118
Fax: (916) 796-2112

Casino Morongo
P.O. Box 366
Cabazon, CA 92230
(909) 849-3080
(800) 775-4386
Fax: (909) 849-3181
Fax: (909) 849-4425

Sher-Ae Heights Bingo
P.O. Box 635
Trinidad, CA 95570
(707) 677-3611
(800) 684-BINGO
Fax: (707) 677-1653

Chicken Ranch Bingo
16929 Chicken Ranch Rd.
P.O. Box 1699
Jamestown, CA 95327
(800) 75-BINGO

Colusa Bingo & Casino
P.O. Box 1267
3770 Hwy. 45
Colusa, CA 95932
(916) 458-8844
(800) 655-UWIN
Fax: (916) 458-2018

Commerce Casino
6131 East Telegraph Rd.
Commerce, CA 90040
(800) 287-7758
(213) 721-2100
Fax: (213) 728-8874

El Dorado
15411 S. Vermont Ave.
Gardena, CA 90247
(310) 323-2800
Fax: (310) 719-9753

Fantasy Springs Casino
84-245 Indio Springs Dr.
Indio, CA 92203-3499
(619) 342-5000
(800) 827-2-WIN
Fax: (619) 347-7880

Hi-Desert Casino
11711 Air Base Rd.
Adelanto, CA 92301
(619) 246-8624
Fax: (619) 246-7846

Hollywood Park Casino
1088 S. Prairie Ave.
Inglewood, CA 90301
(310) 330-2800
(800) 888-HWPC
Fax: (310) 671-4117

Jackson Indian Bingo & Casino
12222 New York Ranch Rd.
Jackson, CA 95642
(209) 223-1677
(800) 822-WINN

Normandie Casino & Showroom
1045 W. Rosenthans Ave.
Gardena, CA 90427
(310) 352-3400
Fax: (310) 532-0316

Palace Bingo
17225 Jersey Ave.
P.O. Box 308
Leemore, CA 93245
(209) 924-7751
(800) 942-6886
Fax: (209) 924-7526

Robinson Rancheria Bingo & Casino
1545 E. Hwy 20
Nice, CA 95464
(800) 809-3636
(707) 275-9000
Fax: (707) 275-9100

San Manuel Indian Bingo & Casino
5797 N. Victoria Ave.
Highland, CA 92346
(800) 359-2464
Fax: (909) 862-3405

Spa Hotel & Casino
Resort and Mineral Springs
Palm Springs, CA

Spotlight 29 Casino
46-200 Harrison St.
Coachella, CA 92236
(619) 775-5566
Fax: (619) 775-4638

Sycuan Gaming Center
5469 Dehesa Rd.
El Cajon, CA 92019
(800) 2-SYCUAN
(619) 445—6002
Fax: (619) 445-1961

Table Mountain Rancheria Casino & Bingo
8184 Friant Rd.
P.O. Box 445
Friant, CA 93626
(800) 541-3637
Fax: (209) 822-2081

Viejas Valley Casino & Turf Club
5000 Willows Rd.
Alpine, CA 91901
(800) POKER
(619) 455-5400
Fax: (619) 455-9187

Win-River Casino Bingo
2100 Rancheria Rd.
Redding, CA 96001
(800) 280-8946
Fax: (916) 243-0337

Colorado
Aspen Mine & Casino
P.O. Box 158
166 E. Bennett Ave.
Cripple Creek, CO 80813
(719) 689-0770
Fax: (719) 689-0747

Baby Doe's Silver Dollar Casino
P.O. Box 607
102 A Lawrence St.
Central City, CO 80427
(303) 582-5510
Fax: (303) 582-0819

Black Diamond Casino
P.O. Box 752
425 E. Bennett Ave.
Cripple Creek, CO 80813
(719) 689-2898
Fax: (719) 689-3988

Black Hawk Station
P.O. Box 477
141 Gregory St.
Black Hawk, CO 80422
(303) 582-5582
Fax: (303) 582-5590

Blazing Saddles Casino
139 Main St.
Black Hawk, CO 80422
(303) 582-0707
Fax: (303) 422-0424

Bronco Billy's Sports Bar & Casino
233 E. Bennett Ave.
Cripple Creek, CO 80813
(719) 689-2142
Fax: (719) 689-2869

Bronco Billy's Sports Bar & Casino
125 Gregory St.
Black Hawk, CO 80422
(303) 825-0907
(800) 298-RICH

Bull Durham Saloon & Casino
P.O. Box 486
110 Main St.
Black Hawk, CO 80422
(303) 582-0810
Fax: (303) 534-5715

Bullwhackers Casino Black Hawk
P.O. Box 308
101 Gregory St.
P.O. Box 308
Black Hawk, CO 80422
(303) 271-2500
Fax: (303) 271-2501

Bullwhackers Casino Central City
130 Main St.
Central City, CO 80427
(303) 271-2500
(800) 426-2855
Fax: (303) 271-2501

Central Palace Casino
P.O. Box 577
132 Lawrence St.
Central City, CO 80427
(303) 477-7117
(800) 822-7466
Fax: (303) 582-5464

Colorado Central Station Casino
340 Main Street Box 22
Black Hawk, CO 80422
(303) 582-3000

Colorado Grand Gaming Parlour
P.O. Box 569
300 E. Bennett Ave.
Cripple Creek, CO 80813
(719) 689-3517
Fax: (719) 689-2644

Creeker's Casino Bar & Grill
274 E. Bennett Ave.
Cripple Creek, CO 80813
(719) 689-7851
Fax: (719) 689-7851

Crooks Palace
P.O. Box 203
200 Gregory St.
Black Hawk, CO 80422
(303) 582-5094
Fax: (303) 271-2501

Doc Holliday Casino
101 Main St.
Central City, CO 80427
(303) 582-1400
Fax: (303) 582-3800

Dostal Alley Saloon & Gambling Emporium
P.O. Box 189
1 Dostal Alley
Central City, CO 80427
(303) 582-1610
Fax: (303) 582-0143

Eureka! Casino
211 Gregory St.
Black Hawk, CO 80422
(303) 582-0140
Fax: (303) 582-5988

Famous Bonanza Pete's Place
P.O. Box 771
107 Main St.
Central City, CO 80427
(303) 582-5914
Fax: (303) 582-0447

Gilipin Hotel Casino
P.O. Box 689
119 Main St.
Black Hawk, CO 80422
(303) 582-1183
Fax: (303) 582-1154

Gold Mine Casino
P.O. Box 317
130 Clear Creek
Black Hawk, CO 80422
(303) 582-0711
Fax: (303) 582-0739

Gold Rush Hotel & Casino
P.O. Box 279
209 E. Bennett
Cripple Creek, CO 80813
(800) 235-8239, (719) 689-2646
Fax: (719) 689-0712

Golden Gates Casino
P.O. Box 8
261 Main St.
Black Hawk, CO 80422
(303) 277-1650
Fax: (303) 277-1712

Golden Rose Casino
P.O. Box 157
102 Main St.
Central City, CO 80427
(303) 582-5060, (800) 929-0255
Fax: (303) 825-1440

Gregory Street Casino
P.O. Box 644
380 Gregory St.
Black Hawk, CO 80422
(303) 582-1006

Grubstake Inn Casino
P.O. Box 101765
Central City, CO 80250
(303) 582-5449
Fax: (303) 582-5708

Harrah's Casino Black Hawk
131 Main St.
Black Hawk, CO 80422
(303) 777-1111
Fax: (303) 582-0441

Harrah's Glory Hole Casino Central City
131 Main St.
Central City, CO 80427
(303) 582-1171
Fax: (303) 582-0441

Harvey's Wagon Wheel Hotel/Casino
10075 W. Colfax Ave.
Lakewood, CO 80215
(303) 582-0800, (303) 231-9200

Imperial Hotel & Casino
P.O. Box 869
123 N. 3rd St.
Cripple Creek, CO 80813
(719) 689-7777
Fax: (719) 689-0416

Independence Hotel & Casino
151 E. Bennett Ave.
Cripple Creek, CO 80813
(719) 689-2925
Fax: (719) 689-3758

Jazz Alley
P.O. Box 389
321 Main St.
Black Hawk, CO 80422
(303) 426-1337
Fax: (303) 582-1125

**Johnny Nolon's Saloon &
Gambling Emporium**
P.O. Box 805
301 E. Bennett Ave.
Cripple Creek, CO 80813
(719) 689-3598, (800) 366-2946
Fax: (719) 689-3598

J.P. McGills Hotel & Casino
232 E. Bennett Ave.
Cripple Creek, CO 80813
(719) 689-0303

The Jubilee Casino
P.O. Box 610
351 Myers Ave.
Cripple Creek, CO 80813
(719) 689-2519
Fax: (719) 689-2195

Lady Luck Casino
120 Main St.
Central City, CO 80427
(303) 582-1603
Fax: (303) 582-1607

Legends Casino
200 Bennett St.
Cripple Creek, CO 80813
(719) 689-3242, (800) 528-6533
Fax: (719) 689-3282

Long Branch Saloon & Casino
P.O. Box 391
123 Main St.
Central City, CO 80427
(303) 582-5896

Long Branch Saloon & Casino
200 E. Bennett Ave.
Cripple Creek, CO 80813
(719) 689-3242, (800) 528-6533
Fax: (719) 689-3282

Lucky Lola's Casino
P.O. Box 1006
251 E Bennett Ave.
Cripple Creek, CO 80813
(719) 689-3140
Fax: (719) 689-3368

Lucky Star Casino
221 Gregory St.
Black Hawk, CO 80422
(303) 582-1122
Fax: (303) 582-0327

**Maverick's Casino &
Steakhouse**
411 E. Bennett Ave.
Cripple Creek, CO 80813
(719) 689-2737
Fax: (719) 689-2457

**Midnight Rose Hotel &
Casino**
P.O. Box 976
256 E. Bennett Ave.
Cripple Creek, CO 80813
(719) 689-0303

Narrow Gauge Gaming Depot
418 E. Bennett Ave.
Cripple Creek, CO 80813
(719) 689-3214
Fax: (719) 689-2869

Old Chicago Casino
P.O. Box 245
419 E. Bennett Ave.
Cripple Creek, CO 80813
(719) 689-7880
Fax: (719) 689-7889

Otto's Casino at the Black Forest Inn
P.O. Box 11
260 Gregory St.
Black Hawk, CO 80422
(303) 582-0151
Fax: (303) 582-0151

Palace Hotel & Casino
P.O. Box 400
712 E. Bennett Ave.
Cripple Creek, CO 80813
(719) 689-2992
Fax: (719) 689-0365

Papone's Palace Casino
P.O. Box 306
118 Main St.
Central City, CO 80427
(303) 279-9291
Fax: (303) 582-3318

Pony Express Casino
P.O. Box 742
110 Gregory St.
Central City, CO 80427
(303) 582-0802

Red Dolly Casino
P.O. Box 28
530 Gregory St.
Black Hawk, CO 80422
(303) 582-1435

Rohling Inn Casino
160 Gregory St.
Black Hawk, CO 80422
(303) 582-9343
Fax: (303) 582-3068

Silver Palace Casino
404 E. Bennett
Cripple Creek, CO 80813
(719) 689-3980

Sky Ute Lodge & Casino
Hwy 172 N.
P.O. Box 340
Ignacio, CO 81137
(970) 563-0300
Fax: (970) 563-9546

Star of Cripple Creek
143 E. Bennett
Cripple Creek, CO 80813
(719) 689-7827

Teller House Casino
P.O. Box 8
120 Eureka St.
Central City, CO 80427
(303) 279-3200
Fax: (303) 279-0980

Ute Mountain Casino
3 Weeminuche Dr.
P.O. Drawer V
Cortez, CO 81334
(303) 565-6553
Fax: (303) 565-6553

Virgin Mule
P.O. Box 874
269 E. Bennett Ave.
Cripple Creek, CO 80813
(719) 689-2734
Fax: (719) 689-0367

**Wild Bill's Pub & Gaming
Parlor & Hotel**
P.O. Box 428
220 E. Bennett Ave.
Cripple Creek, CO 80813
(719) 689-2707
Fax: (719) 689-0480

**Wild Wild West Brewpub &
Casino**
P.O. Box 127
443 E. Bennett Ave.
Cripple Creek, CO 80813
(719) 689-3736
Fax: (719) 689-0346

**Womack's Saloon & Gaming
Parlor**
210 E. Bennett Ave.
Cripple Creek, CO 80813
(719) 689-0333
Fax: (719) 689-0320

Connecticut
Foxwoods Resort Casino
P.O. Box 410, Rte. 2
Ledyard, CT 06339-0410
(203) 885-3000
Fax: (203) 885-3329

Illinois
Alton Belle Riverboat Casino
219 Piasa St.
Alton, IL 62002
(618) 474-7500
Fax: (618) 474-7824

Casino Queen
P.O. Box 2198
200 S. Front St.
East St Louis, IL 62201
(618) 874-5000
(618) 474-7500
Fax: (618) 874-5008

Empress Casino
P.O. Box 2789
2300 Empress Dr.
Joliet, IL 60434
(815) 744-9400
(618) 474-7500
Fax: (815) 744-9455

Grand Victoria Casino
250 S. Grove Ave.
Elgin, IL 60120
(708) 888-1000
Fax: (708) 468-7030

**Harrah's Joliet Casino
Harrah's Northern Star
Harrah's Southern Star**
150 N. Scott St.
Joliet, IL 60431
(815) 740-7800
(800) HARRAHS

Hollywood Casino; Aurora City of Lights I and City of Lights II Riverboats
1 New York St. Bridge
Aurora, IL 60506
(708) 801-7000
Fax: (708) 801-7200

Jumer's Casino Rock Island
18th St. and Mississippi River
P.O. Box 7777
Rock Island, IL 61204-7777
(309) 793-4200
Fax: (309) 793-4206

Pair-A-Dice Riverboat Casino
21 Blackjack Blvd.
East Peoria, IL 61611-1742
(309) 698-7711
Fax: (309) 698-7705

Players Casino
207 S. Ferry St.
Metropolis, IL 62960
(618) 524-2628
Fax: (618) 524-2628

Silver Eagle Casino Cruise
19731 R.R. 20 W.
East Dubuque, IL 61025
(815) 747-2455
Fax: (815) 747-6332

Iowa
Ameristar Casino
2200 River Rd.
Council Bluffs, IA 51501
(800) 700-1012

Belle of Sioux City Casino
100 Chris Larsen Prk.
P.O. Box 3775
Sioux City, IA 51102
(712) 255-0080
Fax: (712) 494-3035

Bluffs Run Casino
2701 23rd Ave.
Council Bluffs, IA 51501
(712) 323-2500
Fax: (712) 322-9354

CasinOmaha
1 Blackford Bend Blvd.
P.O. Box 89
Onawa, IA 51040
(712) 423-3700
Fax: (712) 423-3128

Catfish Bend Riverboat
N. Front St. (Nov-Apr)
Burlington, IA 52601
Fort Madison Landing
Riverview Park (May-Oct)
Fort Madison, IA 52627
(319) 372-2946
Fax: (319) 753-9818

Dubuque Diamond Jo
3rd St. Ice Harbor
P.O. Box 1683
Dubuque, IA 52004-1683
(319) 583-7005
Fax: (319) 583-7516

Lady Luck Casino Bettendorf
1821 State Street, Ste. 204
P.O. Box 1166
Bettendorf, IA 52722
(800) 724-5825
Fax: (319) 359-7580

Meskwaki Casino
1504 305th St.
Tama, IA 52339
(515) 484-2108
Fax: (515) 484-3218

**Miss Marquette
Riverboat Casino & Resort**
P.O. Box 28
Marquette, IA 52158
(800) 4-YOU-BET
Fax: (319) 873-3479

**Mississippi Belle II
Riverboat Casino**
311 Riverview Dr.
P.O. Box 1234
Clinton, IA 52732
(319) 243-9000
Fax: (319) 243-4020

**Prairie Meadows Race
Track & Casino**
1 Prairie Meadows Dr.
P.O. Box 1000
Altoona, IA 50009

The President Riverboat
130 W. River Dr.
Davenport, IA 52801
(319) 322-2578
Fax: (319) 322-2583

Winna Vegas Casino
1500 330 St.
P.O. Box AE
Sloan, IA 51055
(712) 428-9466
Fax: (712) 428-4219

Louisiana
Belle of Baton Rouge
103 France St.
Baton Rouge, LA 70802
(504) 378-6000

**Belle of Orleans, Bally's
Casino Lakeshore Resort**
1 Stars and Stripes Blvd.
New Orleans, LA 70126
(504) 248-3200

Boomtown Casino
4132 Peters Rd.
P.O. Box 1385
Harvey, LA 70059
(504) 366-7711
Fax: (504) 364-8752

Casino Rouge
1717 River Rd. N.
Baton Rouge, LA 70802
(504) 381-7777
Fax: (504) 381-7770

Cypress Bayou Casino
832 Martin Luther King Rd.
P.O. Box 519
Charenton, LA 70523
(318) 923-7284
Fax: (318) 923-7882

**Flamingo Casino New
Orleans**
Poydras St. Wharf
610 S. Peter St.
New Orleans, LA 70130
(504) 587-7777
Fax: (504) 587-1755

Grand Casino Avoyelles
711 E. Tunica Dr.
Grand Boulevard
Marksville, LA 71351
(318) 253-1946
Fax: (318) 253-2033

Grand Casino Coushatta
711 Carshatta Dr.
Highway 165
P.O. Box 1510
Kinder, LA 70648
(318) 738-7263
Fax: (318) 738-7340

Harrah's Casino New Orleans
One Canal Pl. Ste. 2800
365 Canal St.
New Orleans, LA 70130
(504) 533-6000
Fax: (504) 533-6150

Harrah's Shreveport Casino
315 Clyde Fant Pkwy.
401 Market St. Ste. 800
Shreveport, LA 71101
(318) 424-7777
Fax: (318) 424-5650

Horseshoe Casino & Hotel
P.O. Box 71111
711 Horseshoe Blvd.
Bossier City, LA 71111-1111
(318) 742-0711
Fax: (318) 741-7703

Isle of Capri Casino
711 Isle of Capri Blvd.
P.O. Box 5637
Bossier City, LA 71111
(318) 678-7777
Fax: (318) 226-1782

Players Casino
507 North Lakeshore Dr.
800 Bilbo St.
Lake Charles, LA 70601
(318) 437-1500
Fax: (318) 437-1505

River City Casino
Grand Palais Riverboat
Crescent City Riverboat
1400 Annunciation
New Orleans, LA 70130
(504) 524-4422
Fax: (504) 556-5515

Star Casino
507 N. Lakeshore Dr.
800 Bilbo St.
Lake Charles, LA 70601

Treasure Chest Casino
5050 Williams Blvd.
Kenner, LA 70065
(504) 433-8000
Fax: (504) 443-2458

Michigan
Chip-In Casino/Motel & Hannahville Bingo
P.O. Box 351
W399 Hwy. 2 and 41
Harris, MI 49845-0351
(906) 466-2941
Fax: (906) 466-2949

Kewadin Shores Casino
3039 Mackinac Tr.
St. Ignace, MI 49781
(906) 643-7071
Fax: (906) 643-8472

Kewadin Slots
102 Candy Cane Ln.
Christmas, MI 49862
(906) 387-5475
Fax: (906) 387-5475

Kewadin Slots
US Hwy. 2
P.O. Box 126
Manistique, MI 49854
(906) 341-5510
Fax: (906) 341-2951

Kewadin Slots
P.O. Box 189
3 Mile Rd.
Hessel, MI 49745
(906) 484-2903
Fax: (906) 484-3248

Kings Club Casino & Bay Mills Indian Community Bingo
RR 1 Box 313
Lakeshore Dr.
Brimley, MI 49715
(906) 248-3241
Fax: (906) 248-3283

Lac Vieux Desert Casino
P.O. Box 249
Choate Rd.
Watersmeet, MI 49969
(906) 358-4226
Fax: (906) 358-0288

Leelanau Sands Casino
2521 N.W. Bayshore Dr.
Suttons Bay, MI 49682
(616) 271-4104
Fax: (616) 271-4136

Leelanau Super Gaming Palace
2521 N.W. Bayshore Dr.
Suttons Bay, MI 49682
(616) 271-6852
Fax: (616) 271-4208

Ojibwa Casino Resort
R.R. 1 Box 284A
Baraga, MI 49908
(906) 353-6333
Fax: (906) 353-6838

Soaring Eagle Card Room
7498 E. Broadway
Mt. Pleasant, MI 48858
(517) 772-0827
Fax: (517) 772-0372

Soaring Eagle Casino
2395 S. Leaton Rd.
Mt. Pleasant, MI 48858
(517) 772-8900

Vegas Kewadin Casino
2186 Skunk Rd.
Sault Ste. Marie, MI 49783
(906) 632-0530
Fax: (906) 635-4959

Minnesota
Black Bear Casino
601 Hwy. 210
Carlton, MN 55718
(218) 878-2327
Fax: (218) 878-2414

Firefly Creek Casino
P.O. Box 96
R.R. 2
Granite Falls, MN 56241
(612) 564-2121
Fax: (612) 564-2121

Fond-du-Luth Casino
129 E. Superior St.
Duluth, MN 55802
(218) 722-0280
Fax: (218) 722-7505

Fortune Bay Casino
Chippewa Reservation
1430 Bois Forte Rd.
Tower, MN 55790
(218) 753-6400
Fax: (218) 753-6404

Grand Casino Hinkley
R.R. 3 Box 15
777 Lady Luck Dr. (Hwy. 48)
Hinkley, MN 55037
(612) 384-7777
Fax: (612) 449-7757

Grand Casino Mille Lacs
P.O. Box 240 HCR 67 Hwy. 169
777 Grand Ave.
Onamia, MN 56359
(800) 626-LUCK
Fax: (612) 449-5992

Grand Portage Lodge & Casino
P.O. Box 107
Hwy. 61 and Marina Rd.
Grand Portage, MN 55605
(218) 475-2401
Fax: (218) 475-2309

Jackpot Junction Casino
P.O. Box 420
Morton, MN 56270-0420
(507) 644-7800
Fax: (507) 644-2645

Lake of the Woods Lodge & Casino
1012 E. Lake St.
Warroad, MN 56763
(218) 386-3381
Fax: (218) 386-2969

Mystic Lake Casino & Dakota Country Casino
2400 Mystic Lake Blvd.
Prior Lake, MN 55372
(612) 445-9000
Fax: (612) 496-7280

Northern Lights Casino
Box 1003 HCR 73
Walker, MN 56484
(218) 547-2744
Fax: (218) 547-1368

Palace Bingo & Casino
Bingo Palace Dr.
R.R. 3 Box 221
Cass Lake, MN 56633
(218) 335-6787
Fax: (218) 335-6899

Red Lake Casino & Bingo
P.O. Box 574 Hwy. 1
Red Lake, MN 56671
(218) 679-2500
Fax: (218) 679-2666

River Road Casino
R.R. 3 Box 168A
Thief River Falls, MN 56701
(218) 681-4062
Fax: (218) 681-8370

Shooting Star Casino
777 Casino Rd.
P.O. Box 418 Hwy. 59
Mahnomen, MN 56557-0418
(218) 935-2206
Fax: (218) 935-2701

Treasure Island Casino and Bingo
P.O. Box 75
5734 Sturgeon Lake Rd.
Welch, MN 55089
(612) 388-6300
Fax: (612) 385-2560

Mississippi
Ameristar Casino Vicksburg
4146 S Washington St.
Vicksburg, MS 39180
(601) 638-1000
Fax: (601) 630-4037

Bally's Saloon, Gaming Hall
1450 Bally's Blvd.
Casino Center
P.O. Box 215
Robinsville, MS 38664
(601) 363-5600
Fax: (601) 363-5650

Bayou Caddy's Jubilee Casino
P.O. Box 659
Lakeshore, MS 39558-0659
(800) 552-0707
Fax: (601) 467-2054

Biloxi Belle Casino & Resort
P.O. Box 1900
Biloxi, MS 39530
(601) 436-7777
Fax: (601) 374-5051

Boomtown Casino
P.O. Box 369
676 Bayview Ave.
Biloxi, MS 89439
(601) 435-7000
Fax: (601) 435-7964

Casino Magic, Bay St. Louis
711 Casino Magic Dr.
Bay St. Louis, MS 39520
(601) 467-9257
Fax: (601) 466-6661

Casino Magic, Biloxi
195 E. Beach Blvd.
Biloxi, MS 39530
(800) 5-MAGIC-5
Fax: (601) 435-1559

Circus Belle Casino
P.O. Box 299
1010 Casino Center Dr.
Robinsonville, MS 38664
(601) 357-1111
Fax: (601) 435-1559

Copa Casino
777 Copa Blvd.
Gulfport, MS 39502
(601) 863-3330
Fax: (601) 863-3127

Cotton Club Casino
P.O. Box 1777
Greenville, MS 38702
(601) 335-1111
Fax: (601) 378-8953

Fitzgerald's Casino
P.O. Box 327
Robinsonville, MS 38664
(601) 363-5825
Fax: (601) 363-7160

Grand Casino, Biloxi
265 Beach Blvd.
Biloxi, MS 39530
(601) 436-2946
Fax: (601) 436-2801

Grand Casino, Gulfport
3215 W. Beach Blvd.
Gulfport, MS 39501
(601) 867-5583
Fax: (601) 864-6969

Harrah's Casino Hotel, Vicksburg
1310 Mulberry St.
Vicksburg, MS 39180
(601) 636-3423
Fax: (601) 630-4217

Harrah's Casino, Tunica
R.R. 1 P.O. Box 223
711 Harrahs Dr.
Robinsonville, MS 38664
(601) 363-7200
Fax: (601) 363-7230

Hollywood Casino Tunica Commerce Landing
P.O. Box 218
Robinsonville, MS 38664
(601) 357-7700
Fax: (601) 357-7800

Isle of Capri Casino Crown Plaza Resort
151 Beach Blvd.
Biloxi, MS 39530
(601) 435-5400
Fax: (601) 435-5998

Isle of Capri Casino, Vicksburg
P.O. Box 820668
3990 Washington St.
Vicksburg, MS 39180
(601) 636-5700
Fax: (509) 422-3907

Lady Luck, Biloxi
1848 Beach Blvd.
P.O. Box 142
Biloxi, MS 39531
(601) 388-1364
Fax: (601) 388-6401

Lady Luck, Natchez
21 Silver St.
Natchez, MS 39121
(601) 445-0605
Fax: (601) 442-3242

**Lady Luck Rhythm & Blues
Casino Hotel**
P.O. Box 447
777 Lady Luck Pkwy.
Lula, MS 38644
(601) 363-4600
Fax: (601) 337-4492

Las Vegas Casino
242 Walnut St.
Greenville, MS 38701
(601) 335-5800
Fax: (601) 335-2700

Palace Casino
182 E. Howard Ave.
P.O. Box 3500
Biloxi, MS 39533
(601)432-8888
Fax: (601) 432-7345

President Casino Biloxi
2110 Beach Blvd.
Biloxi, MS 39533
(601) 385-3500
Fax: (601) 385-3510

Rainbow Casino
1380 Warrenton Rd.
Vicksburg, MS 39180
(601) 636-7575
Fax: (601) 630-0392

**Sam's Town Hotel &
Gambling Hall**
R.R. 1, Box 224
Robinsonville, MS 38664
(601) 363-0700
Fax: (601) 363-0890

Sheraton Casino
1107 Casino Center Dr.
Robinsonville, MS 38664
(601) 363-4900
Fax: (601) 363-4925

Silver Star Hotel & Casino
P.O. Box 6048
Philadelphia, MS 39350
(601) 656-3400
Fax: (601) 650-1351

Splash Casino
P.O. Box 1888
Tunica, MS 38676
(601) 363-4300
Fax: (601) 363-6621

Treasure Bay Casino
One Treasure Bay Dr.
P.O. Box 298
Robinsonville, MS 38664
(601) 363-6600
Fax: (601) 363-6621

Treasure Bay Casino Resort
1980 Beach Blvd.
Biloxi, MS 39531
(602) 385-6000
Fax: (601) 385-6038

Missouri
Argosy Casino at Riverside
777 N.W. Argosy Pkwy.
Riverside, MO 64150
(816) 746-3100
Reservations (800) 270-7711
Fax: (816) 741-5423

City of Caruthersville Casino Aztar
P.O. Box 1135
Caruthersville, MO 63830
(573) 333-1000
Fax: (573) 333-1177

Harrah's North Kansas City Casino
1 Riverboat Dr.
N. Kansas City, MO 64116
(816) 472-7777
Fax: (816) 472-7778

President Casino on the Admiral
800 N. First St.
St Louis, MO 63102
(314) 622-1111
Fax: (314) 622-3043

St. Charles Riverfront Station
1355 Fifth St.
P.O. Box 720-633302
St Charles, MO 63301
(314) 940-4300
Fax: (314) 940-4323

St. Jo Frontier Casino
77 Francis St.
Riverfront Park
St. Joseph, MO 64501
(816) 279-7577
Fax: (816) 279-9619

Nevada

Las Vegas
49er Saloon & Casino
1556 N. Eastern Ave.
Las Vegas, NV 89101
(702) 649-2421

Aladdin Hotel & Casino
3667 Las Vegas Boulevard S.
P.O. Box 93958
Las Vegas, NV 89193-3958
(702) 736-0111
(800) 634-3424
Fax: (702) 736-0287

Arizona Charlie's Inc.
704 S. Decatur Blvd.
Las Vegas, NV 89107
(800) 342-2695
Fax: (702) 258-5196

Aztec Inn Casino
2200 S. Vegas Blvd.
Las Vegas, NV 89104
(702) 385-4566
Fax: (702) 385-1334

Barbary Coast Hotel & Casino
3595 S. Las Vegas Blvd.
Las Vegas, NV 89109
(702) 737-7111
(800) 634-6755
Fax: (702) 369-3055

Barcelona Hotel & Casino
5011 E. Craig Rd.
Las Vegas, NV 89115
(702) 644-6300
Fax: (702) 644-6510

Beano's Casino
7200 W. Lake Mead Blvd.
Las Vegas, NV 89128
(702) 255-9150
Fax: (702) 363-3211

Best Western
Main St.
1000 N. Main
Las Vegas, NV 89101
(702) 382-3455
Fax: (702) 382-1428

Best Western Mardi Gras Inn
3500 Paradise Rd.
Las Vegas, NV 89109
(702) 731-2020
(800) 634-6051
Fax: (702) 733-6994

Big Dog's Bar & Grill
1511 N. Nellis Blvd.
Las Vegas, NV 89110
(702) 459-1099
Fax: (702) 459-7730

Big Dog's Cafe & Casino
6390 W. Sahara Ave.
Las Vegas, NV 89102
(702) 876-3647
Fax: (702) 876-4453

The Big Game Club
4747 Faircenter Park
Las Vegas, NV 89102
(702) 870-0087

Bill Ladd's Silver Dollar Saloon
2501 E. Charleston Blvd.
Las Vegas, NV 89104
(702) 382-6921

Binion's Horseshoe Club Hotel & Casino
P.O. Box 520
128 E. Fremont St.
Las Vegas, NV 89109
(702) 382-1600
(800) 937-6537

Boardwalk Hotel & Casino
Holiday Inn
3750 Las Vegas Blvd. S.
Las Vegas, NV 89109
(702) 735-2400
Fax: (702) 739-8152

Bonanza Lounge
4300 E. Bonanza Rd.
Las Vegas, NV 89110

Boomtown Las Vegas
3333 Blue Diamond Rd.
Las Vegas, NV 89139
(702) 263-7777
(800) 588-7711
Fax: (702) 896-4925

Boulder Station Hotel & Casino
4111 Boulder Hwy.
Las Vegas, NV 89121
(800) 683-7777
Fax: (702) 221-6510

Bourbon Street Hotel & Casino
120 E. Flamingo Rd.
Las Vegas, NV 89109
(702) 737-7200
(800) 634-6956
Fax: (702) 734-9155

Caesars Palace
3570 Las Vegas Blvd S.
Las Vegas, NV 89109
(702) 731-7110
(800) 634-6001
Fax: (702) 731-6636

Cal's Jackpot Casino
3012 Griswold St.
North Las Vegas, NV 89030
(702) 399-2269

Captains Quarters
2610 Regatta Dr.
Las Vegas, NV 89128
(702) 256-6200
Fax: (702) 256-4372

Casino Royale & Hotel
3411 Las Vegas Blvd S.
Las Vegas, NV 89109
(702) 737-3500
Fax: (702) 737-9216

Castaways Casino
3132 S. Highland Dr.
Las Vegas, NV 89109
(702) 735-1212
Fax: (702) 735-1510

Charlie's Lakeside Bar & Grill
8603 W. Sahara Ave.
Las Vegas, NV 89117
(702) 258-5170

**Circus Circus Hotel & Casino,
Las Vegas**
P.O. Box 14967
2880 Las Vegas Blvd. S.
Las Vegas, NV 89109
(702) 734-0410
(800) 634-3450

Continental Hotel & Casino
4100 Paradise Rd.
Las Vegas, NV 89109
(702) 737-5555
Fax: (702) 369-8776

Dan's Royal Flush Casino
3049 Las Vegas Blvd. S.
Las Vegas, NV 89109
(702) 735-7666
Fax: (702) 735-2619

Dann's Slot Country
4213 Boulder Hwy.
Las Vegas, NV 89121
(702) 451-4974

Days Inn/Town Hall Casino
4155 Koval Ln.
Las Vegas, NV 89101
(702) 731-2111
Fax: (702) 731-1113

**Debbie Reynolds Hotel Casino
and Hollywood Movie Museum**
305 Convention Center Dr.
Las Vegas, NV 89109
(702) 734-0711
(800) 633-1666
Fax: (702) 791-0753

Desert Inn Hotel, Las Vegas
3145 Las Vegas Blvd S.
Las Vegas, NV 89109
(702) 733-4444
Fax: (702) 733-4676

Draft House Bar & Casino
4543 N. Rancho Dr.
Las Vegas, NV 89130
(702) 645-1404
Fax: (702) 645-7173

El Cortez Hotel & Casino
600 E. Fremont St.
P.O. Box 680
Las Vegas, NV 89101
(702) 385-5200
(800) 634-6703
Fax: (702) 385-1554

Ellis Island Casino
4178 Koval Ln.
Las Vegas, NV 89109
(702) 733-8901
Fax: (702) 733-9781

Ernie's Casino
1901 N. Rancho Dr.
Las Vegas, NV 89106
(702) 646-4855
Fax: (702) 648-1182

Eureka Casino
595 E. Sahara Ave.
Las Vegas, NV 89104
(702) 794-3464
Fax: (702) 794-3464

Excalibur Hotel & Casino
P.O. Box 96778
3850 Las Vegas Blvd. S.
Las Vegas, NV 89193
(800) 937-7777
Fax: (702) 597-7009

Fiesta Hotel & Casino
2400 N. Rancho Drive
Las Vegas, NV 89130
(800) 731-7333

Fitzgerald's Casino Hotel
301 E. Fremont St.
Las Vegas, NV 89101
(702) 388-2400
(800) 274-5825
Fax: (388-8032

Flamingo Hilton Hotel & Casino
3555 Las Vegas Blvd S.
Las Vegas, NV 89109
(702) 733-3111
(800) 732-2111
Fax: (702) 785-7034

Foothills Express
714 N. Rainbow Blvd.
Las Vegas, NV 89108
(702) 878-2281

Foothills Ranch
3377 N. Rancho Dr.
Las Vegas, NV 89130
(702) 658-6360

Four Queens Hotel & Casino
202 E. Fremont St.
Las Vegas, NV 89101
(702) 385-4011
(800) 634-6182
Fax: (702) 387-5133

Friendly Fergie's Casino & Saloon
2430 S. Las Vegas Blvd.
Las Vegas, NV 89104
(702) 598-1985

Frontier Hotel & Gambling Hall
3120 Las Vegas Blvd. S.
Las Vegas, NV 89109
(702) 794-8200
(800) 634-6966
Fax: (702) 755-8013

Gloria's II
1966 N. Rainbow Blvd.
Las Vegas, NV 89108
(702) 647-0744
Fax: (702) 647-2058

Gold Coast Hotel & Casino
4000 W. Flamingo Rd.
Las Vegas, NV 89103
(703) 367-7111
Fax: (702) 367-6312

Gold Spike Hotel & Casino
400 E. Ogden Ave.
Las Vegas NV 89101-4239
(702) 384-8444
(800) 634-6703
Fax: (702) 384-8768

The Golden Gate Hotel & Casino
1 Fremont St.
Las Vegas, NV 89101
(702) 382-6300
Fax: (702) 383-9681

Golden Nugget Hotel & Casino
129 E. Fremont St.
P.O. Box 610
Las Vegas, NV 89101
(702) 385-7111
(800) 634-3454
Fax: (702) 386-8170

Hacienda Resort Hotel & Casino
3950 Las Vegas Blvd.
Las Vegas, NV 89119
(702) 739-8911
Fax: (702) 798-8288

Hard Rock Hotel & Casino
4455 Paradise Rd.
P.O. Box 70387
Las Vegas, NV 89170-0387
(702) 693-5000
(800) 473-7625
Fax: (702) 693-5000

Harrah's Casino Hotel
3475 Las Vegas Blvd. S.
P.O. Box 15000
Las Vegas, NV 89109
(702) 369-5000
(800) 634-6765
Fax: (702) 369-5008

Holy Cow! Casino Cafe and Brewery
3025 Sheridan St.
2423 Las Vegas Blvd. S.
Las Vegas, NV 89041
(702) 732-2697
Fax: (702) 732-1413

Hotel San Remo Casino & Resort
115 E. Tropicana Ave.
Las Vegas, NV 89109
(702) 739-9000
(800) 522-7366
Fax: (702) 736-1120

Howard Johnson Hotel & Casino on Tropicana
3111 W. Tropicana Ave.
Las Vegas, NV 89103
(702) 798-1111
Fax: (702) 798-7138

Imperial Palace Hotel & Casino
3535 Las Vegas Blvd. S.
Las Vegas, NV 89109-8935
(702) 731-3311
(800) 634-6441
Fax: (702) 794-3347

Jackie Gaughan's Plaza Hotel & Casino
P.O. Box 760
1 Main St.
Las Vegas, NV 89010
(702) 386-2110
(800) 634-6575
Fax: (702) 382-8281

King 8 Hotel & Gambling Hall
3330 W Tropicana Ave.
Las Vegas, NV 89103
(702) 736-8988
Fax: (702) 736-7106

Klondike Inn & Casino
5191 Las Vegas Blvd. S.
Las Vegas, NV 89119
(702) 739-9351
Fax: (702) 794-8710

Lady Luck Casino/Hotel
206 N. 3rd St.
Las Vegas, NV 89101
(702) 477 3000
(800) 523-9582
Fax: (702) 477-3005

Las Vegas Club Hotel & Casino
18 E. Fremont Ave.
P.O. Box 1719
Las Vegas, NV 89101
(702) 385-1664
(800) 634-6532
Fax: (702) 387-6071

Las Vegas Hilton Hotel & Casino
P.O. Box 93147
3000 Paradise Rd.
Las Vegas, NV 89109
(702) 732-5111
(800) 732-7117
Fax: (702) 732-5675

LeRoy's Horse & Sports Place
114 S. First St.
Las Vegas, NV 89101
(702) 382-1561

Longhorn Casino
5288 Boulder Hwy.
Las Vegas, NV 89122
(702) 435-9170
Fax: (702) 435-9729

Loose Caboose Saloon
15 N. Nellis Blvd. A1
Las Vegas, NV 89110
(702) 452-4500

Luxor Hotel & Casino
3900 Las Vegas Blvd. S.
Las Vegas, NV 89119-1000
(702) 262-4000
(800) 288-1000
Fax: (702) 262-4857

Mad Matty's Bar Casino & Grille
8100 W. Sahara Ave.
Las Vegas, NV 89117
(702) 254-9997
Fax: (702) 255-9798

Maxim's Hotel & Casino
160 E. Flamingo Rd.
Las Vegas, NV 89109
(702) 731-4300
(800) 634-6987
Fax: (702) 735-3252

MGM Grand Hotel, Casino and Theme Park
3799 Las Vegas Blvd. S.
Las Vegas, NV 89109
(702) 891-1111
(800) 929-1111

The Mirage
P.O. Box 7777
3400 Las Vegas Blvd. S.
Las Vegas, NV 89109
(702) 791-7111
Fax: (702) 791-7446

Mizpah Casino
4380 Boulder Hwy.
Las Vegas, NV 89121
(702) 323-5194

Monte Carlo Resort & Casino
3770 Las Vegas Blvd. S.
Las Vegas, NV 89109
(702) 730-7777
(800) 311-8999

Moulin Rouge Hotel & Casino
900 W. Bonanza Rd.
Las Vegas, NV 89106
(702) 648-5040
Fax: (702) 648-5541

Nevada Palace Hotel & Casino
5255 Boulder Hwy.
Las Vegas, NV 89122
(800) 634-6283

New York New York Hotel and Casino
3790 Las Vegas Blvd. S.
Las Vegas, NV 89109
(800) NY-FOR-ME (800-693-6763)

One-Eyed Jacks
4380 Boulder Hwy.
Las Vegas, NV 89121
(702) 434-9777

Opera House Saloon & Casino
2542 N. Las Vegas Blvd.
North Las Vegas, NV 89030
(702) 649-8801
Fax: (702) 649-8435

P.J. Russo's
2300 S. Maryland Pk.
Las Vegas, NV 89104
(702) 735-5454

P.T.'s Pub
347 N. Nellis
Las Vegas, NV 89110
(702) 646-6657
Fax: (702) 564-5489

Palace Station Hotel & Casino
P.O. Box 26448
2411 W. Sahara Ave.
Las Vegas, NV 89102
(702) 367-2411
(800) 634-3101
Fax: (702) 367-6138

Peppermill Coffee Shop & Lounge
2985 Las Vegas Blvd. S.
Las Vegas, NV 89109
(702) 735-7635
Fax: (702) 735-4185

Pioneer Club
25 E. Fremont St.
Las Vegas, NV 89101

Port Tack Restaurant
3190 W. Sahara Ave.
Las Vegas, NV 89102
(702) 873-3345
Fax: (702) 873-6472

Quality Inn Casino
377 E. Flamingo Rd.
Las Vegas, NV 89109
(702) 733-7777
(800) 634-6617
Fax: (702) 734-0902

Queen of Hearts Hotel & Casino
19 E. Lewis Ave.
Las Vegas, NV 89101
(702) 382-8878
(800) 835-6005

R-Bar
6000 W. Charleston Blvd.
Las Vegas, NV 89102
(702) 259-0120

Rainbow Vegas Hotel & Casino
401 S. Casino Center Blvd.
Las Vegas, NV 89101
(702) 386-6166
(800) 634-6635
Fax: (702) 385-9864

Rio Suite Hotel & Casino
3700 W. Flamingo Rd.
Las Vegas, NV 89103
(702) 252-7777
(800) 752-9746
Fax: (702) 247-7918

Riviera
2901 Las Vegas Blvd.
Las Vegas, NV 89109
(800) 634-6753

Royal Hotel Casino
99 Convention Center Dr.
Las Vegas, NV 89109
(702) 735-6117
(800) 634-6118
Fax: (702) 735-2546

Sahara Hotel & Casino
2535 Las Vegas Blvd. S.
Las Vegas, NV 89109
(702) 737-2111
(800) 634-6666
Fax: (702) 737-2575

Sam Boyd's California Hotel, Casino & RV Park
12 Ogden Ave.
Las Vegas, NV 89101
(702) 385-1222

Sam Boyd's Fremont Hotel & Casino
P.O. Box 940
200 E. Fremont St.
Las Vegas, NV 89101
(800) 634-6460

Sam's Town Hotel & Gambling Hall
5111 Boulder Hwy.
P.O. Box 12001
Las Vegas, NV 89122
(702) 456-7777
(800) 634-6371
Fax: (702) 454-8087

Sands Hotel Casino
3355 Las Vegas Blvd. S.
Las Vegas, NV 89109
(702) 733-5000
Fax: (702) 733-5301

Sante Fe Hotel & Casino
4949 N. Rancho Dr.
Las Vegas, NV 89130
(702) 658-4900
Fax: (702) 658-4191

Sassy Sally's
32 Fremont St.
115 N. 1st St.
Las Vegas, NV 89101
(702) 382-5777
Fax: (702) 385-4934

Sheraton Desert Inn
3145 Las Vegas Blvd. S.
Las Vegas, NV 89109
(800) 634-6906

Showboat Hotel & Casino
2800 Fremont St.
Las Vegas, NV 89104
(800) 634-3484
Fax: (702) 385-9163

Silver City Casino
3001 Las Vegas Blvd. S.
Las Vegas, NV 89109
(702) 732-0866

Skinny Dugan's Pub
4127 W. Charleston Blvd.
Las Vegas, NV 89102
(702) 877-0522

Slots-A Fun Casino
3890 Las Vegas Blvd. S.
Las Vegas, NV 89109
(702) 794-3814
Fax: (702) 734-6253

Stage Door Casino
4000 S. Audrie St.
Las Vegas, NV 89109
(702) 733-0124
Fax: (702) 733-9876

Stardust Resort & Casino
3000 Las Vegas Blvd. S.
Las Vegas, NV 89109
(702) 732-6111
(800) 634-6757
Fax: (702) 732-6296

Treasure Island Hotel & Casino
3300 Las Vegas Blvd. S.
Las Vegas, NV 89109
(702) 894-7444
(800) 944-7444
Fax: (702) 792-7646

Triple Play
1875 S. Decatur Blvd.
Las Vegas, NV 89102
(702) 364-0808

Tropicana Resort & Casino
3801 Las Vegas Blvd. S.
Las Vegas, NV 89109
(702) 739-2222
(800) 634-4000
Fax: (702) 739-2323

Union Plaza Hotel
1 Main St
Las Vegas, NV 89101
(702) 386-2110
Fax: (702) 382-8281

**Vacation Village Hotel &
Casino**
P.O. Box 96958
6711 Las Vegas Blvd. S.
Las Vegas, NV 89119
(702) 897-1700
(800) 338-0608
Fax: (702) 361-6726

Vegas World Hotel & Casino
2000 Las Vegas Blvd. S.
Las Vegas, NV 89104
(702) 382-2000

Western Hotel & Casino
899 E. Fremont St.
Las Vegas, NV 89101-4239
(702) 384-4620
Fax: (702) 385-4047

Westward Ho Hotel & Casino
2900 Las Vegas Blvd. S.
Las Vegas, NV 89109
(702) 731-2900

Whistle Stop
2839 W. Sahara Ave.
Las Vegas, NV 89102
(702) 873-2086

Nevada (not Las Vegas)
49er Club
1241 N. Boulder Hwy.
670 S. Hwy. 95
Searchlight, NV 89406
(702) 297-1479

**Alpine Lodge & Nevada Club
Casino**
P.O. Box 96
Hwy. 50
Eureka, NV 89316
(702) 237-5365

Baldini's Sports Casino
865 S. Rock Blvd.
Sparks, NV 89431
(702) 358-0116
Fax: (702) 358-5362

Barton's Club 93
P.O. Box 323
Hwy. 93
Jackpot, NV 89825
(702) 755-2341
Fax: (702) 755-2362

**Best Western Bonanza Inn &
Casino**
P.O. Box 1530
855 W. Williams Ave.
Fallon, NV 89407-1530
(702) 423-6031
Fax: (702) 423-6282

**Bill's Casino Lake Tahoe—
Harrah's**
P.O. Box 8
Hwy. 50 and Stateline
Stateline, NV 89449
(702) 588-2455
Fax: (702) 588-1390

Billy's East Lounge
4563 E. Sunset Rd.
Henderson, NV 89014
(702) 454-1887

Bird Farm
128 E. Williams Ave.
Fallon, NV
(702) 423-7877

**Bob Cashell's Horseshoe
Club & Casino**
P.O. Box 1871
229 N. Virginia St.
Reno, NV 89502
(702) 323-7900
Fax: (702) 323-7185

Bonanza Casino
4720 N. Virginia St.
Reno, NV 89503
(702) 323-2724
Fax: (702) 323-5788

Bonanza Saloon
P.O. Box 95
Virginia City, NV 89440
(702) 847-0655
Fax: (702) 847-0789

Border Inn
Hwy. 50
Baker, NV 89311
(702) 234-7300

Bordertown
19575 Hwy. 395 N.
Reno, NV 89506
(702) 972-1309

**Bruno's Country Club &
Casino**
P.O. Box 70
445 Main St.
Gevlach, NV 89412
(702) 557-2220

Bucket of Blood Saloon
P.O. Box E.
1 S. C St.
Virginia City, NV 89440
(702) 847-0322

Buffalo Bill's Resort & Casino
I-15, Southern CA/NV border
Jean, NV 89019
(702) 382-1111

Burro Inn
P.O. Box 3
Beatty, NV 89003
(702) 553-2892
Fax: (702) 553-2892

**Cactus Jack's Senator
Club Casino**
420 N. Casson St.
Carson City, NV 89701
(702) 822-8770
Fax: (702) 882-9147

Cactus Pete's Resort Casino
P.O. Box 508
US Hwy. 93
Jackpot, NV 89825
(702) 755-2321
Fax: (702) 7552737

Caesars Tahoe Resort
P.O. Box 5800
Stateline, NV 89449
(702) 588-3515

**Cal-Nev-Ari Casino/Blue Sky
Motel**
P.O. Box 430
1 Spirit Mountain Rd.
Cal-Nev-Ari, NV 89039
(702) 297-1118
Fax: (702) 297-1217

Cal-Neva Lodge & Casino, Crystal Bay
P.O. Box 368
Crystal Bay, NV 89402
(702) 832-4000
Fax: (702) 831-9007

Carson Horseshoe
402 N. Carson St.
Carson City, NV 89701
(702) 883-2211

Carson Nugget Casino
P.O. Box 2027
507 N. Carson St.
Carson City, NV 89701
(702) 882-1626
Fax: (702) 883-1106

Carson Station Hotel/Casino
P.O. Box 1966
Carson City, NV 89702-1966
(702) 883-0900

Carson Valley Inn Hotel & Casino
1627 US Hwy. 395
Minden, NV 89423
(702) 782-9711
Fax: (702) 782-7472

Casino West
11 N. Main St.
Yerington, NV 89447
(702) 463-2481
Fax: (702) 463-2481

Cheers Hotel & Casino
567 W. 4th St.
Reno, NV 89503
(702) 322-8181
Fax: (702) 324-5905

Circus Circus Hotel & Casino, Reno
P.O. Box 5880
500 N. Sierra St.
Reno, NV 89508
(702) 329-0711
Fax: (702) 329-0599

Clarion Hotel Casino
3800 S. Virginia St.
Reno, NV 89502
(702) 825-4700
Fax: (702) 825-1170

Club Cal-Nevada Casino, Carson City
P.O. Box 2071
30 N. Virginia
38 E. 2nd St.
Reno, NV 89505
(702) 323-1046
Fax: (702) 785-3299

Colonial Inn Hotel & Casino
250 N. Arlington Ave.
Reno, NV 89501
(702) 322-3838
Fax: (702) 323-4588

Colorado Belle Hotel & Casino
P.O. Box 2304
2100 South Casino Dr.
Laughlin, NV 89028
(702) 298-4000
Fax: (702) 229-0032

Colt Service Center & Casino
650 W. Front St.
Battle Mountain, NV 89820
(702) 635-5424
Fax: (702) 635-5699

Commercial Hotel Casino
345 4th St.
Elko, NV 89801
(702) 738-3181
Fax: (702) 753-9247

Comstock Hotel & Casino
200 W. 2nd St.
Reno, NV 89501
(702) 329-1880
Fax: (702) 348-0539

Copper Queen Hotel & Casino
701 Ave. 1
Ely, NV 89301
(702) 289-4884
Fax: (702) 289-1495

Country Club
P.O. Box 176
Gerlach, NV 89412
(702) 557-2220
Fax: (702) 557-2320

Crystal Bay Club Casino
P.O. Box 37
Hwy. 28
Crystal Bay, NV 89402
(702) 831-0512
Fax: (702) 831-5065

Delta Saloon
P.O. Box 158
18 S. C St.
Virginia City, NV 89440
(702) 827-0789
Fax: (702) 847-9613

Don Laughlin's Riverside Resort Hotel & Casino
P.O. Box 500
1650 Casino Dr.
Laughlin, NV
(702) 298-2535
Fax: (702) 298-2612

Ed's Tahoe Nugget
P.O. Box 4740
Stateline, NV 89449
(702) 588-7733

Eddie's Fabulous 50's
45 W. 2nd St.
Reno, NV 89501
(702) 329-1950

Edgewater Hotel and Casino
2020 S. Casino Dr.
P.O. Box 642
Laughlin, NV 89028
(702) 298-2453
Fax: (702) 298-5606

El Capitan Lodge & Casino
P.O. Box 1000
540 F St.
Hawthorne, NV 89415
(702) 945-3322
Fax: (702) 324-6229

Eldorado Casino
140 S. Water St.
Henderson, NV 89015
(702) 564-1811
Fax: (702) 564-5369

Eldorado Hotel Casino
P.O. Box 3399
345 N. Virginia St.
Reno, NV 89505
(702) 786-5700
Fax: (702) 348-7513

Exchange Club of Beatty
P.O. Box 607
604 Main St.
Beatty, NV 89003
(702) 553-2368
Fax: (702) 553-2441

Fallon Nugget
P.O. Box 1530
70 S. Main St.
Fallon, NV 89407
(702) 423-3111
Fax: (702) 423-6338

Fiesta Hotel & Casino
333 N. Rancho Dr.
N. Las Vegas, NV 89106
(702) 631-7000

Fitzgerald's Casino & Hotel
255 N. Virginia St.
Reno, NV 89501
(702) 785-3300
Fax: (702) 785-7180

Flamingo Hilton Laughlin
1900 S. Casino Dr.
Laughlin, NV 89129
(702) 298-5111
Fax: (702) 298-5129

Flamingo Hilton, Reno
255 N. Sierra St.
Reno, NV 89501
(702) 322-1111
Fax: (702) 795-7057

Fort Mojave Casino
P.O. Box 77011
Laughlin, NV 89028-7011
(702) 535-5555

Four Jacks Hotel & Casino
P.O. Box 468
Hwy. 93
Jackpot, NV 89825
(702) 755-2491
Fax: (702) 755-2934

Fourway Bar, Cafe & Casino
P.O. Box 515
US Hwy. 93 and I-80
Wells NV 89835
(702) 752-3344

Gambler
211 N. Virginia St.
Reno, NV 89502
(702) 322-7620

The Gambler
1324 Victorian Ave.
Sparks, NV 89431
(702) 322-7620

Giudici's Victorian Gambling Hall
1324 Victorian Ave.
Sparks, NV 89431
(702) 359-8868
Fax: (702) 359-8955

Gold 'N' Silver Inn
790 W. 4th St.
Reno, NV 89503
(702) 323-2696

Gold Country Motor Inn
2050 Idaho St.
Elko, NV 89801
(702) 738-8421

Gold Dust West Casino
P.O. Box 2759-89504
444 Vine St.
Reno, NV 89503
(702) 323-2211

Gold Ranch
P.O. Box 160
Verdi, NV 89439
(702) 345-0556
Fax: (702) 345-2356

Gold Strike Hotel & Gambling Hall
P.O. Box 19278
1 Main St.
Jean, NV 89109
(702) 477-5000
Fax: (702) 574-1583

Gold Strike Inn & Casino
US Hwys. 93 and 466
Boulder City, NV 89005
(702) 293-5000

Golden Nugget, Laughlin
P.O. Box 77111
Laughlin, NV 89029
(702) 298-7111
Fax: (702) 398-7646

Harrah's Casino Hotel, Lake Tahoe
P.O. Box 8
Stateline, NV 89449
(702) 588-6611
Fax: (702) 586-6606

Harrah's Casino Hotel, Laughlin
P.O. Box 33000
Laughlin, NV 89029
(702) 298-4600
Fax: (702) 298-3023

Harvey's Resort Hotel & Casino
P.O. Box 128
Stateline, NV 89449
(800) 553-1022
Fax: (702) 588-0489

Headquarters Bar & Casino
1345 S. Maine St.
Fallon, NV 89406
(702) 423-6355

Hideaway Casino
21 Scobie Dr.
W Wendover, NV 89883
(702) 664-9971

Hobey's Casino
5195 Sun Valley Dr.
Sun Valley, NV 89433
(702) 673-0683

Holiday Hotel Casino
111 Mill St.
Reno, NV 89501
(702) 329-0411
Fax: (702) 329-3627

Holiday Inn Elko
3015 Idaho St.
Elko, NV 89801
(702) 738-8425

Horseshoe Casino
P.O. Box 508
US Hwy. 93
Jackpot, NV 89825
(702) 755-7777
Fax: (702) 755-2737

Horseshoe Casino, Reno
P.O. Box 1871
229 N. Virginia St.
Reno, NV 89505
(702) 323-7900
Fax: (702) 323-7185

Hotel Nevada & Gambling Hall
P.O. Box 209
501 Aultman St.
Ely, NV 89301
(702) 289-6665
Fax: (702) 289-4715

Hyatt Regency Lake Tahoe Resort & Casino
P.O. Box 3239
111 Country Club Dr.
Incline Village, NV 89450
(702) 832-1234
Fax: (702) 831-7508

Indian Springs Hotel & Casino
P.O. Box 298
Hwy. 95
Indian Springs, NV 89018
(702) 384-7449
Fax: (702) 879-3457

Jackpot Owl Club Casino Restaurant & Motel
72 E. Front St.
Battle Mountain, NV 89820
(702) 635-2444
Fax: (702) 635-5155

Jailhouse Motel & Casino
211 5th St.
Ely, NV 89301
(702) 289-3033
Fax: (702) 289-8709

Jax Casino
P.O. Box 1196
485 Cornell Ave.
Lovelock, NV 89419
(702) 273-2288

Jerry's Nugget
1821 Las Vegas Blvd. N.
North Las Vegas, NV 89030
(702) 399-3000
Fax: (702)399-1959

Jim Kelly's Nugget
P.O. Box 1248
Crystal Bay, NV 89402-1248
(702) 831-0455

JJ's Sierra Gambling Hall & Saloon
4350 Las Vegas Blvd. N.
North Las Vegas, NV 89115
(702) 643-1955

Joe's Longhorn Casino
3016 E. Lake Mead Blvd.
North Las Vegas, NV 89030
(702) 642-1940
Fax: (702) 642-5256

Joe's Tavern
P.O. Box 1630
537 Sierra Way
Hawthorne, NV 89415
(702) 945-2302

John Ascuaga's Nugget
1100 Nugget Ave.
Sparks, NV 89431
(702) 356-3300
Fax: (702) 356-3434

Jokers Wild
920 Boulder Hwy.
Henderson, NV 89015
(702) 564-8100

Kactus Kate's Casino
Interstate Hwy. 15
Jean, NV 89109
(702) 477-5000

Keystone Club
Hwy. 351
Gabbs, NV 89409
(702) 285-4031

Lake Mead Lounge & Casino
846 E. Lake Mead Blvd.
Henderson, NV 89015
(702) 565-0297
Fax: (702) 565-0304

Lake Tahoe Horizon Casino/Resort
Hwy. 50
P.O. Box C
Stateline, NV 89449
(702) 588-6211
Fax: (702) 588-3110

Lakeside Inn & Casino
P.O. Box 5640
Hwy. 50
Lake Tahoe, NV 89449
(702) 588-7777
Fax: (702) 588-4902

Ligouri's Bar & Casino
1133 N. Boulder Hwy.
Henderson, NV 89015
(702) 565-1688

Lucky Club
45 Main St.
Yerington, NV 89477
(702) 463-2868

Lucky Strike Mining Company Casino
642 S. Boulder Hwy.
Henderson, NV 89015
(702) 564-7118

Mac's Casino & Nevada Crossing Hotel
P.O. Box 2000
1045 Wendover Blvd.
West Wendover, NV 89883
(702) 664-4000
Fax: (702) 664-2900

Mark Twain Saloon
P.O. Box 392
63 S. C St.
Virginia City NV 89440
(702) 847-0599

Mint Casino
1130 B St.
Sparks, NV 89427
(702) 359-4944

Mizpah Hotel & Casino
P.O. Box 952
100 Main St.
Tonopah, NV 89049
(702) 482-6202

Model-T Casino & Hotel
P.O. Box 3500
1130 W. Winnemucca Blvd.
Winnemucca, NV 89445
(702) 623-2588
Fax: (702) 623-5547

Mr. B's Casino
Hwy. I-80
Star Route, Box 210
Ryepatch, NV 89419
(702) 538-7318
Fax: (702) 538-7374

Mr. B's Casino
Hwy I-80
6000 E. Frontage Rd.
Mill City, NV 89418
(702) 538-7306
Fax: (702) 538-7448

Mugshots Eatery & Casino
1120 N. Boulder Hwy.
Henderson, NV 89015
(702) 566-6577

Nevada Club Casino
224 N. Virginia St.
Reno, NV 89505
(702) 329-1721
Fax: (702) 786-7180

Nevada Hotel Casino
36 E. Front St.
Battle Mountain, NV 89820
(702) 635-2453

The Nugget
233 N. Virginia St.
Reno, NV 89501
(702) 323-0716
Fax: (702) 323-3254

Old Reno Casino
P.O. Box 3343
44 W. Commercial Row
Reno, NV 89505
(702) 322-6971

Old West Inn Lounge & Casino
P.O. Box 384
456 6th St.
Wells, NV 89835
(702) 752-3888

Owl Club & Steak House
P.O. Box 159
Main St. and Hwy. 50
Eureka, NV 89316
(702) 237-5280
Fax: (702) 237-5285

Owl Club Casino & Motel
72 E. Front St.
Battle Mountain, NV 89820
(702) 635-5155

P.T.'s Slot Casino
44 Water St.
Henderson, NV 89105
(702) 564-4994

Peanut House Saloon
2292 S. Carson St.
Carson City, NV 89701
(702) 882-8252

Peppermill Hotel Casino
2707 S. Virginia St.
Reno, NV 89502
(702) 826-2121
Fax: (702) 826-5205

Peppermill Inn & Casino
P.O. Box 100
I-80 Exit 410
West Wendover, NV 89883
(702) 664-2255
Fax: (702) 664-3756

Petrelli's Fireside Inn & Casino
P.O. Box 2
Star Route 1
Ely, NV 89301
(702) 289-3765

Pioneer Hotel & Gambling Hall
2200 S. Casino Dr.
Laughlin, NV 89029
(702) 298-2442
Fax: (702) 298-5256

Pioneer Inn Casino
221 S. Virginia St.
Reno, NV 89501
(702) 324-7777
Fax: (702) 323-5343

Plantation Station Gambling Hall
2121 Victorian Ave.
Sparks, NV 89431
(702) 359-9440
Fax: (702) 359-9440

Player's Island Resort Casino Spa
930 West Mesquite Blvd.
P.O. Box 2737
Mesquite, NV 89024
(702) 346-7529

Poker Palace Casino
2757 N. Las Vegas Blvd.
North Las Vegas, NV 89030
(702) 649-3799
Fax: (702) 649-9375

Polar Palace Casino
2757 N. Las Vegas Blvd.
North Las Vegas, NV 89030
(702) 649-3799

Ponderosa Club & Arcade
P.O. Box 158
Virginia City, NV 89440
(702) 847-0757

Popo's Gambling Hall
2501 E. Lake Mead Blvd.
North Las Vegas, NV 89030
(702) 649-8022

Primadonna Resort & Casino
Exit 1 I-15 on CA/NV state line
Jean, NV 89109
(702) 382-1212
(800) 367-7383
Fax: (702) 874-1749

Railroad Pass Hotel & Casino
2800 S. Boulder Hwy.
Henderson, NV 89015
(702) 294-5000
Fax: (702) 294-0129

Rainbow Club & Casino
122 S. Water St.
Henderson, NV 89015
(702) 565-9777
Fax: (702) 565-4809

Ramada Express Hotel & Casino
2121 S. Casino Dr.
P.O. Box 77771
Laughlin, NV 89028
(702) 298-4200
Fax: (702) 298-6431

Red Garter Saloon & Gambling Hall
80 S. C St.
Virginia City, NV 89440
(702) 874-0665

Red Lion Inn & Casino
741 W. Winnemucca Blvd.
Winnemucca, NV 89445
(702) 623-2565
Fax: (702) 623-5702

Red Lion Inn II & Casino
P.O. Box 1389
Elko, NV 89801
(702) 738-2111
Fax: (702) 738-2628

Regency Casino
P.O. Box 525
Laughlin, NV 89029
(702) 298-2439
Fax: (702) 298-3977

Renata's Supper Club
4451 E. Sunset Rd.
Henderson, NV 89014
(702) 435-4000
Fax: (702) 435-5510

Reno Cannon International Airport
P.O. Box 10580
Reno, NV 89510
(702) 328-6400

Reno Hilton Resort
2500 E. 2nd St.
Reno, NV 89595
(702) 789-2000

Reno Turf Club
P.O. Box 2071
Reno, NV 89505
(702) 323-1046
Fax: (702) 785-3288

Riverboat Hotel & Casino
34 W. 2nd St.
Reno, NV 89501
(702) 323-8877
Fax: (702) 348-0926

Saddle West Resort Hotel & Casino
P.O. Box 234
Pahrump, NV 89041
(800) 522-5953
Fax: (702) 727-5315

Sam's Town Gold River Hotel & Gambling Hall
P.O. Box 77700
Laughlin, NV 89102
(702) 298-2242
Fax: (702) 298-2129

Sands Regency Hotel & Mr. C's
345 N. Arlington Ave.
Reno, NV 89501
(702) 348-2200
Fax: (702) 348-2226

Say When
P.O. Box 375
McDermott, NV 89421-0375
(702) 532-8515

Searchlight Nugget Casino
P.O. Box 187
100 N. Hwy. 95
Searchlight, NV 89046
(702) 297-1201

Sharkey's Nugget
P.O. Box 625
1440 Hwy. 395
Gardnerville, NV 89410
(702) 782-3133

Si Redde's Oasis
P.O. Box 360
897 Mesquite Blvd.
Mesquite, NV 89024
(702) 346-5232
Fax: (702) 346-2969

Silver Club Hotel Casino
1040 Victorian Sq.
Sparks, NV 89432
(702) 358-4771
Fax: (702) 358-5643

Silver Dollar Saloon & Casino
4848 Idaho St.
Elko, NV 89801
(702) 738-2217

Silver Legacy Resort & Casino
P.O. Box 3920
407 N. Virginia St.
Reno, NV 89501
(702) 322-3933

Silver Queen Hotel & Casino
28 N. St.
Virginia City, NV 89440
(702) 847-0440

Silver Smith Casino Resort
P.O. Box 729
100 Wendover Blvd.
Wendover, NV 89883
(702) 664-2231

Silver Strike Casino
P.O. Box 3133
Tonopah, NV 89049
(702) 482-9490

Skyline Restaurant & Casino
1741 N. Boulder Hwy.
Henderson, NV 89015
(702) 565-9116
Fax: (702) 564-3540

Stagecoach Hotel & Casino
P.O. Box 836
Hwy 95 N.
Beatty, NV 89003
(702) 553-2419
Fax: (702) 553-2548

Starlite Bowl
1201 Stardust St.
Reno, NV 89503
(702) 747-3522

Stateline Casino, Inc.
P.O. Box 730
490 Mesquite Blvd.
Mesquite, NV 89024
(702) 346-5752
Fax: (702) 346-5751

Station House Casino
P.O. Box 1351
100 Erie Main
Tonopah, NV 89409
(702) 482-8762
Fax: (702) 482-9777

Stockman's Bar, Restaurant & Casino
1604 W. Williams Ave.
Fallon, NV 89406
(702) 423-2117
Fax: (702) 423-3066

Stockmen's Motor Hotel & Casino
340 Commercial St.
Elko, NV 89801
(702) 738-5141
Fax: (702) 738-9363

Sturgeon's Log Cabin Best Western
1420 Cornell St.
Lovelock, NV 89419
(702) 273-2971
Fax: (702) 273-2278

Sundance Casino
P.O. Box 2607
Winnemucca, NV 89445
(702) 623-3336
Fax: (702) 623-3336

Sundowner Hotel & Casino
450 N. Arlington Ave.
Reno, NV 89503
(702) 786-7050
Fax: (702) 348-6074

Tahoe Biltmore Lodge & Casino
P.O. Box 115
Hwy. 28
Crystal Bay, NV 89402
(702) 831-0660
Fax: (702) 832-7675

Tamarack Grill & Bar
13101 S. Virginia St.
Reno, NV 89511
(702) 853-4567

Tom's Sunset Casino
444 W. Sunset Rd.
Henderson, NV 89015
(702) 564-5551
Fax: (702) 564-5305

Topaz Lodge & Casino
Hwy. 395
Topaz Lake, NV 89410
(702) 266-3338
Fax: (702) 266-3338

Treasure Club Casino
1144 B St.
Sparks, NV 89531
(702) 356-7177

Treasury Club
P.O. Box 10750
Reno, NV 89510
(702) 356-7177
(702) 356-7177

Triple-J Bingo Hall & Casino
725 S Racetrack Rd.
Henderson, NV 89015
(702) 566-5555
Fax: (702) 566-1111

Truck Inn 7-Z's Motel
I-80 Exit 48
485 Truck Inn Way
Fernley, NV 89408
(702) 351-1000
Fax: (702) 575-6002

Valley Inn Club
P.O. Box 419
Mesquite, NV 89024
(702) 346-2955

Virgin River Hotel, Casino & Bingo
P.O. Box 1620
915 Mesquite Blvd.
Mesquite, NV 89024
(702) 346-7777
Fax: (702) 346-7780

Virginian Hotel & Casino
140 N. Virginia St.
Reno, NV 89501
(702) 329-4664
Fax: (702) 329-3673

Wells Chinatown Casino
P.O. Box 96
455 S. Humboldt Ave.
Wells, NV 89835
(702) 752-2101

Western Village Inn & Casino
P.O. Box 3267
815 E. Nichols Blvd.
Sparks, NV 89432
(702) 331-1069
Fax: (702) 331-4834

Whiskey Pete's Hotel & Casino
P.O. Box 93716
Jean, NV 89019
(702) 382-4388
Fax: (702) 874-1554

Winners Hotel & Casino
185 W. Winnemucca Blvd.
Winnemucca, NV 89445-3456
(702) 623-2511
Fax: (702) 623-1207

New Jersey
Bally's Park Place Casino Hotel & Tower
Park Place and Boardwalk
Atlantic City, NJ 08401
(609) 340-2000
Fax: (609) 340-1058

Caesar's Atlantic City
2100 Pacific Ave.
Atlantic City, NJ 08401
(609) 348-4411
Fax: (609) 348-8830

Claridge Casino Hotel
Boardwalk and Park Place
Atlantic City, NJ 08401
(609) 340-3400

The Grand, A Bally's Casino Resort
Boston and Pacific Ave.
Atlantic, NJ 08401
(609) 347-7111
Fax: (609) 340-4858

Harrah's Casino Hotel
777 Harrah's Blvd.
Atlantic City, NJ 08401
(609) 441-5000
Fax: (609) 345-8651

Merv Griffin's Resort Casino Hotel
North Carolina Ave.
Atlantic City, NJ 08401-7329
(609) 344-6000
Fax: (609) 340-7684

Sands Hotel & Casino
Indiana Ave. and Brighton Prk.
Atlantic City, NJ 08041
(609) 441-4000

TropWorld Casino and Entertainment Resort
Brighton Ave. and Boardwalk
Atlantic City, NJ 08401-6390
(609) 340-4000
Fax: (609) 340-4124

Trump Plaza Hotel & Casino
Boardwalk at Mississippi Ave.
Atlantic City, NJ 08401
(609) 441-6000
Fax: (609) 441-7881

Trump Taj Mahal Casino Resort
1000 Boardwalk
Atlantic City, NJ 08401
(609) 449-1000
Fax: (609) 449-6818

Trump's Castle Casino Resort
Huron Ave. and Brigantine Blvd.
Atlantic City, NJ 08401
(609) 441-2000
Fax: (609) 345-4091

New Mexico
Camel Rock Casino
R.R. 11 Box 3A
Santa Fe, NM 87501
(505) 984-8414
Fax: (505) 989-9234

Casino Sandia
P.O. Box 10188
Albuquerque, NM 87184
(505) 897-2173
Fax: (505) 897-1117

Inn of the Mountain Gods Casino
P.O. Box 269
Carrizzo Canyon
Mescalero, NM 88340
(505) 257-5141
Fax: (505) 257-6173

Isleta Gaming Palace Casino
11000 Broadway S.E.
Albuquerque, NM 87105
(505) 869-2614
Fax: (505) 869-0152

Jicarilla Inn Bingo
P.O. Box 233
Dulce, NM 87528
(505) 759-3663
Fax: (505) 759-3130

Oh-Kay Casino & Bingo
P.O. Box 1270
San Juan Pueblo, NM 87566
(505) 747-1668
Fax: (505) 753-8283

Pojoaque Gaming, Inc.
R.R. 11 Box 21B
Santa Fe, NM 87501
(505) 455-3313
Fax: (505) 455-7188

Santa Ana Star Casino
Box 9201
54 Jemez Canyon Dam Road
Bernalillo, NM 87004
(505) 867-0000
Fax: (505) 867-1472

Sky City Tribal Casino
P.O. Box 310
Acoma, NM 87034
(505) 522-6017
Fax: (505) 552-9256

New York
Turning Stone Casino
P.O. Box 126
5218 Patrick Rd.
Verona, NY 13478
(315) 361-7711
Fax: (315) 361-7901

North Dakota
Big "O" Casino
512 Dakota Ave.
Wahpeton, ND 58705
(701) 642-2407

Blue Wolf Casino
I-94 and University
US Hwy. 81
Fargo, ND 58102
(701) 232-2019

Borrowed Buck's Roadhouse
1201 Westrac Dr.
Fargo, ND 58103
(701) 232-7861

**Brass Mint Casino &
Lounge/Holiday Inn**
3803 13th Ave. S.
Fargo, ND 58103
(701) 282-2700

Bun Lounge Casino
P.O. Box 12420
1708 State Mill Rd.
Grand Forks, ND 58201
(701) 746-1290

**Cactus Jack's Gold Rush
Casino**
3402 Interstate Blvd.
Fargo, ND 58103
(701) 280-0400

Charlie Brown's Casino
414 Gateway Dr.
Grand Forks, ND 58201
(701) 852-5795

Cheers Lounge Restaurant
1309 N. Broadway
Minot, ND 58701
(701) 852-5795

Dakotah Lounge
1014 S 12 St.
Bismarck, ND 58504
(701) 223-3514

Dakotah Sioux Casino-Tokio
P.O. Box 133
Tokio, ND 58379
(701) 294-2109
Fax: (701) 294-2910

Dakotah Sioux Casino, St. Michael
P.O. Box 23
St. Michael, ND 58370
(701) 766-4612
Fax: (701) 766-4877

Doublewood Inn
Casino Lounge
3333 13th Ave S.
Fargo, ND 58103
(701) 235-3333

Doublewood Ramada Inn Casino
I-94, Exit 36
Bismarck, ND 58501
(701) 258-7000

El Rancho Motel Casino
1623 2nd Ave. W.
Williston, ND 58801
(701) 572-6321

El Roco
1730 13th Ave. N.
Grand Forks, ND 58201
(701) 772-8613

Flying J Travel
3150 39th St.
Fargo, ND 58103
(701) 282-7766

Four Bears Casino & Lodge
P.O. Box 579
Hwy. 23 W.
New Town, ND 58763
(701) 627-4018
Fax: (701) 627-3714

Jailhouse Rock Casino
901 40th St. S.W.
Fargo, ND 58103
(701) 282-7766

Nickels Lounge
800 S. 3rd St.
Bismarck, ND 58504
(701) 258-7700

Off Broadway Lounge & Casino
605 E. Broadway Ave.
Bismarck, ND 58501
(701) 255-6000

Penquin's Casino
2100 Burdick Expwy. E.
Minot, ND 58701
(701) 839-0406

Perspectives Lounge & Casino-Radisson Hotel Fargo
201 5th St. N.
Fargo, ND 58102
(701) 232-7363

Pete's Lounge & Casino
710 1st Ave. N.
Grand Forks, ND 58203
(701) 746-5411

Prairie Knights Casino & Lodge
HC1 Box 36A
Fort Yates, ND 58538
(701) 854-7777
Fax: (701) 854-7785

Ramada Inn Casino
P.O. Box 13757
1205 N. 43rd St.
Grand Forks, ND 58203
(701) 775-3951

Rick's Bar
2721 Main Ave.
Fargo, ND 58103
(701) 232-8356

Sheraton Riverside Inn
2100 Burdick Expwy. E.
Minot, ND 58701
(701) 852-2504

Silver Spur
501 Pleasant Ave.
Surry, ND 58785
(701) 838-3616

Southgate Casino
2525 Washington St. S.
Grand Forks, ND 58203
(701) 775-6174

Stooge's Casino
10 3rd St. N.
Grand Forks, ND 58102
(701) 746-7189

Super-8 Lounge
2324 2nd Ave.
Williston, ND 58801
(701) 572-8371
Fax: (701) 572-8048

Turtle Mountain Chippewa Casino
P.O. Box 1449
Hwy. 5 W.
Belcourt, ND 58316
(701) 477-3281
Fax: (701) 477-5331

Upper Deck Casino
707 28th Ave. N.
Fargo, ND 58102
(701) 235-1171

West End Casino
4220 5th Ave. N.
Grand Forks, ND 58102
(701) 775-9775

South Dakota
76 Motel & Restaurant
68 Main St.
Deadwood, SD 57732
(605) 578-3476

Agency Bingo & Casino
Box 569
Veterans Memorial Dr.
Agency Village, SD 57262
(605) 698-4273
Fax: (605) 698-4271

B.B. Cody's
681 Main St.
Deadwood, SD 57732
(605) 578-3430
Fax: (605) 578-2397

Best Western Hickock House
137 Charles St.
Deadwood, SD 57732-1304
(800)-873-8174
Fax: (605) 578-1855

Big Jake's Card Room
639 Main St.
Deadwood, SD 57732-1123
(605) 578-3631

Black Jack
270 Main St.
Deadwood, SD 57732-1124
(605) 578-9777

Bodega Bar & Cafe
662 Main St.
Deadwood, SD 57732-1124
(605) 578-1996

Buffalo Saloon
658 Main St.
Deadwood, SD 57732-1124
(605) 578-9993
Fax: (605) 578-1537

Bullock Hotel & Casino
633 Main St.
Deadwood, SD 57732-1123
(605) 578-1745
Fax: (605) 578-1382

Carnival Queen
606 Main St.
Deadwood, SD 57732
(605) 578-1574

Carrie Nation Temperance Saloon
605 Main St.
Deadwood, SD 57732-1106
(605) 578-2036

Casey's
557 Main St.
Deadwood, SD 57732-1117
(605) 578-1207

Deadwood Livery
605 Main St.
Deadwood, SD 57732-1106
(605) 578-2036

Decker's Food Center Gaming
124 Sherman St.
Deadwood, SD 57732-1309
(605) 578-2722
Fax: (605) 578-1887

The Depot and Mother Lode Gaming Saloon
155 Sherman St.
Deadwood, SD 57732-1337
(605) 578-2699
Fax: (605) 578-2305

Durty Nelly's
700 Main St.
Deadwood, SD 57732
(605) 578-2241

Fairmont Hotel
The Oyster Bay
626-628 Main St.
Deadwood, SD 57732-1111
(605) 578-2205

First Gold Hotel Gaming & Restaurant
270 Main St.
Deadwood, SD 57732
(800) 274-1876
Fax: (605) 578-3979

Fort Randall Casino Hotel
P.O. Box 756
R.R. 1
Wagner, SD 57380
(605) 487-7871
Fax: (605) 487-7354

Four Aces
531 Main St.
Deadwood, SD 57732
(605) 578-2323
Fax: (605) 578-2718

Fraternal Order of Eagles
409 Cliff St.
Deadwood, SD 57732-0533
(605) 578-1064

French Quarter
680 Main St.
Deadwood, SD 57732-1124
(605) 578-2100

Gold Dust Gaming & Entertainment Complex
688 Main St.
Deadwood, SD 57732
Fax: (605) 518-2272

Gold Nugget Inn, Diner & Casino
801 Main St.
Deadwood, SD 57732
(800) 287-1251

Goldberg Gaming
670 Main St.
Deadwood, SD 57732-1124
(605) 578-1515
Fax: (605) 578-2812

Golden Buffalo Casino
P.O. Box 204
Lower Brule, SD 57548
(650) 473-5577
Fax: (605) 473-9270

Goldigger's Hotel & Gaming Establishment
629 Main St.
Deadwood, SD 57732-0131
(605) 578-3213
Fax: (605) 578-3762

Grand River Casino
P.O. Box 639
Mobridge, SD 37601
(800) 475-3321
Fax: (605) 845-7260

Hickock's Saloon
685 Main St.
Deadwood, SD 57732-1135
(605) 578-2222
Fax: (605) 578-3163

Historic Franklin Hotel
700 Main St.
Deadwood, SD 57732
(605) 578-2241
Fax: (605) 578-3452

Jackpot Charlie's Green Door Club
616 Main St.
Deadwood, SD 57732-1111
(605) 578-2014
Fax: (650) 578-SLOT

Lady Luck
660 Main St.
Deadwood, SD 57732-1124
(605) 578-1162

Lariat Motel
360 Main St.
Deadwood, SD 57732-1236
(605) 578-1500

Legends
678 Main St.
Deadwood, SD 57732-1123
(605) 578-3141
Fax: (605) 642-2623

Lillie's
671 Main St.
Deadwood, SD 57732-1122
(605) 578-3104

Lode Star Casino
P.O. Box 140
Fort Thompson, SD 57339-0050
(605) 245-6000
Fax: (605) 245-2240

Lucky-8 Casino and Super-8 Hotel
196 Cliff
Deadwood, SD 57732-3363
(605) 578-2535
Fax: (605) 578-3604

Lucky Miner
651 Main St.
Deadwood, SD 57732-1123
(605) 578-3363
Fax: (605) 578-3364

Lucky Wrangler
638 Main St.
Deadwood, SD 57732
(605) 578-3260

Midnight Star Gaming Emporium
677 Main St.
Deadwood, SD 57732-1122
(605) 578-1555
Fax: (605) 578-2739

Mineral Palace Hotel & Gaming Complex
6607 Main St.
Deadwood, SD 57732-1106
(605) 578-2036
Fax: (605) 578-2037

Miss Kitty's Chinatown Cafe
649 Main St.
Deadwood, SD 57732-1123
(605) 578-1811
Fax: (605) 578-1818

Mustang
556 Main St.
Deadwood, SD 57732-1105
(605) 578-1715

Old Style Saloon #10
657 Main St.
Deadwood, SD 57732-1123
(605) 578-3346
Fax: (605) 578-1944

Painted Pony Gaming
692 Main St.
Deadwood, SD 57732-1124
(605) 578-1012
Fax: (605) 578-3130

Peacock Club
634 Main St.
Deadwood, SD 57732-1124
(605) 578-2025

Pink Palace
673 Main St.
Deadwood, SD 57732-1122
(605) 578-1276

Prairie Wind Casino
HC 49 Box 10
Pine Ridge, SD 57770
(605) 535-6300
Fax: (605) 535-6211

Rosebud Casino
P.O. Box 21
Mission, SD 57555-0021
(605) 378-3800
Fax: (605) 378-3870

Royal River Casino
P.O. Box 326
Veterans St.
Flandreau, SD 57028-0326
(605) 997-3746
Fax: (605) 997-9998

Silver Dollar
686 Main St.
Deadwood, SD 57732-1124
(605) 578-2100

Silverado
709 Main St.
Deadwood, SD 57732-1011
(605) 578-3670
Fax: (605) 578-1366

Slots of Luck
668 Main St.
Deadwood, SD 57732
(605) 578-1979

Star of the West Casino
700 Main St.
Deadwood, SD 57732
(605) 578-2241
Fax: (605) 578-3452

Thunder Cove
P.O. Box 326
Hwy. 85 S.
Deadwood, SD 57732-0326
(605) 578-3045

Tin Lizzie Gambling Hall
555 Main St.
Deadwood, SD 57732-1105
(800) 643-4490
Fax: (605) 578-1751

Wild Bill's Bar & Gambling Hall
608 Historic Main St.
Deadwood, SD 57732
(605) 578-2177
Fax: (605) 578-2179

Washington
Colville Tribal Bingo
41 Apple Way Rd.
Okanogan, WA 98840
(509) 42-BINGO
Fax: (509) 422-3907

Double Eagle Casino
Box 961
Chewlah, WA 99109
(509) 935-4406
Fax: (509) 935-6790

Lummi Casino
2559 Lummi View Dr.
Bellingham, WA 98226
(360) 758-7559
Fax: (360) 758-7545

Mill Bay Casino
455 E. Wapato Lake Rd.
Manson, WA 98831
(509) 687-2102
Fax: (509) 687-4501

Muckleshoot Indian Casino
2402 Auburn Way S.
P.O. Box 795
Auburn, WA 98002
(206) 804-4444
Fax: (206) 939-7702

Nooksack River Casino
P.O. Box
5048 Mt. Baker Hwy.
Deming, WA 98244-0248
(206) 592-5472
Fax: (206) 592-5542

Quileute Tribe Casino
P.O. Box 279
La Push, WA 98350
(206) 374-6739
Fax: (206) 374-9484

Seven Cedars Casino
27056 Hwy. 101
Sequim, WA 98382
(360) 683-7777
Fax: (360) 681-6711

**Spokane Tribal Indian
Bingo & Casino**
P.O. Box 1106
S. Hwy. 395 and Smith Rd.
Chewelah, WA 99109
(509) 935-6167
Fax: (509) 935-4554

Swinomish Casino & Bingo
837 Casino Dr.
P.O. Box 628
Anacortes, WA 98221
(360) 293-2691
Fax: (360) 293-2691

Tulalip Bingo & Casino
6410 33rd Ave. N.E.
Marysville, WA 98271
(360) 651-1111
Fax: (360) 651-2234

Two Rivers Casino
6828 B Hwy. 25 S.
Davenport, WA 99122
(509) 722-4000
Fax: (509) 722-4015

Wisconsin

Bad River Bingo & Casino
P.O. Box 8
Hwy. 2
Odanah, WI 54861
(715) 682-7121
Fax: (715) 862-7149

Ho-Chunk Casino
S-3214A Hwy. 12
Baraboo, WI 53913
(600) 356-6210
Fax: (608) 355-4046

Hole-in-the-Wall Casino & Hotel
P.O. Box 98
Hwys. 77 and 35
Danbury, WI 54830
(800) BET-UWIN
Fax: (715) 656-3434

Isle Vista Casino
P.O. Box 1167
Hwy. 13 N.
Bayfield, WI 54814
(715) 779-3712
Fax: (715) 779-3715

Lake of the Torches Casino
P.O. Box 550
562 Peace Pipe Rd.
Lac du Flambeau, WI 54538
(715) 588-7070
Fax: (715) 588-9508

LCO Casino
R.R. 5 Box 5003
Hwys. B & K
Hayward, WI 54843
(715) 634-5643
Fax: (715) 634-8110

Majestic Pines Casino
R.R. 5 Hwy. 54
Black River Falls, WI 54615-0433
(715) 284-9098
Fax: (715) 284-9739

Menominee Casino, Hotel & Bingo
P.O. Box 760
Hwy. 47 and 55
Keshena, WI 54135-0760
(715) 799-3600
Fax: (715) 799-4051

Mohican North Star Casino & Bingo
W12180A County Rd. A
Bowler, WI 54416
(715) 787-3110
Fax: (715) 787-3129

Mole Lake Casino
P.O. Box 277
Hwy. 55
Crandon, WI 54520
(715) 478-5290
Fax: (715) 478-5735

Oneida Bingo & Casino
2020 Airport Dr.
Green Bay, WI 54313
(414) 494-4500
Fax: (414) 497-5003

Potawatomi Bingo Casino
1721 W. Canal St.
Milwaukee, WI 53233
(414) 645-6888
Fax: (414) 645-6866

**Potawatomi Bingo &
Northern Lights Casino**
P.O. Box 140 Hwy. 32 S.
Wabeno, WI 54566
(715) 473-2021
Fax: (715) 473-6104

Rainbow Casino
949 Co. Trunk G
Nekoosa, WI 54457
(715) 886-4500
Fax: (715) 886-4551

St. Croix Casino & Hotel
777 US Hwy. 8
Turtle Lake, WI 54889
(715) 986-4777
Fax: (715) 986-2800

Canada
Cash Casino
6350 67th St.
Red Deer, Alberta T4P 3L7
(403) 346-3339

Casino ABS
1251 3rd Ave. S.
Lethbridge, Alberta T1J 0K8
(403) 381- WINS

Casino ABS South
7055 Argyll Road
Edmonton, Alberta T6C 4A5
(403) 463-9467

Casino De Charlevoix
183 Avenue Richelieu
Pointe-Au-Pic, Quebec G0T 1M0
(418) 665-5300

Casino De Montreal
1 Avenue du Casino
Montreal, Quebec H3C 4W7
(514) 392-2746

Casino Roma Resort
Orilla, Ontario
(705) 329-3325

Casino Windsor
445 Riverside Dr. W.
Windsor, Ontario N9A 6T8
(519) 258-7878

Club Regent
1425 Regency Ave. W.
Winnipeg, Manitoba R2C 3B2
(204) 957-2700

The Crystal Casino
7th Floor Hotel Garry
222 Broadway Ave.
Winnipeg, Manitoba R3C 0R3
(204) 957-2500

**Diamond Tooth Gertie's
Gambling Hall**
Queen St. and 4th Ave.
Dawson City, Yukon Territories
Y0B 1G0
(403) 993-5575

Digger's Territorial Casino
Exhibition Grounds
North Battleford,
Saskatchewan S9A 2Y9
(306) 665-9434

Emerald Casino
Saskatoon Prairieland Exhibition
Centre
Ruth St. & Herman St.
Saskatoon, Saskatchewan S7K
4E4
(306) 665-9434

Gold Dust Casino
24 Boudreau Rd.
St. Albert, Alberta T8N 6K3
(403) 460-8092

Golden Nugget Casino
250 Thatcher Dr. E.
Moose Jaw, Saskatchewan
(306) 692-2723

Grand Casino
725 Southeast Marine Dr.
Vancouver, British Columbia
V5X 2T9
(604) 437-1696

Great Canadian Casino
115 Chapel St.
Nanaimo, British Columbia
(604) 303-1000

Great Canadian Casino
8440 Bridgeport and No. 3 Rd.
Richmond, British Columbia
(604) 303-1000

Great Canadian Casino
15330 - 102A Ave.
Surrey, British Columbia
(604) 303-1000

Great Canadian Casino
2477 Heather St.
Vancouver, British Columbia
(604) 303-1000

Great Canadian Casino
Renaissance Hotel Downtown
1133 West Hastings St.
Vancouver, British Columbia
(604) 303-1000

Great Canadian Casino
Red Lion Inn
3366 Douglas St.
Victoria, British Columbia
(604) 303-1000

Hull Casino/Casino De Hull
1 Boulevard du Casino
Hull, Quebec J8Y 6W3
(819) 772-2100

McPhillips Street Station
484 McPhillips St.
Winnipeg, Manitoba R2X 2H2
(204) 957-3900

Northern Belle Casino
350 Riverside Dr. E.
Windsor, Ontario

Palace Casino
1335 West Edmonton Mall
8770 170th St.
Edmonton, Alberta T5T 4M2
(403) 444-2112

Royal Casino
308 Maclean St.
Quesnel, British Columbia V2J 2N9
(604) 992-7763

Royal Diamond Casino
B106-750 Pacific Blvd. S.
Plaza of Nations
Vancouver, British Columbia V6
5E7
(604) 685-2340

Sheraton Casino
1969 Upper Water St.
Halifax, Nova Scotia B3J 3J5
(902) 425-7777

Sheraton Casino
525 George St.
Sydney, Nova Scotia B1P 1K5
(902) 563-7777

Silver Sage Casino
1800 Elphinstone St.
Regina, Saskatchewan S4P 2Z6
(306) 777-0777

HOW TO REACH OTHER CASINOS

If you are traveling to other parts of the world and want to see if they have a casino near where you are going, then check either of these two Internet sites:

The Casino Net

http://the-casino-net.com/index.htm

Casino City
http://www.casinocity.com

Chapter Nineteen
GAMBLING ON THE INTERNET

You don't need to visit Las Vegas or Atlantic City to gamble the night away. The Internet has plenty of places to play your favorite casino games. Slots! Blackjack! Craps! Poker! Sports! If a casino has a game, it's offered by an on-line casino somewhere. This chapter will show you a few of the many places you can go on the Internet to gamble. Some of these sites offer the opportunity to gamble with real money while others are just for fun.

Before gambling on the Internet, make sure you stay legal. A lawsuit was filed earlier this year by the Minnesota attorney general against a Las Vegas Internet firm that planned to create an on-line sports betting parlor. The company claimed that its service is legal, but the attorney general said such activity is covered by federal law prohibiting "a wire communication facility for the transmission of interstate or foreign commerce bets and wagers." The lawsuit charged the company with fraud for saying in its ads that such betting is legal. The state court ruled that Minnesota had jurisdiction to enforce its laws against the Internet gambling business.

Many Internet gambling parlors operate legally outside the United States, but that doesn't mean it's legal for an Internet user in the United States to gamble on-line. The parlor may be operating legally, but the gambler is breaking the law. How can you be sure that what you're doing is legal? Good question! Attorneys and politicians are wrestling over enforcing federal laws and state laws. In late 1997, legislation was introduced to expressly prohibit Internet gambling. The two bills would allow fines and prison sentences for those who operate on-line gambling businesses and for players. If either bill becomes law, enforcement against businesses could be very difficult; catching and prosecuting players would be virtually impossible and exorbitantly expensive for authorities. What's a player to do? Keep informed about the laws that govern gambling and interstate commerce and remember that there's a whole world of gambling opportunities beyond the borders of the United States, no matter what the politicians in Washington, D.C. decide to do. Whatever you do, play it safe.

There are no government regulations of games on the Internet. However, there are plenty of sites that offer the excitement of gambling without any financial risk. Some sites will even offer great prizes for tournaments. A particular favorite is Blackjack Time, which offers week-long blackjack tournaments with prizes tied to hotels in Las Vegas. Play at the sites you like and be careful if you decide to gamble for real on the Internet.

REAL SITES TO GAMBLE ON THE INTERNET

The sites listed below offer "real gambling"—that is, gambling for money. These sites will require you to submit a credit card number in order to properly credit and debit transactions. Use caution when giving out your credit card to anyone on the Internet.

American Sports Betting
http://www.pananet.com/sports/

Fallons Casino
http://www.fcasino.com/

Global Casinos
http://www.gamblenet.com/global-casino/

Golden Jackpot Casino
http://www.jetnet.ag/

Intercasino
http://www.intercasino.com/about/index.html

InterKeno
http://www.interkeno.com/

International Casino
http://www.iwe.com/intcasino/

Internet Casino
http://www.casino.org/

On-line Casinos
http://www.lecasino.com/

Real Sports
http://www.realsports.com/

Sports International On-Line Sports Betting
http://www.gamblenet.com/bet/

World Wide Telesports On-Line Sports Betting
http://www.cpscaribnet.com/wwts/wwts.html

World Wide Web Casinos
http://www.netcasino.com/english/index.html

PLAY-MONEY GAMBLING SITES

The sites listed below are places where you can practice your gambling skills without risking any real money. These sites can be just as exciting as the sites offering real gambling. Some of these sites have tournaments that offer great prizes to those of you who are lucky at the tables.

2 Play Fantasy Sports
http://www.2play.com

The Betting Parlor
http://www.boston.com/bookie/

Blackjack Time
http://test.blackjacktime.com

Casinos of the South Pacific
http://marble.net:8081/casino.html

Dor-Cino
http://www.dorcino.com/dorcino.html

Fox Casino
http://www.foxcasino.com

Tiffany Video Poker
http://tiffany.indirect.com/cgi-bin/poker

Virtual Vegas
http://www.virtualvegas.com

There are a few casino-related Internet sites that don't offer games but provide excellent information on casino gambling.

"Casino News!!!" (http://www.geocities.com/SunsetStrip/5424/) is a site that has current news regarding the casino industry plus an excellent source of links to Las Vegas casinos. You can also note any questions or comments regarding this book at this site.

"Casino Center" is the home page for the monthly publication *Casino Player Magazine*. Its Internet address is: http://www.casinocenter.com. This is an excellent source for information on the casino industry for both the players and the workers in the industry.

Another site to check out is "Rolling Good Times On-Line." The Internet address is: http://www.RGTonline.com/. This is a thorough site on casinos and the Internet that includes a listing of sites mentioning casino gambling along with a rating for each.

If you can't find the information you're looking for at any of these sites, do a search using Yahoo or one of the other search engines. Yahoo is a directory for the Internet. Its site address is: http://www.yahoo.com. Any time you need to find any subject on the Internet, Yahoo should be your first stop. Search engines are popping up all the time, each promising to be better than the others—or at least different. The following list should help you find Web sites related to casino gambling:

Dogpile
http://www.dogpile.com

HotBot
http://www.hotbot.com

AltaVista
http://altavista.digital.com

MetaFind
http://www.metafind.com

Web sites can be fun places to practice your casino games, but there's no comparison with playing in a casino. Web sites can help you practice different strategies, so when you go to Las Vegas or other casinos, you can play as smart as possible. Have fun surfing the Internet and dropping in on these casino sites!

APPENDIX

GAMBLING PUBLICATIONS

Below is a list of publications on the casino industry. If you would like to check out a copy of one of these publications, call or write them and they'll gladly send you a free copy.

Casino Player Magazine
8025 Black Horse Pike
Suite 470
Atlantic City, NJ 08232
1-800-969-0711

This publication is a monthly with nice glossy pages. It covers all aspects of casino gaming for the players and has excellent contributing writers with good knowledge of the games they're advising. Contains a monthly directory of upcoming casino entertainment and tournaments. Each month's issue is around seventy pages.

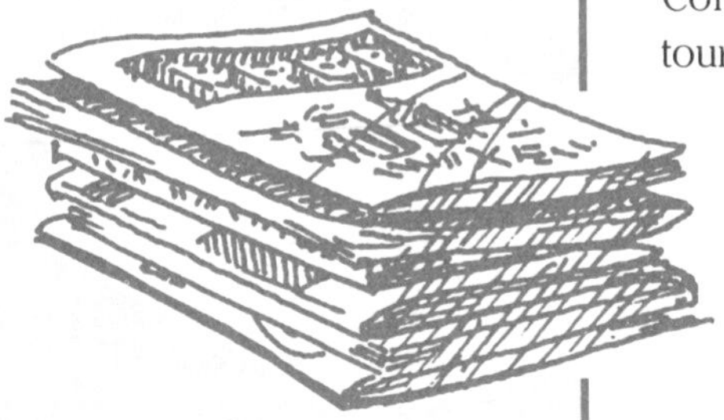

Casino Journal
3100 W. Sahara Avenue
Suite 207
Las Vegas, NV 89102
(702) 253-6230

A monthly publication geared toward the executives of the casino industry. Has a lot of good information on what's happening on the business side of casinos. This large magazine format publication has about 100 pages per issue.

Las Vegas Adviser
3687 South Procyon Avenue
Las Vegas, NV 89103
1-800-244-2224

The best monthly publication for the Las Vegas area casinos. Contains a monthly top ten list of Las Vegas values. A small publication of only ten pages, but it's the best source of information for planning to visit Las Vegas.

Casino Executive
2655 South Rainbow Boulevard
Suite 410
Las Vegas, NV 89102
1-800-950-9467

A monthly publication for the casino executives. Each month has a theme (i.e. July is a guide to North America's casinos). Excellent coverage for the investors of gaming stocks. Each issue is around fifty-five pages.

Card Player Magazine
3140 South Polaris Avenue #8
Las Vegas, NV 89102
(702) 871-1720

A monthly publication mostly devoted to the game of poker. Has excellent coverage of the game of poker. Contains coverage of big poker tournaments and each issue lists a directory of upcoming tournaments. Each issue contains help from professional poker players. Each issue is about 100 pages.

GAMBLING BOOK CLUBS

1. Gambler's Book Club and Book Shop
   GBC Press
   630 South 11th Street
   Las Vegas, NV 89101
   1-800-634-6243
   Call to request your free catalog.

2. Gambler's General Store
   800 South Main
   Las Vegas, NV
   1-800-322-CHIP

3. Paulson Dice and Card
   2121 Industrial Road
   Las Vegas, NV
   (702) 384-2425

GAMBLING BOOKS

1. *Guerrilla Gambling—How to Beat the Casinos at Their Own Game,*
   by Frank Scoblete
   Bonus Books Inc.
   160 East Illinois Street
   Chicago, IL 60611

2. *Comp City: A Guide to Free Las Vegas Vacations,*
   by Max Rubin
   Huntington Press
   5280 South Valley View Boulevard
   Suite B
   Las Vegas, NV 89118

3. *Bargain City: Booking, Betting and Beating the New Las Vegas,*
   by Anthony Curtis
   Huntington Press
   5280 South Valley View Boulevard
   Las Vegas, NV 89118

4. *Professional Blackjack,*
   by Stanford Wong
   Pi Yee Press
   7910 Ivanhoe Avenue, #34
   La Jolla, CA 92037

5. *Best Blackjack,*
   by Frank Scoblete
   Bonus Books Inc.
   160 East Illinois Street
   Chicago, IL 60611

6. *Beat the Craps Out of the Casinos,*
   by Frank Scoblete
   Bonus Books Inc.
   160 East Illinois Street
   Chicago, IL 60611

7. *Las Vegas Behind The Tables,*
   by Barney Vinson
   Gollehon Press
   Grand Rapids, MI

8. *Big Deal—A Year as a Professional Poker Player,*
   by Anthony Holden
   Viking Penguin
   375 Hudson Street
   New York, NY 10014

9. *Casino,*
   by Nicholas Pileggi
   Simon & Schuster
   Rockefeller Center
   1230 Avenue of the Americas
   New York, NY 10020

10. *Fool's Die,*
    by Mario Puzo
    G.P. Putnam's Sons
    200 Madison Avenue
    New York, NY

GAMBLING MOVIES

This movie list includes films that have a gambling theme or extended scenes shot in a casino.

1. *Casino*
   Starring Robert De Niro, Joe Pesci, and Sharon Stone

2. *National Lampoon's Vegas Vacation*
   Starring Chevy Chase, Beverly D'Angelo, and Randy Quaid

3. *Indecent Proposal*
   Starring Robert Redford, Demi Moore, and Woody Harrelson

4. *Honeymoon in Vegas*
   Starring Nicolas Cage, Sarah Jessica Parker, and James Caan

5. *Bugsy*
   Starring Warren Beatty, Annette Bening

6. *Rain Man*
   Starring Dustin Hoffman and Tom Cruise

7. *Heat*
   Starring Burt Reynolds

8. *Lost in America*
   Starring Albert Brooks

9. *Diamonds Are Forever*
   Starring Sean Connery

10. *Viva Las Vegas*
    Starring Elvis Presley

11. *Ocean's Eleven*
    Starring Frank Sinatra, Sammy Davis Jr., Dean Martin and Peter Lawford

GAMBLING ADDICTION

Gambling can be a very fun form of entertainment. However, a small percentage of the people who gamble are compulsive gamblers. This is a very sad situation that can ruin careers, families, friendships and lives. Below is a listing of groups to contact if you feel you have a gambling problem or if you have a friend or family member who you think has a gambling problem.

1. Gamblers Anonymous
   P.O. Box 17173
   Los Angeles, CA 90017
   (213) 386-8789

2. The National Council on Problem Gambling, Inc.
   445 West 59th Street
   Room 1521
   New York, NY 10019
   1-800-522-4700

3. The Council on Compulsive Gambling of New Jersey, Inc.
   1315 West State Street
   Trenton, NJ 08618
   1-800-GAMBLER

For help for family members and friends of compulsive gamblers contact:

Gam-Anon
P.O. Box 157
Whitestone, NY 11357
(718) 352-1671

Below is a set of guidelines to follow to reduce the risk of developing a gambling problem.

1. The decision to gamble is a personal choice.
   Don't let anyone pressure you to gamble. Many people will choose to gamble socially for a limited period of time or for a limited amount of money. This is the only way to gamble. Set limits for yourself (both time and an amount of money to lose). Never gamble alone. Always gamble to socialize with friends, family, or co-workers, never to make money.

2. Gambling isn't essential to having a good time.

    Gambling can be an enjoyable complement to other activities, but shouldn't be seen as the only reason for socializing. The real value of socializing is being with friends and taking time out from the pressures of daily living.

3. Acceptable losses need to be established before starting to gamble.

    People need to expect that they will lose more than they will win. The odds are always against winning. Any money spent on gambling needs to be considered entertainment. Money that's needed for basics, like food, shelter, clothing, education, etc. should not be used for gambling. For those who choose to gamble, it's essential to know when to stop.

4. Borrowing money to gamble should be avoided and discouraged.

    Borrowing money from a friend, writing bad checks, taking out loans, or borrowing from any other source of funds with the intention of repayment with gambling winnings is always high-risk and inappropriate.

5. There are times when people shouldn't gamble.

    ♠ When gambling interferes with work or family responsibilities.
    ♠ When in recovery from compulsive/pathological gambling.
    ♠ When the money bet exceeds a predetermined limit.
    ♠ When the form of gambling is illegal.
    ♠ When in the early stages of recovery from other addictions such as chemical dependency.

6. Use of alcohol or drugs when gambling is risky.

    Alcohol or other drug use can affect a person's judgment and can interfere with his/her ability to control gambling and adhere to predetermined limits.

7. There are certain reasons for gambling that present a high risk for problems.

♠ Gambling to relieve stress, loneliness, anger or depression.
♠ Gambling to make up for a loss or series of losses (chasing).
♠ Gambling to impress others.
♠ Gambling to cope with the death or loss of a loved one.

WHAT TO SAY IF SOMEONE'S GAMBLING CONCERNS YOU

It's possible that you will experience times when someone else may be gambling in ways that do not follow these guidelines and seem risky. What should you do when a friend or family member is gambling too much, at inappropriate times, or is acting in some ways that are upsetting?

A simple and straightforward approach to letting someone know you are concerned is often the most helpful. While there is no foolproof way to share a concern with another person, the following process has worked well for many people.

1. Tell the person that you care about him/her and that you feel concerned about the way you see him/her acting.
2. Tell the person *exactly* what he/she has done that concerns you.
3. After you tell the person that you care, how you feel, and what you've seen, it's important to be willing to listen to what he/she says.
4. Tell the person what you would like to see him/her do.
5. Tell the person what you are willing and able to do to help.

Keep in mind that gambling can be a great way to socialize and have fun, but keep your gambling under strict control and you'll have a much better time at the casinos. Enjoy being with your friends and view being at the casino as a secondary reason for entertainment. If you set a period of time with which you are going to gamble and a predetermined set amount of money you can lose, then you'll have a much better time enjoying a night out with your friends and family.

GLOSSARY

aces and eights—In poker this is considered "the Dead Man's Hand" because it was the hand held by Wild Bill Hickok when he was shot.

ace high—A hand in poker which contains odd cards, the highest of which is an ace.

across the board—A bet on all the numbers (4, 5, 6, 8, 9, and 10) in craps.

action—The amount of money wagered at any given moment.

ante—Chips or cash put up by the players in poker before the dealing of the hands.

baccarat—An adaptation of a card game that originated in France.

back line—A don't-pass bet in craps. Any bet placed against the shooter.

bank—The person who covers the bet in a game. In most casino games, the bank is the casino itself.

bank hand—The second of the two hands dealt in baccarat.

bank roll—The total amount of money a gambler sets aside to gamble with.

barber pole—A bet consisting of different colored chips all mixed together.

basic strategy—In blackjack, the best possible play of any given hand based on the dealer's up card and the two cards you posses. In other games, the best play available.

betting limits—In a table game, the betting limits establish the minimum and maximum amounts of money that can be wagered on one bet. You can't wager less or more than the amounts posted.

bet the pot—In poker, betting an amount equal to the amount in the pot.

biased wheel—A roulette wheel that has an imperfection which shows up by certain numbers appearing out of proportion to their probability.

black action—A bet made with a black $100 chip.

blackjack—A natural—ten-value card and an ace. Pays off at three to two.

blind—In hold'em or other poker games, an ante put up by one or two players. Rotates with each hand.

bluff—In poker, the attempt to take the pot by making the other players think you have a superior hand.

boxcars—A roll of twelve or double sixes in craps.

boxman—The person who sits at the center of the craps table and supervises the game.

bring in—A mandatory bet in seven-card stud made by the player with the lowest up-card in the first round of betting.

bust—To go over twenty-one in blackjack. If you bust you lose. If the dealer busts and you don't, you win. If both you and the dealer bust, you lose anyway.

button—A small marker that is moved from player to player after each hand of hold'em poker to designate the dealer position.

buy bet—In craps, betting the point numbers four and ten by paying a five percent commission.

buy in—Exchanging cash for chips at a table.

cage—The cashiers area of a casino where chips are exchanged for cash.

call—In poker, a call is when a player makes a bet equal to the previous bet. Sometimes referred to as seeing a bet.

caller—The dealer in charge of the game in baccarat.

cancellation betting system—A betting system using a series of numbers that cancels numbers after a winning bet and adds numbers after a loss. Also called the Labouchere system.

capping a bet—Adding more chips to a bet that has already won. Also called past posting.

card counting—Keeping track of which cards have been played since the last shuffle.

carousel—A group of slot machines that are positioned in a circle or ring.

casino rate—A reduced hotel room rate that casinos offer good customers.

center bets—The proposition bets in the center of a craps table.

check—Another term for a casino chip. In poker, a player can check in order to stay in the game but not bet. This can only be done when no previous player in the round has made a bet.

chip tray—The tray in front of a dealer which holds the table's chips.

color up—To exchange smaller denomination chips for larger denomination chips.

column bet—In roulette, a bet made on one of the columns of twelve numbers on the layout.

combination bet—In roulette, a bet with one chip on two or more numbers.

combination ticket—In keno, a bet on a number of different propositions.

come bet—Similar to a pass line bet in craps, a wager that the next point number rolled will come up before another seven.

come-out roll—The roll that establishes the shooter's pass line point in craps.

come point—The number that must be repeated before a seven is thrown.

commission—The percentage that the casino takes out of winning card hands or for buy bets in craps, usually five percent.

comp—Freebies that casinos give out for certain levels of betting.

corner bet—In roulette, a bet that four numbers in a given segment of the layout will win. Also known as a square bet or a quarter bet.

crap out—To roll a two, three, or twelve in craps on the come-out roll.

craps—The numbers two, three and twelve. A dice game played in the casino.

credit line—The amount of credit a player is allowed by a given casino.

cut card—A card of a different color that is used to cut a deck of cards.

cut the deck—To divide the deck before dealing. Usually done by a player.

dealer—The casino employee who staffs the games in the casino.

dice—Two identical numbered cubes used by a shooter in a crap game.

dice tray—The small tray that holds the dice that are not being used. Sometimes known as the dice boat.

discard rack—The plastic, upright receptacle for cards that have already been played in some games.

don't come—A bet at craps that the next point number rolled will not be repeated before a seven is thrown. One of the best bets in the casino.

don't pass—A bet at craps that the shooter will not make his point before the seven is thrown.

double down—In blackjack, to double the size of your bet and receive only one card. You can also double for less than the initial wager.

double odds—The right to place a free-odds bet up to double the original pass line or come bet. The best bet in the casino because you are paid true odds (no casino advantage).

double-up system—Player attempts to get all his previous losses back by increasing (doubling) his previous bet. This is also known as the Martingale system.

double zero—Another term for the American roulette wheel. The area of the American roulette wheel that contains the 00.

draw—The second round of cards that are dealt in draw poker.

drop—The casino term for the total amount of money and markers wagered at the tables.

drop box—Where the money is dropped after a player cashes in.

dumping—A casino table that is losing money to the players.

early surrender—Rarely found rule in blackjack that allows players to forfeit half their bet, even if the dealer has a blackjack.

even—A wager in roulette that one of the even numbers will come up on the next spin.

even money—A bet that pays back the same amount of money wagered plus the original wager.

face cards—The king, queen, and jack. Also known as picture cards.

favorable deck—A deck whose remaining cards favor the player.

field bet—A wager at craps that wins if the number 2, 3, 4, 9, 10, 11, or 12 is rolled. Player loses on a 5, 6, 7, and 8. It's a one roll bet.

first base—The seat at the table immediately to the dealer's left.

flat bet—Bet that is paid off at even money in craps. Also, any player who bets the same amount hand after hand.

flop—The three cards dealt face up in the center of the table in a game of hold'em poker.

flush—In poker, five cards of the same suit.

fold—In poker, to drop out of play.

four of a kind—Four cards of the same rank.

fourth street—The second round of betting in seven-card stud because the player has four cards. In hold'em it's the third round of betting and occurs when the fourth card is showing on the board.

free odds—Wager placed behind the pass line bet or the come bet that is paid off at the true odds. The best bet in the casino because there's no casino advantage.

front line—Another name for the pass line in craps.

full house—A poker hand consisting of three of a kind and a pair.

full odds—The maximum odds allowed on a given craps table.

gambling stake—Amount of money reserved for gambling. Same as a bankroll.

george—A casino player who is a good tipper.

greens—Chips valued at $25.

hard hand—A blackjack hand that cannot use the ace as an eleven. Any hand in blackjack that doesn't have an ace is a hard hand.

hard way bets—A bet in craps that the shooter will roll the 4, 6, 8, or 10 as doubles before a 7 shows or any other combination of that number.

high roller—A player who plays for larger than normal stakes.

high pair—A pair of jacks, queens, kings, or aces.

hit—To receive another card on your hand in blackjack.

hole card—The card face down that is dealt to the dealer in blackjack. Also, any cards dealt face down in poker.

hot—A player who has been winning. Also, a slot machine that is paying out.

hot dice—Dice that have been passing and making numbers.

hot table—A table where the players have been winning.

house edge—The mathematical edge that the casino has on a given bet. Also known as the casino advantage.

inside numbers—In craps, the numbers 5, 6, 8, or 9.

inside straight—A straight that can only be completed by one card on the inside. For example, 5, 6, X, 8, 9.

insurance—A side wager at blackjack for up to half the original wager that the dealer has a blackjack when he has an ace showing.

jackpot—A grand payout, either on a machine or at a table game.

juice—The five percent commission that the house charges on buy bets in craps. Also known as vigorish.

keno board—Large electronic board that displays the winning numbers drawn in keno.

keno lounge—The main area within a casino where keno is played.

keno runner—A casino employee who shuttles your keno bet from wherever you are to the keno lounge counter, and who also delivers payment for winning tickets.

kicker—In poker, an extra card, usually a high card, that is kept with a pair.

lay bet—A wrong bet (that is, a bet against the shooter) on a number at craps that is paid off at true odds after the casino extracts a five percent commission.

laying odds—To bet against the shooter by making an odds bet.

line—The sports book's method of dealing with the inequality of teams in order to attract equal amount of money on each team.

loose machine—A slot machine or video poker machine that is paying off more than other machines of its type. A machine that is winning for a player.

making a point—Having your pass line number repeat before the appearance of a seven.

markers—Establishing credit with a casino.

Martingale system—Doubling a bet after a loss in an attempt to make back all your losses and a small win.

mini-baccarat—Baccarat played on a regular baccarat table for lower stakes.

money line—The betting line quoted in some sports. When you bet on the favorite with the money line you'll lay more money than you'll win. If you bet the underdog, you'll win more money than you bet.

money management—The methods a player uses to avoid losing his or her bankroll.

multiple coin machine—Slot and video poker machines that require more than one coin in order to win the jackpot.

multiple-deck game—Blackjack played with more than one deck, which gives the house more of an advantage over the player. Also, any shoe game with more than one deck.

natural—A perfect hand. In blackjack, an ace and a ten-value card. In baccarat, an eight or a nine total.

nickel—A five dollar chip.

no action—A call made by a dealer that the casino will not cover a particular bet or that a particular deal or roll doesn't count.

odd bet—A bet at roulette that one of the odd number will hit on the next spin.

odds—The bet that pays off at true odds in craps. Also, the likelihood of a given event happening.

one-armed bandits—The term given to slot machines.

open—In poker, to make the first bet.

outside bets—One of the two to one or even money bets at roulette. They appear on the outside of the layout.

outside numbers—The box numbers 4, 5, 9, and 10 on the craps layout.

paint—A picture card. When a player says "Paint me," he is asking for a face card.

pair—In poker, two cards of the same rank.

parlay—To double one's bet after a win.

pass line—A wager with the shooter that he will make his point.

past posting—Placing a winning wager after a decision has been reached. Usually leads to being escorted out of the casino.

pat hand—Any hand in a card game that does not require additional cards.

pay line—The line upon which a player is paid at slots. Generally corresponds to the number of coins played.

penetration—How deeply a dealer deals into a deck or a shoe at blackjack.

pit—An area consisting of a number of gaming tables.

pit boss—The individual in charge of a pit.

place bet—Going directly up on a number in craps. The house pays the bet at house odds, not true odds.

player hand—The first of two hands dealt at baccarat.

point—The number 4, 5, 6, 8, 9, or 10) which the shooter must repeat before a seven is rolled in order to win on the pass line at craps.

point spread—The betting line quoted for football, basketball, and hockey, where the favorite gives up points or the underdog takes points in order to equalize the attractiveness of bets on either side.

pot—The total amount of money at stake in a deal.

premium players—A casino term meaning big bettors or players with big credit lines.

press—To increase the amount wagered, usually by doubling, after a win.

progressive jackpots—The grand prize offered on certain kinds of slot and video poker machines that keeps growing as more and more money is played. Grows until it is hit by a player.

proposition bet—Bets in the center of the craps layout (figure 4-1), on certain combinations of the dice.

puck—A marker used to indicate the point in a craps game.

push—A tie hand between the dealer and a player. No money changes hands.

quarters—Chips valued at $25. Also known as greens.

rail—The high border that encloses a craps table where the players keep their chips.

raise—In poker, to increase the amount previously bet by another player.

rake—The commission the card rooms take out of a pot.

rating—Evaluating a player's play for the purpose of comps.

reds—Casino chips worth $5.

reel—One of the loops inside a slot machine upon which the symbols are located.

RFB—Complimentary room, food and beverage.

risk-time—The amount of time you are at a table with your money at risk.

river—Staying until the fifth and final round of betting in seven-card stud.

roll—To toss the dice in craps.

royal flush—An ace, king, queen, jack, and ten of the same suit.

session—A given period of time at play in a casino. Usually terminated at a predetermined time, or at a certain level of wins or losses.

seven out—For a shooter at craps to roll a seven before repeating the point number.

shill—An individual employed by the casino to play games that are being underplayed.

shoe—The box that holds the decks for a card game.

showdown—In poker, the final betting of the players who remain, followed by the showing of the cards.

shuffle tracking—Watching as the cards are being shuffled to memorize and later locate groups of cards.

single-deck blackjack—Blackjack played with one deck. The best game in the casino if the rules are standard.

snake eyes—The two at craps.

soft hand—Any hand at blackjack where the ace can be used as one or eleven.

split—To make two hands from a pair at blackjack.

sports book—A facility that accepts wagers on sporting events.

spot—The number on a keno ticket that has been crossed out for betting purposes.

spread—The difference between the minimum and maximum bets a player makes.

stand—To keep the cards you have. Not to draw any more cards.

stickman—Crap dealer who uses the thin stick and pushes the dice to the shooter.

stiff—In blackjack, a total of twelve through sixteen. Also a player who doesn't tip.

straight—Five cards in sequence.

straight flush—Five cards in sequence and all in the same suit.

straight ticket—A keno ticket that has only one wager and that involves the selection from one to fifteen different numbers.

street bet—A bet in roulette that one of three particular numbers will hit on the next spin.

the Strip—Las Vegas Boulevard. Three miles of casinos.

surrender—A blackjack option where the player may give up half his bet. Player loses full bet if the dealer has a blackjack.

table game—Any game in a casino that is played at a table.

taking the odds—To back up a pass line or a come bet in craps by making a wager that pays off at true odds or (if allowed by the casino) double odds.

tapped out—To lose your entire bankroll.

teaser—A sports parlay that uses different spreads than those that are used for regular parlays.

third base—The spot directly to the dealer's right; the last person to play before the dealer.

three of a kind—Three cards of the same denomination.

tight machine—A slot machine that is not paying back a good percentage. A machine that a player is losing at.

toke—A tip to a casino employee.

tom—A poor tipper.

true odds—The actual probability of an event happening.

twenty-one—Another name for blackjack,

two pair—A hand consisting of two separate pairs.

under—A sports bet that the combined total of points scored by both teams during a game will be under a specified total.

vigorish—The casino tax on a bet. Also known as vig or juice.

wheel of fortune—A carnival game that has found its way into the casinos. Also known as Big Six Wheel.

wrong bet—A bet in craps that the shooter will lose.

INDEX

Internet
gambling on, 250-52
software downloads, 92
See also World Wide Web
Iowa, casinos in, 204-5

J
jackpots, 266
See also progressive jackpots
juice, 266
See also vigorish

K
keno, 136
cards, 138
decisions per hour, 183
etiquette, 142
expected losses, 13
house advantage, 9, 136, 139
rules, 136-40
strategy, 140-42
video, 142
keno boards, 138, 266
keno lounges, 136, 266
keno runners, 138, 266
kickers, 266

L
Las Vegas, 6-7, 12-13
casinos in, 212-21
World Series of Poker, 83
lay bets
craps, 45-46, 266
sports, 151
laying odds, in craps, 43, 266
Let It Ride poker, 96
decisions per hour, 183
etiquette, 101-2
house advantage, 9, 100
rules, 97-99
strategy, 99-101
table, 96
tournaments, 101

lines, sports betting, 48-51, 267
loose slot machines, 267
losses
expected, 13
limiting, 184, 189
lotteries, 5, 130
Louisiana
casinos in, 205-6
New Orleans, 5-6
low bets, 59
Lowe, Edwin S., 120

M
magazines, 256-57
making a point, 267
markers, 267
Martingale system, 187-88, 267
MegaBucks progressive slot
machine jackpot, 166, 169
Michigan, casinos in, 206-7
mini-baccarat, 114, 267
decisions per hour, 183
etiquette, 118
house advantage, 9, 114
rules, 114-17
strategy, 117-18
Minnesota, casinos in, 207-9
Mississippi, casinos in, 209-11
Missouri, casinos in, 211-12
money line bets, 151, 267
money management, 182-84, 267
in bingo, 131-32
expected losses, 13
limiting losses, 184, 189
movies, with gambling themes, 259
multiple coin machines,
167-68, 267
multiple-deck blackjack games,
19, 267

N
natural
in baccarat, 115

in blackjack, 20, 263, 267
in craps, 37
Nevada, 7
casinos in, 221-34
progressive slot machine
jackpot, 166, 169
See also Las Vegas
New Jersey, Atlantic City, 7-8,
234-35
New Mexico, casinos in, 235-36
New Orleans, 5-6, 205, 206
nickels (chips), 267
no action call, 267
North Dakota, casinos in, 236-38

O
odd bets (roulette), 58, 267
odds, 267
odds bets (craps), 40-42, 267
one-armed bandits. *See* slot
machines
online gambling, 250-52
opening, in poker, 267
outside bets, 54, 58-59, 267
outside numbers, 267

P
Pai Gow poker, 104
banking games, 109-10
decisions per hour, 183
etiquette, 112
house advantage, 9, 104-5
rules, 105-10
strategy, 110-12
table, 104
paint, 267
pairs, 267
parlaying, 267
in sports betting, 152-53
pass line bets, 37-38, 267
past posting, 267
pat hands, 23, 267
pay line, 164, 267